Welcome to

THE

EVERYTHING

Family Guides ®

THESE HANDY, PORTABLE BOOKS are designed to be the perfect traveling companions. Whether you're traveling within a tight family budget or feeling the urge to splurg, you will find all you need to create a memorable family vacation.

Use these books to plan your trips, and then take them along with you for easy reference. Does Jimmy want to c   ? Or maybe Jane wants to go to the local hobby shor   ng® *Family Guides* offer many ways to entertain ki   so ensuring you get the most out of your ti

Review this book cover-   as before you travel, and stick it in y   ag to use as a quick reference guide for act.   and excursions you want to experience. Let *The   amily Guides* help you travel the world, and you'll disco   vacationing with the whole family can be filled with fun and exciting adventures.

TRAVEL TIP

Quick, handy tips

TRAVEL ESSENTIAL

Don't leave home without . . .

FAST FACT

Details to make your trip more enjoyable

JUST FOR PARENTS

Appealing information for moms and dads

THE EVERYTHING
— Family Guide —
to Las Vegas

Dear Reader,

Thanks for picking up this copy of *The Everything® Family Guide to Las Vegas*. This book was written to help you and your family get the most out of your vacation, no matter how large or small your travel budget happens to be. Throughout this book, not only will you find detailed information about all there is to see and do on or near the world-famous Las Vegas Strip, but you'll also discover dozens of money-saving tips you can utilize when booking airfares, making hotel reservations, and planning how you'll actually spend your time in Las Vegas.

This book was written for families, which is what sets it apart from other travel guides. Instead of describing the best places to gamble, then providing strategies for winning at the casinos, this guide focuses on all of the mega-resorts, hotels, activities, shows, attractions, restaurants, shops, and day spas located on or near the Strip.

You'll soon discover the best ways to spend your time and find out what's most suitable for you *and* your kids or teens. All of the mega resorts, attractions, and shows, for example, are rated based not just on the quality of entertainment offered and overall value, but on age appropriateness as well. This will quickly help you identify the best place to stay and the most exciting and appropriate things to see and do.

If you want to share your vacation experiences, please visit my We site at *www.JasonRich.com* or drop me an e-mail at *jr7777@aol.co* My goal has been to provide the most comprehensive, informative, a fun-to-read travel guide possible. As you read this book, I hope yo agree that I've achieved my objective.

Have a wonderful, memorable, and safe trip!

Jason Rich
(*www.JasonRich.com*)

THE

EVERYTHING

FAMILY GUIDE TO

LAS VEGAS

Hotels, casinos, restaurants, major
family attractions—and more!

Jason Rich

Adams Media
Avon, Massachusetts

Dedication

This book is dedicated to Ferras AlQaisi for making all of
my travel adventures so much fun, as well as to my life-
long friends Mark Giordani and Ellen Bendremer.

• • •

Publishing Director: Gary M. Krebs
Managing Editor: Laura M. Daly
Copy Chief: Brett Palana-Shanahan
Acquisitions Editor: Gina Chaimanis
Development Editor: Karen Johnson Jacot
Production Editor: Casey Ebert

Director of Manufacturing: Susan Beale
Production Director: Michelle Roy Kelly
Cover Design: Paul Beatrice, Matt LeBlanc
Layout and Graphics: Colleen Cunningham
    Holly Curtis, Erin Dawson,
    Sorae Lee

An Everything® Series Book.
Everything® and everything.com® are registered trademarks of F+W Publications, Inc.

Published by Adams Media, an F+W Publications Company
57 Littlefield Street, Avon, MA 02322 U.S.A.
www.adamsmedia.com

ISBN: 1-59337-359-7

Printed in Canada.

J I H G F E D C B A

Library of Congress Cataloging-in-Publication Data
Rich, Jason.
The everything family guide to Las Vegas / Jason Rich.
    p. cm. -- (An everything series book)
    ISBN 1-59337-359-7
    1. Family recreation--Nevada--Las Vegas--Guidebooks. 2. Las
Vegas (Nev.)--Guidebooks. I. Title. II. Series: Everything series.

F849.L35R53 2005
917.93'1350434--dc22
                                            2005011013

This publication is designed to provide accurate and authoritative information with regard to the
subject matter covered. It is sold with the understanding that the publisher is not engaged in ren-
dering legal, accounting, or other professional advice. If legal advice or other expert assistance
is required, the services of a competent professional person should be sought.
             —From a *Declaration of Principles* jointly adopted by a Committee of the
    American Bar Association and a Committee of Publishers and Associations

Many of the designations used by manufacturers and sellers to distinguish their products are
claimed as trademarks. Where those designations appear in this book and Adams Media was
aware of a trademark claim, the designations have been printed with initial capital letters.

Visit the entire Everything® series at www.everything.com

Contents

Top 10 Las Vegas Shows
Definitely Worth Seeing

1. *Avenue Q*

2. *Blue Man Group Live*

3. *Celine Dion: A New Day . . .*

4. Cirque du Soleil's "O"

5. Cirque du Soleil's *Mystère*

6. Lance Burton: Master Magician

7. *Mamma Mia!*

8. Penn & Teller

9. *Phantom of the Opera* (starting in 2006)

10. Rita Rudner

Acknowledgments

Thanks to everyone at Adams Media, especially Gina Chaimanis, for inviting me to work on this exciting book. I'd also like to thank all of the owners, operators, and public relations professionals at the various Las Vegas area mega-resorts, hotels, attractions, shows, restaurants, activities, and day spas for their assistance on this project. A special thank you also goes out to Mimi Tilton . . . (you rock!)

On a personal note, the love and support I receive on an ongoing basis from my closest and dearest friends is extremely important to me. For this, I am truly grateful. Thanks to Ferras AlQaisi and Chris Coates, who have shared in my Las Vegas travel adventures, as well as to Mark Giordani and the Bendremer family (Ellen, Sandy, Emily, and Ryan). Finally, thanks to my family for all of their support.

Introduction

As the title of this book suggests, *The Everything® Family Guide to Las Vegas* is an information-packed resource written specifically for families that will help you plan the ultimate vacation to Las Vegas, plus save money in the process! Throughout this book, you will be reading about all of the mega-resorts, hotels, attractions, shows, activities, restaurants, and day spas that the Las Vegas area has to offer.

To help you make the best decisions about where to stay, how to plan your itinerary, and how to choose the most exciting ways to spend your time (based on the people you're traveling with), this book not only provides the information you need but also rates everything based on overall value and age-appropriateness.

After all, because of the casinos, Las Vegas is primarily the ultimate theme park and vacation destination for adults. As you'll discover, however, there's an incredible number of fun, exciting, and memorable ways to spend quality time with your kids and teens as you explore all that Las Vegas has to offer. While some shows, attractions, and activities are family-friendly and suitable for people of all ages, some are more appropriate for just teens or are exclusively for adults. The ratings this book offers will help you decide what's appropriate for the people you're traveling with, whether they're toddlers, kids, teens, adults, or senior citizens.

Later in this book, you'll be reading detailed information about all of the mega-resorts, hotels, and casinos on or near the Las Vegas Strip. For each detailed hotel or resort description, the following information is offered:

- The resort's name.
- The resort's address, toll-free and local phone numbers, and Web site.
- The number of rooms and the average room rates.
- An overview of the resort and what the resort offers.

- The resort's overall family-friendliness rating, which is based on the value it offers plus the types of people the property caters to.
- A description of the resort's guest room accommodations, including what amenities you can expect to find within the rooms and suites.
- Details about the main activities and attractions offered within the resort, including ratings for each to help you determine its family-friendliness and value.
- Information about the shows and entertainment offered within the resort, including ratings for each to help you determine if it's suitable for your kids and teens.
- A look at the resort's day spa, a place that adults traveling to Las Vegas can go to relax, work out, or be pampered.
- Details about all of the fine-dining and casual-dining options offered within the resort, as well as information about the nightclubs, bars, and lounges at the resort that cater to the over-twenty-one crowd.
- An overview of the shopping opportunities that the resort offers.
- Information about the resort's casino.

By the time you're done reading *The Everything® Family Guide to Las Vegas*, you will have the knowledge you need to plan and experience the ultimate family vacation!

CHAPTER 1

Viva Las Vegas

GET READY TO EXPERIENCE an incredible vacation, as you discover what fabulous Las Vegas has to offer. In this chapter, you'll learn what's new in Las Vegas, find out why Las Vegas appeals to virtually everyone, and get a peek into the city's history. Most importantly, you'll find out why Las Vegas is the fastest-growing city in America and why more than 35 million people visit each year.

Welcome to Las Vegas

Over the past few years, Las Vegas has once again undergone expansion and a significant transformation. In addition to continuing its reign as America's fastest-growing city, this is a vacation destination visited by more than 35 million tourists every year. In an effort to keep up with this growth, many existing hotels and resorts have recently expanded and remodeled. There are also several new properties that have recently found a home on or near the world-famous Las Vegas Strip.

If you're planning a vacation or trip to Las Vegas, you're in for an amazing and memorable experience! There's no place else like it on the planet. Las Vegas is situated smack in the middle of the desert, yet this amazing oasis is filled with some of the largest, flashiest, and most opulent casinos, resorts, and hotels you'll find anywhere. Within these properties are world-class restaurants; theaters, which are the homes to many incredible shows; countless attractions and activities (many suitable for the entire family); amazing shopping opportunities; all of the amenities you'd expect from top-notch resorts; golf courses; day spas; plus, of course, casinos.

More than 70 percent of those traveling to Las Vegas come to experience a memorable vacation. Millions of others come for business or to attend a convention. Yet of the more than 35 million visitors each year, upward of 11 percent bring their families, including children under the age of twenty-one.

Despite the fact that the casino properties tend to target adults who enjoy gambling, there continues to be plenty for families to see, do, and experience throughout the Las Vegas area.

Las Vegas Attracts Family Vacationers

Las Vegas is a mecca for everything that's trendy, exciting, and entertaining, especially for the over-twenty-one crowd. Properties such as the Palms, the Rio, and the Hard Rock Hotel & Casino have become popular hangouts and vacation destinations of the young, rich, and famous.

Considering the history of Las Vegas and its current focus on adult-oriented entertainment, you're probably asking yourself, "Is this really a place you should bring your kids for vacation?" The answer to this is both an unequivocal "yes" and "no," depending on how well you plan your vacation and the activities you choose to partake in, especially with your children.

Making the Right Choice

Many resort and casino properties that catered to young people in the past have refocused their efforts and now cater mainly to the over-twenty-one crowd. If you've previously visited Las Vegas, you may recall that the MGM Grand, for example, offered the Grand Adventures theme park. This theme park, and attractions like it at a few other properties, no longer exist. However, there is still plenty for families traveling with kids and teens to see and do throughout the Las Vegas area.

The trick is to select the ideal place to stay, and then to seek out the very best family-oriented attractions, rides, shows, shopping, and dining experiences that Las Vegas has to offer. Even if you don't gamble, you can still occupy every minute of the day and night with countless memorable and fun activities.

▲ A prime view of the Las Vegas Strip.   Photo © The Las Vegas News Bureau.

The Las Vegas Appeal

Recently, a multitude of network television shows, including *CSI: Crime Scene Investigation, Las Vegas, The Casino*, and MTV's *The Real World*, along with several major motion pictures, have put the spotlight on Las Vegas, depicting it as the fun and exciting vacation destination that it's become. This has definitely boosted interest among tourists, especially after the tragic events of September 11 when tourism in America slowed down for a while.

So, what's the incredible appeal that keeps people coming back to Las Vegas? Well, in addition to its rich history as a gaming town and its reputation for being a hangout for mega-popular entertainers, Las Vegas continues to offer people a fun and memorable escape from reality. No matter what your travel budget is, Las Vegas offers a vacation experience the likes of which no place else on the planet can offer.

Satisfaction Guaranteed

In recent years, many world-class chefs have made a home in Las Vegas, which now offers some of the finest dining experiences you'll find anywhere. In addition, this city has become the home for many Broadway-style and high-budget production shows (such as *Mamma Mia!* and *Blue Man Group Live*), plus it's where you can see world-famous recording artists such as Celine Dion and Elton John performing almost nightly.

 TRAVEL TIP

While *Siegfried & Roy* was one of the best production shows ever presented in Las Vegas, it is no longer at The Mirage. There are still, however, dozens of incredible Broadway-style and full production shows to choose from. You won't want to leave Las Vegas without experiencing one of the Cirque du Soleil shows, for example. Each of these unusual and exciting shows is well worth the price of admission.

When it comes to shopping, between the Forum Shops at Caesars Palace, the Fashion Show Mall (located along the Strip), the Galleria at Sunset Mall, and the hundreds of shops and boutiques within the hotels, resorts, and casinos themselves, you can shop for several days straight, until you literally collapse from exhaustion.

After reaching that point of exhaustion, consider dropping into one of the world-class day spas within the various mega-resorts. At places such as the Canyon Ranch SpaClub (located within The Venetian), you can experience a relaxing and rejuvenating massage, body wrap, or any of over 120 other spa services, plus enjoy the top-notch spa facilities and incredible hospitality as you're being pampered. These spas cater to male and female clientele.

Something for Everyone

Along with dining, seeing shows, and shopping, you'll also find dozens of world-class golf courses, exciting nightclubs, and museums, plus many utterly unique activities you can enjoy as part of your vacation.

For example, there's indoor skydiving for those who are adventurous. If you want to explore beyond the Las Vegas Strip, you can take a helicopter tour of the Hoover Dam and/or the Grand Canyon and experience one of the seven Wonders of the World in a way you'll never forget.

If you're a fan of the *Star Trek* television shows and movies, you won't want to miss *The Star Trek Experience* at the Las Vegas Hilton. It's a state-of-the-art ride/attraction that's suitable for the entire family.

Museums and Galleries

In terms of museums, people of all ages will enjoy spending an hour or two exploring Madame Tussauds wax museum, which offers photo-realistic, life-size replicas of hundreds of famous celebrities. The Guinness World Record Museum is the home of many wacky, weird, and wonderful displays that bring the popular *Guinness Book of Records* to life.

Several of the resorts along the Strip, such as the Bellagio, also offer exquisite art collections and galleries, showcasing famous, one-of-a-kind works from Monet, Picasso, and many other renowned artists whom you'd typically see on display only at the world's most prestigious museums.

Action-Adventure

If you're traveling with young people, just some of the things you won't want to miss include a visit to Circus, Circus, where you can experience the Adventuredome theme park, offering more than twenty rides and attractions, plus ongoing circus acts performed under the giant indoor big top.

In front of Treasure Island, there's also the free twenty-minute show called *Sirens of TI*, during which visitors will see pirates, pyrotechnics, and high-diving acrobatics. In front of Caesars Palace, The Mirage, and the Bellagio, there are shooting fountain shows, synchronized to music, that are presented throughout the day and night.

Several of the major resort/casinos offer one-of-a-kind roller coasters, including New York-New York, the Stratosphere Tower, and Sahara Hotel & Casino. There's also Wet 'n Wild, a sixteen-acre water park that's open between May and September.

If you want to see lions, tigers, sharks, dolphins, and other exotic creatures, be sure to stop by the Flamingo Wildlife Habitat (the Flamingo Las Vegas), the Lion Habitat (MGM Grand), the Shark Reef (Mandalay Bay Resort & Casino), and Siegfried & Roy's Secret Garden & Dolphin Habitat (The Mirage).

A few other family-oriented activities and attractions you'll soon be learning more about include GameWorks Las Vegas (an indoor arcade and virtual-reality experience with more than 300 interactive video games and the world's largest indoor rock-climbing structure), the IMAX theater at the Luxor, the Las Vegas Cyber Speedway (Sahara Hotel & Casino), M&M's Academy (located near the MGM Grand), the Volcano at The Mirage, and King Tut's Tomb and Museum (the Luxor). Any of these fun and one-of-a-kind attractions will help make your Las Vegas vacation something you'll always remember.

Planning Ahead

Aside from all there is to see and do throughout Las Vegas, many people wind up spending countless hours or even full days simply exploring the various resort hotels and casinos located along the Strip. Each of these larger-than-life properties offers a distinctive theme, incredible architecture, and an ambiance you need to experience to believe.

As you prepare for your trip to Las Vegas, be sure to read all about what this incredible city has to offer *before* you arrive; then plan your itinerary carefully, to ensure that you're able to experience everything that interests you. Preplanning your trip will also help you stay within your budget, plus allow you to make advance reservations for some of the most popular restaurants, shows, and attractions, which often sell out. Celine Dion's *A New Day . . .* concert, for example, often sells out several weeks or even months in advance.

Perhaps it's because Las Vegas offers so much variety that it appeals to people of all ages and from all walks of life. Whatever the reason for Las Vegas's popularity, it's no surprise that more than 82 percent of those who travel here each year are repeat visitors. Unless you're planning to spend several weeks on vacation in Las Vegas, it's virtually impossible to see and do everything during a single visit.

A Quick Look at Las Vegas's Past

Before you experience firsthand the vacation destination Las Vegas has transformed itself into, let's take a quick look at its past. For many centuries Nevada was inhabited only by the Paiute, Shoshone, and Washoe Indian tribes. Back in the early 1700s, this area was popular among Spanish traders en route to Los Angeles along the Spanish Trail. Back then, the Spaniards referred to the route through the valley as *jornada de muerte*, or "journey of death." The discovery of a valley, with its abundant wild grasses and water supply, reduced the journey to Los Angeles by several days. The valley was ultimately named Las Vegas, which in Spanish means "the Meadows."

In 1855, a group of thirty Mormon missionaries built the first non-Indian settlement in the region. The missionaries' primary purpose was to teach the Paiute Indians farming techniques. The Paiutes rejected the teachings and periodically wound up raiding the fort until it was ultimately abandoned in 1857.

In the late nineteenth century, the discovery of minerals and precious metals established the area's mining industry. In 1905, the completion of a railway, which linked Southern California with Salt Lake City, helped to establish Las Vegas as a railroad town. The availability of water made Las Vegas an ideal rest stop. The railroad was the principal industry in Las Vegas for the next quarter century.

On May 15, 1905, Las Vegas was founded as a city. At the time of incorporation, the city encompassed just under twenty square miles, and had a mere 800 inhabitants.

In 1931, Las Vegas took the first step toward evolving into the mecca tourist destination it has become today. On March 19, 1931, gambling was legalized in the state of Nevada. One month later, the city issued six gambling licenses. In addition, the state's divorce laws were liberalized and state residency was made easier to attain. Thus, a "quickie" divorce could be attained after six weeks of residency. Short-term residents waiting for their divorce to be finalized typically stayed at "dude ranches," which represented the first generation of the world-famous Las Vegas Strip hotels. The area continued to grow dramatically in the early 1930s, as the construction of the Hoover Dam brought into the area an influx of construction workers.

By 1940, Las Vegas's population had grown to more than eight thousand. With the start of World War II, the defense industry began populating the valley. To this day, the defense industry continues to employ a significant number of valley residents. Following World War II, lavish resort hotels and gambling casinos began showcasing top-name entertainment.

Outgrowing Its Roots

Tourism and entertainment soon took over as the largest employer in the valley. By 1960, Las Vegas encompassed twenty-five square miles and had a population of more than 64,000. During the 1960s, Howard Hughes, along with a handful of large corporations, began building and buying hotel/casino properties, which resulted in dramatic growth. In Las Vegas, the term "gambling" evolved into "gaming," which soon became a very profitable and totally legitimate business. Throughout the 1970s and into the 1980s, large and well-known corporations continued to invest in the hotel/casino industry. By 1980 Las Vegas's population was more than 160,000 people.

≡ FAST FACT

The latest population prediction for Las Vegas is 2 million permanent residents and over 40 million annual visitors in 2005. In 2003, more than 35 million tourists generated over $32.8 billion in revenue for Las Vegas.

Starting in the mid-1980s, a period of unprecedented growth began. Annual population increases, averaging nearly 7 percent, caused the city's population to almost double between 1985 and 1995. This incredible growth continues to this day.

Happy 100th Birthday, Las Vegas!

On December 31, 2004, Las Vegas kicked off a massive, year-long centennial celebration. For a listing of scheduled events, point your Web browser to ✐*www.lasvegas2005.org.* According to the Web site, "The Centennial Celebration Committee has promised to commemorate our 100th Birthday as only Las Vegas can, by hosting a party that is bigger and brighter than the neon lights on the Las Vegas Strip! Our 100th Birthday will pay tribute to the people, places, things, and events that helped our city carve a rich and dynamic place in American and world history."

Las Vegas Builds Its Own "Walk of Fame"

One of the new attractions to open in conjunction with the Centennial event is the Las Vegas Walk of Fame. This attraction is part of the downtown Las Vegas revitalization project. It features 18-inch bronze gaming chips cemented into the walkways around the area by the Fremont Street Experience.

The bronze gaming chips feature well-known Vegas celebrities (such as Frank Sinatra, Dean Martin, Bugsy Siegel, and Howard Hughes) and all the celebrated performers, characters, and local historical figures who helped build and transform Las Vegas into the tourist destination it's become today.

≡ FAST FACT

Elvis Presley's first appearances in Vegas took place at the Frontier Hotel on May 5, 1956. Among the songs he performed were "Heartbreak Hotel," "Blue Suede Shoes," "Long Tall Sally," and "Money Honey." For nearly a decade after that, Elvis stayed away from concert appearances, so he could concentrate on making movies. In 1969, Elvis returned to Las Vegas, where he became a fixture at the Las Vegas Hilton.

Every month in 2005, eight to ten new gaming chips will be made a permanent part of the history of Las Vegas. In the future, new gaming chips will be added each year, expanding upon this new tradition that will be of interest to tourists visiting the downtown area.

Las Vegas Evolves and Expands

One thing you'll notice when you visit Las Vegas is the ever-present construction. This city is always expanding and evolving. As older or less profitable resorts and casinos close down, they're demolished and quickly replaced with bigger, more extravagant, and fancier mega-resorts located on or near the Strip.

During the time this book was written, in addition to many of the popular resorts and casinos undergoing massive expansion (including Caesars Palace, the Hard Rock Hotel & Casino, and the Bellagio), the Wynn Las Vegas Resort & Casino was being built. Scheduled to open in April 2005, this $2.5 billion property, built where the Desert Inn Casino used to stand, will contain fifty floors housing 2,701 guest rooms, eighteen restaurants, a 110,000-square-foot casino, plus 200,000 square feet of convention space, making it one of the largest (and most expensive to build) properties on the Strip.

FAST FACT

In 2003, more than 4,063 new hotel rooms and 1,045 time-share or condo/hotel units were added to resort and hotel properties in the Las Vegas area. By 2006, there will be more than 139,133 hotel rooms available to vacationers in Las Vegas.

Meanwhile, plans were underway to transform the Aladdin Resort & Casino into the Planet Hollywood Resort & Casino. Modeled after the famous theme restaurant chain, which displays authentic Hollywood memorabilia, this resort will ultimately become a new "hot spot" for those in search of the trendiest places in the world to stay.

The New Way to Ride

With so much expansion along the Strip), in July 2004 a state-of-the-art, above-ground monorail system opened to help transport people quickly from one end of the Strip to the other and avoid traffic. This was a privately funded $650 million construction project.

Phase one of the Disney World–like monorail system transports travelers from the MGM Grand to the Sahara, with additional stops along the way at Bally's/Paris, the Flamingo/Caesars Palace, Harrah's, the Las Vegas Convention Center, and the Las Vegas Hilton.

Eventually this transportation system will offer a direct route to and from the McCarran International Airport, as well as other destinations in downtown Las Vegas (Fremont Street) and along the Strip. Initially operating from 6:00 A.M. to 2:00 A.M., the monorail is expected to carry upward of 20 million people per year and will eventually run twenty-four hours per day.

▲ The Las Vegas Monorail system.   Photo provided by PR Newswire Photo Service.

The per-ride cost for the monorail is $3 per person; however, several discounted ticket options are available that make this a cost-effective mode of transportation as you explore Las Vegas (see Table

1-1). Especially at night when traffic along the Strip is at its worst and a taxi ride could cost upward of $15 to go from one end of the Strip to the other, the monorail system offers a fast and relatively inexpensive alternative.

TABLE 1-1
LAS VEGAS MONORAIL TICKET PRICES (SUBJECT TO CHANGE)

Number of Rides	Price per Person
1	$3.00
2	$5.75
10 (Usable over any period of days)	$25.00
1-Day Pass (unlimited rides)	$15.00
3-Day Pass (unlimited rides)	$40.00

 TRAVEL TIP

The Las Vegas Monorail can save you time and money as you travel around Las Vegas. The monorail glides above the often bumper-to-bumper traffic along Las Vegas Boulevard, at speeds reaching fifty miles per hour. The initial four-mile route (from one end of the Strip to the other) takes approximately fourteen minutes. For additional information about the monorail, point your Web browser to www. lvmonorail.com.

Las Vegas Is Unlike Any Other Vacation Destination

You've probably already discovered that Las Vegas is unlike any other vacation destination in the world. How memorable and exciting your own vacation will ultimately be, however, will be determined by how you decide to spend your time and money.

As you read this book, you'll discover the best places to stay; learn about exciting and memorable ways to spend your time; find out how to save money when booking your trip and experiencing all that Las Vegas has to offer; and discover the secrets for making your vacation as memorable as possible, based on your own interests (and what the people you're traveling with like to do).

From *The Everything® Family Guide to Las Vegas*, you'll discover how you and your family can best enjoy your vacation. But what's a family, exactly? For the purpose of this book, a "family" is defined as:

- Parents and/or grandparents traveling with young kids (preteens)
- Parents and/or grandparents traveling with teenagers (under twenty-one)
- Parents traveling with their adult children (age twenty-one and older)
- An adult couple traveling alone
- Adults traveling with their own parents or in-laws (senior citizens)

What this book doesn't offer are tips for getting rich quick by gambling at the various casinos. Sorry, you won't discover the ultimate secret for winning at blackjack here, but you will learn which of the casinos are best for you, based upon the type of gambling you enjoy.

The next chapter will speed your vacation planning by helping you get ready for your trip, pack your bags, and book your travel. Unlike many other tourist destinations, Las Vegas is open twenty-four hours per day, seven days per week, 365 days per year, so there will be plenty to see and do no matter when you arrive. Based on the activities you have in mind, things to consider when choosing your travel dates include the temperature and what conventions are taking place at the time of your visit. These and other considerations will also be explored in the next chapter.

CHAPTER 2

Planning Your Trip to Las Vegas

YOUR FIRST STEP IN PLANNING a Las Vegas vacation is to determine the timing and length of your trip and your overall budget. Once you know when your trip will begin and how many days you have to enjoy yourself, you can plan your itinerary and choose which of Las Vegas's many resorts, casinos, shows, and other attractions you want to experience firsthand. Then you can book your airfare and hotel accommodations, and possibly reserve a rental car.

The Weather in Las Vegas

In the summer, the temperature in Las Vegas can reach well over 100 degrees. Luckily—unless you're planning to play golf, spend time at your hotel's pool, or take a sightseeing tour to the Grand Canyon, for example—most of the activities surrounding the Las Vegas Strip are indoors, requiring you to be outdoors very little.

Before packing your suitcase, determine what the weather forecast will be during your visit. The following Web sites offer up-to-date weather forecasts for the Las Vegas area:

- *Las Vegas Review-Journal* newspaper—*www.lvrj.com*
- *Las Vegas Sun* newspaper—*www.lasvegassun.com*
- LasVegas.com Weather—*www.vegas.com*
- The National Weather Service—*www.wrh.noaa.gov*

- The Weather Channel—*www.weather.com*
- Yahoo! Weather—*http://weather.yahoo.com*

TRAVEL TIP

When it's hot outside, it's an excellent strategy to take a taxi or another form of transportation to get from one area of the Strip to another. In the evening or when it's cooler, walking between resort properties is a popular option. Distances between resort properties, even if they're located next door to each other along the Strip, can be considerable, so pace yourself.

Average Temperatures in Las Vegas

Table 2-1 lists the average temperatures throughout the year in the Las Vegas area. Keep in mind that even when the temperature is extremely hot outside, all of the hotels, restaurants, casinos, theaters, and indoor activities are air-conditioned, so pack and dress accordingly.

TABLE 2-1
LAS VEGAS TEMPERATURES

Month	High Temperature (°F)	Low Temperature (°F)
January	58°	34°
February	63°	39°
March	69°	44°
April	78°	51°
May	88°	60°
June	100°	69°
July	106°	74°
August	103°	74°
September	95°	66°
October	82°	54°
November	67°	43°
December	58°	34°

≡FAST FACT

The coldest day on record in Las Vegas was on January 13, 1963. The temperature dropped to a mere 8°F. The hottest day in Las Vegas was on July 24, 1985, when the temperature rose to 116°F.

The Best and Worst Times to Visit Las Vegas

Las Vegas is well known for hosting some of the world's largest conventions, concerts, and sporting events. When one of these major events is taking place, people from all over the world flock to Las Vegas to participate. In addition, Las Vegas has become a popular destination to celebrate certain holidays, such as New Year's Eve and Valentine's Day. During these times, Las Vegas's hotels and resorts are at or near capacity.

Unlike other tourist destinations, the price you'll pay for hotel accommodations in Las Vegas, especially at the mega-resorts located on or near the Strip, is directly related to how crowded Las Vegas is. For example, during a slow week or during the off-season, a room at a luxury resort may go for under $100 per night. That same room during a popular convention or holiday period could go for $500 or more per night. Thus, you'll often find the best travel deals during non-convention and non-holiday (non–peak travel) periods. Travel-related Web sites are among the very best places for finding the lowest-priced travel deals and discounted packages.

Peak Travel Times

Some of the most popular times to visit Las Vegas coincide with holidays, special events, and conventions. (See Table 2-2.) As a general rule, any three-day holiday weekend throughout the year is going to be a popular time to visit Las Vegas, so expect the city to be at or near capacity in terms of hotel availability. Plan on paying higher hotel and airfare rates, having to deal with larger crowds, and finding shows and attractions crowded or sold out.

If you'll plan to visit Las Vegas during a peak time, book early. For a list of special events, visit ✐*www.vegas.com.*

TABLE 2-2
THE MOST POPULAR TIMES TO VISIT LAS VEGAS

Holiday or Special Event	Date(s)
New Year's Eve	Late December/Early January
Consumer Electronics Show (CES)–Convention	First week of January
Super Bowl weekend	January
Valentine's Day	Mid-February
Men's Apparel Guild of CA (MAGIC)—Convention	Third week in February
President's Day weekend	February
NASCAR Winston Cup	Early March
ShoWest—Convention	Early to mid-March
St. Patrick's Day	March
March Madness (college basketball)	March
Spring break/Easter	March
National Association of Broadcasters Convention	Early April
Cinco de Mayo	May
Memorial Day weekend	May
CineVegas—Convention	Mid-June
July 4th weekend	Early July
Men's Apparel Guild of CA (MAGIC)—Convention	Mid- to late August
Labor Day weekend	September
Columbus Day weekend	October
Halloween	October 31
Thanksgiving weekend	Late November
Billboard Music Awards—Convention and televised awards show	Early December
National Finals Rodeo (NFR)	Early December
Christmas	December 25

Choosing Your Activities

If you'll be traveling with other people, including family members (adults or children), it's an excellent idea to have everyone help select which attractions and activities you want to check out. If everyone gets to share his or her own input in the itinerary planning, you're more likely to have a relaxing and enjoyable experience.

While the majority of your time in the Las Vegas area may be spent visiting the many resorts, casinos, theme parks, shows, restaurants, shops, spas, and attractions located on or near the Strip, you may also want to check out the Hoover Dam and Grand Canyon tours.

Perhaps you're traveling to Las Vegas to pamper yourself at one of the world-class spas the city has recently become famous for, or maybe you prefer to spend time relaxing at your resort's swimming pool or playing tennis or golf. If you enjoy exploring malls and unique shops, the shopping opportunities in Las Vegas are also well worth experiencing.

Based on the information in this book, you should be able to plan an itinerary that is designed just for you and your traveling companions. As the title suggests, this book describes just about *everything* you can see, do, and experience along the Las Vegas Strip and nearby. Keep pen and paper handy to take notes as you plan the ultimate trip!

Packed and Ready to Go: Choosing Your Luggage

Knowing what you want to bring with you to Las Vegas is the first step, but choosing your luggage and then actually packing your bags can be a challenging and somewhat cumbersome task, especially if you're traveling with kids.

Not everyone owns luggage that is suitable for airplane travel. If you need to buy luggage before your trip, the first step is to determine how you'll be using the luggage. The pieces of luggage a business traveler might purchase are very different from the luggage a family going on vacation would use. A family that takes just one trip per year doesn't need to spend as much on their luggage as an individual or family that travels often.

No matter who you are, it's an excellent strategy to purchase good-quality luggage. Luggage needs to be durable, especially if it will be checked at the airport, as opposed to being carried on an airplane. Some luggage is specifically designed to keep clothing, such as suits and dresses, wrinkle free, while other luggage pieces are designed to hold large amounts of casual clothing.

When you go shopping for new luggage, look carefully at the quality of the fabric or the leather. Tumi luggage (✍*www.tumi.com*), for example, is manufactured using Napa leather, which is a wonderfully soft, yet incredibly strong leather, or Tru-Ballistic nylon, which was originally developed for the military for use in bulletproof vests.

Some less-expensive luggage materials simply can't hold up to repeated abuse, which means it'll have to be fixed or replaced much sooner. No matter what style or brand of luggage you purchase, choosing luggage manufactured with durable fabric is critical.

Luggage Considerations

If you're buying luggage with wheels, evaluate the quality of those wheels. Do they spin smoothly? Do they wobble? This is important when you're dragging thirty to sixty pounds of luggage behind you through the airport—a trek that often requires walking over half a mile as you navigate your way around the busy airport concourses. The construction of the handle is also important. Look for handles that are strong, comfortable, and durable.

Overall, luggage needs to be strong and lightweight. All of the stitching should be tight, with no loose threads visible. Examine how well it's laid out. Are the compartments where you'd want to put them? Do the compartments provide added efficiency? Also, is all of the space in the bag usable for packing? Can any of the pockets be accessed from the outside?

When shopping for luggage, visit a specialty luggage store or a major department store that carries a lot of luggage styles from different manufacturers. Purchase luggage from a retailer that will fix or replace your luggage if it gets damaged or has a manufacturer's defect. Be sure you understand the manufacturer's warranty.

For families going on vacation together, the best pieces of luggage to purchase are large, soft-body suitcases that are on wheels. A large duffle bag on wheels (such as Tumi's style #6452 or #2252, either of which measures 30" × 14.5" × 13") aren't great for fancy suits or dresses, but they can hold a tremendous amount of casual clothing (and other items), and they're easy to carry or roll around an airport. Travelers planning to take along several formal outfits (dresses, gowns, sport jackets, tuxedos, or suits) should pack those garments in a garment bag. Suitcases with special suit compartments are only designed to hold one or two formal garments. Overpacking formal garments will cause them to wrinkle.

Dozens of different manufacturers offer luggage in a wide range of colors and styles, and at a variety of price points. Keep in mind that quality varies greatly between manufacturers. While two bags from different manufacturers might look similar, their overall quality level and price might be very different, which is why examining each bag before you purchase it is important.

Popular luggage manufacturers include Atlantic, American Tourister, Andiamo, Biggs & Riley, Dakota Metro, Hartmann, Kipling, Samsonite, Travelpro, and Tumi.

Stand Out in a Crowd

Since many pieces of luggage look alike, it's up to you to make your bag look different. To achieve this, so that the wrong person doesn't accidentally pick it up off the baggage claim conveyor belt, tie a bright-colored ribbon around the handle. Also, make sure that your identification tags are well attached to each bag. The tag should list your full name, address, and phone number. (Some people choose to use a work address and phone number for security reasons.) In addition to having this information on the outside tag, it's also an excellent idea to include it inside the bag, so that if your bag gets lost and the luggage tag falls off, the person who finds it can still contact you.

Safety First

Those paper luggage tags supplied by the airlines fall off bags too easily, so avoid using them. Many luggage companies will monogram your luggage. This is another way to make your bags more easily identifiable. If you're traveling to Las Vegas from outside of the United States or you're traveling overseas in conjunction with your Las Vegas trip, make a photocopy of your passport and place it inside your luggage, near the top.

 TRAVEL ESSENTIAL

Be sure to place durable identification tags (listing your name, address, and phone number) on all of your baggage, including your laptop computer. It is a good idea to place an identification tag inside your baggage as well.

Once luggage is checked with the airline, there really isn't anything you can do to protect it from receiving physical abuse. The only thing you can do is buy the best-made luggage you can find and afford. Incidents of baggage theft are minimal, but you should never pack jewelry, computer equipment, cameras, or other valuables in the luggage that will be checked at the airport. These items should be carried onto the plane in a carry-on bag.

Locking Your Luggage

One of the newer security measures implemented at all U.S. airports is that you are no longer supposed to lock your luggage before checking it, unless you're using a locking system that's been approved by the TSA (Transportation Security Administration), the organization in charge of security at all U.S. airports.

If you lock your luggage using a traditional lock, and the TSA chooses to hand-search your checked bags, the lock will be broken off. A lock that is "accepted and recognized" by the TSA means that the authorized screeners will be able to open and then relock your bags for security screening.

TRAVEL ESSENTIAL

Never pack anything valuable within your luggage, such as jewelry, camera equipment, consumer electronics, or anything that can't easily be replaced if lost or stolen. The airlines will typically *not* take responsibility for these items.

TSA screeners have tools for all TSA accepted and recognized locks that enable them to open the lock without damaging it if a physical inspection is required. Most locks on the market are *not* TSA-recognized. Even if a luggage lock is accepted and recognized by the TSA, there's still a chance it will be broken off or removed from your bag. Many screeners don't have the patience to remove the locks in the appropriate manner before searching your bag.

Some companies that offer TSA-accepted and -recognized luggage locks include the following:

- American Tourister Accessories
- Atlantic Luggage
- Austin House Travel Essentials
- Brookstone
- Eagle Creek Travel Safe
- EasyGo
- eBags
- Franzus Travel Smart
- Lewis N Clark
- Master Lock
- Prestolock SearchAlert
- Royal Traveller by Samsonite Accessories
- Samsonite Accessories
- Samsonite Luggage
- Sharper Image
- Target Embark
- Voltage Valet

Packing Tips from the Pros

There are several useful packing tips you can employ to ensure that you don't forget anything and that you pack the most efficient way possible. Most important is that you should never check any items that you must have when you get off the plane. This includes prescription medications, your travel documents, your identification and other wallet items, and eyeglasses.

TRAVEL ESSENTIAL

A government-issued ID (driver's license, passport, or military-issued ID) must be kept with each adult traveler at all times. You'll need to present your ID, along with airline ticket (and/or boarding pass), several times during the airport security screening and airport check-in process. Your ID and travel documentation should be kept in your pocket, not in a packed suitcase or within your carry-on.

If you're planning to pack fancy clothes that can't get wrinkled, use a garment bag or a suitcase with a special compartment designed for suits and dresses. To save space, consider rolling casual clothes and placing them in your luggage. This works best with jeans and casual pants, socks, casual shirts, sweaters, and sweatshirts, for example. Place cosmetics, shampoos, perfume bottles, toothpaste, and anything else that could leak in sealable plastic bags.

While packing your luggage, make a list of each bag's contents and leave the list or a copy of it at home. If your bag gets lost or stolen, having a list of missing items will help you get reimbursed by the airline or insurance company. Keep your bags with you at all times until they are safely checked with the airline at a designated baggage check-in location.

Do not pack any items that the TSA has put on its list of things that cannot be checked or carried on to an aircraft. Keep in mind, your luggage will be x-rayed and could also be hand-searched.

Packing Your Carry-On Bag

A carry-on bag is a small piece of luggage you take onboard the airplane with you. You are allowed one carry-on in addition to one personal item, such as a laptop computer, purse, small backpack, briefcase, or camera case.

The TSA will screen any carry-on baggage that will fit through the x-ray machine, however, each airline also has specific size requirements for carry-ons. They must fit under your seat or in the overhead compartment located above your seat. Be sure to have a luggage tag on each of your bags, including your carry-ons, and never leave any bags unattended at the airport, even for a moment.

What to Pack in Your Carry-On Bag

Within your carry-on bag(s), it's important to pack all of your valuables, including your jewelry, camera, video camera, laptop computer, iPod/Walkman, and other electronics you'll be taking to Las Vegas. You'll also want to bring on the airplane with you anything that you can't afford to be without for more than a few hours, such as your eyeglasses, medications/prescriptions, and contact lenses and supplies.

Also, consider packing a book, one or more magazines, and stereo headphones in your carry-on, along with anything else that might help you pass the time on the flight or if the flight is delayed.

TRAVEL ESSENTIAL

Many flights lasting longer than a few hours offer some type of in-flight movie or video entertainment. On most airlines, you can rent a headset for between $2 and $5 to watch this entertainment. You can, however, bring your own Walkman stereo headphones and save the headset rental fee. Noise-reduction headphones work the best on flights.

If you're traveling with kids or teens, bring along a Nintendo Game Boy Advance (or another portable video-game system), books, crayons and paper, and other activities that don't generate a lot of noise and that your kids can use while they're sitting in their seats. Travel-size versions of popular board games also offer plenty of entertainment value and are easy to carry.

 TRAVEL TIP

If you have a laptop computer with a built-in DVD drive or a portable DVD player, you can watch your own movie (which you bring with you) on the flight. NetFlix (*www.netflix.com*), for example, is an excellent service for renting DVDs, without having to pay late fees or return the DVDs to a specific location. Having your kids watch their favorite DVD movies during a flight is a perfect way to pass the time.

Keep in mind that for your kids, the novelty of being onboard an airplane will typically wear off a few minutes after take-off. After take-off your kids will have to stay in their seats during much of the flights to and from Las Vegas. Thus, it's important to have the toys, magazines, books, activities, and snacks they like on hand in order to keep them entertained or at least occupied.

Remember, each ticketed passenger is allowed just one carry-on bag, plus a personal item. Especially if you're traveling with children, consider including a change of clothes, or at least an extra T-shirt and pair of shorts in your carry-on bag. If your other bags get lost or you spill something on yourself during the flight, you'll have something to change into in a pinch.

Some people have problems with excessive pressure in their ears when they fly. If you think you might have an ear problem, bring along chewing gum and consider purchasing earplugs that you can wear during the flight. Most pharmacies and drugstores, as well as many shops in airports, carry a product called EarPlanes (manufactured by Cirrus Air Technologies, *www.cirrushealthcare.com*) for under $5 a pair. These are designed to help travelers who have a head cold or the flu, or who tend to suffer from earaches when flying. Special child-size EarPlanes are also available.

Packing Your Regular Luggage

Checked baggage is luggage you check at the ticket counter or at curbside. It will not be accessible during your flight. The TSA has some tips for packing your checked baggage that will help to speed your trip and ensure that your checked luggage makes the flight with you.

For example, don't put film in your checked baggage, as the screening equipment will damage it. Pack shoes, boots, sneakers, and other footwear on top of other contents in your luggage. Avoid packing food and drink items in checked baggage. And don't stack piles of books or documents on top of each other; spread them out within your baggage.

TRAVEL ESSENTIAL

If your luggage gets damaged or lost by the airline, it's critical that claims be made in person, before leaving the airport. Should a problem arise, visit your airline's lost baggage counter, located near the baggage claim area at the airport.

You should avoid overpacking your bag. The TSA screener must be able to easily reseal your bag if it is opened for inspection. If possible, distribute your clothes and belongings throughout several bags as opposed to overpacking one bag. Be sure to check with your airline or travel agent to determine maximum weight limitations per bag. The maximum weight per bag on domestic flights is typically fifty pounds. Each ticketed passenger can typically check two or three bags, depending on the airline. If your bag is too heavy and exceeds the airline's weight or size limit, or if you try to check too many bags, you will be billed extra by the airline at the time you check in. These fees add up fast and the airlines have become very strict about enforcing their luggage guidelines.

 TRAVEL TIP

Very few airlines still serve meals on flights. Some still offer small snacks, but most now sell meals or snacks, often at rather high prices. Especially if you're traveling with children or have a long flight to or from Las Vegas, it's an excellent idea to bring along your own food on to the plane. Complimentary soft drinks and water, however, are still available on virtually all commercial flights. Alcoholic beverages can be purchased.

Traveling with Infants Just Got Easier

If you'll be traveling with one or more infants, chances are you'll need to pack a wide range of products, including diapers, toys, a child safety seat, etc. While you'll certainly need to bring along all of the products you typically use, a company called Babies Travel Lite (888-450-LITE/☞*www.babiestravellite.com*) offers a wide range of baby products, diapers, meals, formulas, health-care supplies, and other items that can be ordered by phone or online, then shipped directly to your Las Vegas-area hotel room (and be waiting for you upon your arrival).

This service will help you determine exactly what supplies you need and allow you to travel with considerably less baggage. In addition to offering products separately, the company has created diaper, mealtime, and bathtime "baby bundles," which offer everything you'll need, prepackaged.

All products sold are name-brand and offered at discounted prices. You'll pay an extra service charge per order (which gets reduced if you order early, up to fifteen days before your trip), plus any delivery/shipping charges.

Travel Budget Checklist

Use the travel budget checklist in Table 2-3 to help you approximate the cost of your Las Vegas trip in advance. Planning your itinerary before you leave, and setting budgetary spending limits, will help you enjoy your vacation without going into unexpected debt or spending outside of your budget.

TABLE 2-3
CALCULATING YOUR TRAVEL COSTS

Expense	Calculation	Totals
Adult airfares	$_____ per ticket × _____ (# of adults)	$_____
Child airfares	$_____ per ticket × _____ (# of children)	$_____
Rental car	$_____ per day/week × _____ (# of days/weeks)	$_____
Car insurance/gas	$_____ per day × _____ (# of days)	$_____
Transportation	$_____ per trip × _____ (# of people) × _____ (# of trips)	$_____
Hotel/motel	$_____ per night × _____ (# of rooms) × _____ (# of nights)	$_____
Show ticket(s)	$_____ per ticket × _____ (# of people)	$_____
Show ticket(s)	$_____ per ticket × _____ (# of people)	$_____
Show ticket(s)	$_____ per ticket × _____ (# of people)	$_____
Other attraction	$_____ per ticket × _____ (# of people)	$_____
Other attraction	$_____ per ticket × _____ (# of people)	$_____
Other attraction	$_____ per ticket × _____ (# of people)	$_____
Other attraction	$_____ per ticket × _____ (# of people)	$_____
Tours	$_____ per ticket × _____ (# of people)	$_____
Adult nighttime entertainment	$_____ per person × _____ (# of nights)	$_____
Child nighttime entertainment	$_____ per person × _____ (# of nights)	$_____

Expense	Calculation	Totals
Total meal budget	$____ per person × ____ (# of meals) × ____ (# of days)	$____
Snack/drink budget	$____ per person × ____ (# of days)	$____
Souvenir budget	$____ per person	$____
Babysitting	$____ per child (per hour) × ____ (# of hours) × ____ (# of children)	$____
Kennel costs	$____ per day × ____ (# of days) × ____ (# of pets)	$____
Airport parking	$____ per day × ____ (# of days)	$____
Gambling budget		$____
Other		$____
Other		$____
Other		$____
Approximate vacation expenses total:		$____

Getting to and from Las Vegas

People come to Las Vegas from all over the world using every popular mode of transportation, including plane, car, and train. This section describes some of your travel options.

Making Airline Reservations

All of the airlines listed in this chapter offer competitive rates and travel packages to Las Vegas, so be sure to shop around for the best airfares and flights.

As a general rule, you want to book your flight as far in advance as possible. Many airlines offer their best prices if you book and pay for your tickets twenty-one days in advance. You can, however, also obtain good fares if you make your reservations (and pay for your airline tickets) fourteen days or seven days early. When making travel plans, try to have the most flexible schedule possible, and, if your schedule permits, you'll almost always get a better airfare if your stay includes a Saturday night.

Keep in mind that with "discounted" or "special" airfares, the tickets are usually not refundable and not changeable. If you can change the flight, the change fee is usually $50 to $100 per ticket, plus the price difference in the airfare itself. Tickets purchased from a discount online service, such as Priceline.com or Hotwire.com, cannot be changed or refunded.

If you want to use frequent-flier miles to book your airline ticket(s) to Las Vegas, keep in mind that seats may be difficult to reserve during peak travel periods, so make your reservations early. The advantages of using a frequent-flier ticket are that it's free, plus most airlines allow you to change your travel plans at the last minute, with no penalties or fees.

≡FAST FACT

Cross-country, red-eye (overnight) flights are almost always the cheapest flights available. While most people hate flying all night, you can sometimes save up to several hundred dollars when travel-ing between coasts via a red-eye flight on any airline. These flights are typically not ideal if you're traveling with kids, since you'll be flying all night and it will dramatically disrupt their regular sleeping schedule.

When making airline reservations by phone (calling the airline directly), always ask reservation representatives for the absolute best airfares available. After a fare is quoted to you, ask again if it is the best deal. Next, ask if there are other flights to and from Las Vegas at about the same time that are less expensive.

You often won't be quoted the absolute lowest prices the first time you ask. Also, check the travel section of your local newspa-per for advertised special fares and promotions. By calling the air-line directly, you can often make a reservation that will be held for twenty-four hours without having to pay for the ticket, so make an unpaid reservation and then shop around by calling additional airlines and surfing the Web.

There are several alternatives available when it comes to securing the best airfares. You can:

- Contact the airline directly by phone.
- Visit the airline's own Web site.
- Surf the Internet and visit the various travel-related Web sites (such as Hotwire.com, Travelocity.com, Orbitz.com, etc.).
- Call a travel agency and have them do the busywork for you.

Using a Travel Agent or Service

Because Las Vegas is such a popular destination, travel agents and travel services can be helpful when it comes to planning a trip to Las Vegas. You can find a travel agent in the Yellow Pages, but it's always a better idea to use a travel agent who comes highly recommended by a friend, coworker, or relative. Travel agents can be extremely helpful and save you money, but some will purposely quote you higher airfares, since they're receiving a commission from the airline based on the price of the tickets they sell. If you're a member of AAA or have an American Express card, both of these companies offer full-service and reliable travel agencies, available either in person or by telephone.

 TRAVEL TIP

Flight delayed? Track your flights with ease! Be sure to provide people you're meeting (or those who are picking you up) with your appropriate airline, flight number, and departure time/date information. With this information, anyone can contact your airline, visit your airline's Web site or go to ✎http://flighttracker.lycos.com, ✎www.travelocity.com, ✎www.orbitz.com, or ✎www.fly.faa.gov to obtain up-to-the-minute details about your flight and learn about any delays.

Travel agents have computer systems that allow them to search for flight availability on all airlines at once. Most travel agents will be happy to work with you over the telephone, so it's not necessary to take time out of your busy schedule to visit a travel agent's office.

As you choose the actual times of your flights, if you plan on sleeping during the flight and book an early-morning or late-night flight, beware. When it comes to tourism, the Las Vegas airport is one of the busiest in the world, and with tourists and family travelers going to and from Las Vegas come cute babies and adorable young children who tend to spend the first few moments of a flight happy and cheerful, but can wind up screaming and crying through the rest of the trip. Sure, kids are wonderful, but if you're trying to sleep on a plane and you're surrounded by crying babies, you're not going to be a happy traveler.

Save a Fortune: Book Your Vacation Online

One of the cheapest ways to book a Las Vegas vacation is to go online and visit several travel-related Web sites, the Web sites for individual airlines, plus the Vegas.com Web site. By shopping around online, you'll typically find the lowest airfares and the best-discounted travel packages. The more time you invest shopping for the best travel deals, the more likely you are to save money.

Also, the more flexible you are in terms of your travel, the more money you'll save when booking airline tickets. As mentioned, if you book your ticket twenty-one days, fourteen days, or seven days in advance, plus have a Saturday night stay included in your itinerary, you'll probably get the lowest airfares. However, some of the online travel-related Web sites specialize in last-minute travel and can save you up to 60 percent off published airfares, even if you book twenty-four hours before your departure.

While any of the travel-related Web sites listed in this section will save you money as you book your airfare, hotel, and/or rental car (separately or as a package), you'll typically have to make concessions, such as purchasing airline tickets that cannot be changed or refunded. In some situations, in order to save the most money possible, you won't be able to select the exact airline you'll be flying on or your exact travel times.

Before using any of the travel-related Web sites, be sure you understand exactly how they work. Any of these Web sites can be used to find and purchase discounted airfares, hotel accommodations, and a rental car (either separately or as a travel package). In some cases, if you book your airfare and hotel (and/or rental car) at the same time using one of these services, you'll save even more money.

The Ultimate Online Source: Vegas.Com

The Vegas.com (*www.vegas.com*) Web site has become the official clearinghouse for all tourist information having to do with Las Vegas. From this Web site, you can book your airline tickets, hotel accommodations, and rental car, purchase show and attraction tickets, and learn all about what there is to do in the Las Vegas area.

In terms of making your travel arrangements, be sure to check Vegas.com for discounted travel packages (including airfare and hotel), plus last-minute travel deals. On the main page of this Web site is also a listing of upcoming special events, such as concerts.

The Popular Travel-Related Web Sites

Table 2-4 gives a brief description of what each of the popular travel-related Web sites offers. When using any of these services, be sure to indicate the number of adults, children, and senior citizens traveling. To ensure that everyone winds up on the same flights, it's important to book everyone's travel simultaneously. Once the flights are purchased using any of these Web sites, you can contact the airline directly to confirm seat assignments and make any special travel arrangements, such as wheelchair service. You'll want to do this as soon as you book your tickets, to ensure that you and your kids will be seated together on the airplane.

To make sure you're getting the lowest possible airfares, consider pricing out the day prior and the day after your ideal departure and return dates. If there are multiple airports in your city (or nearby), be sure to check each of those departure airports separately. Typically, you'll also find lower rates if you travel on Tuesdays, Wednesdays, and Thursdays.

TABLE 2-4
POPULAR TRAVEL-RELATED WEB SITES

Travel-Related Web Site	Web Site Address (URL)	Description
AOL Travel (Keyword: *Travel*)	*www.aol.com*	Enter your travel dates; then see available flights, their prices, and departure and arrival times displayed.
CheapTickets	*www.cheaptickets.com*	Enter your travel dates; then see available flights, their prices, and departure and arrival times displayed.
Discount Fares	*www.discount fares.com*	Enter your travel dates; then see available flights, their prices, and departure and arrival times displayed.
Expedia	*www.expedia.com*	Enter your travel dates; then see available flights, their prices, and departure and arrival times displayed.
Hotwire	*www.hotwire.com*	You can often get the best deals with Hotwire; however, you won't find out your specific airline or exact flight times until you've purchased your nonrefundable, non-changeable tickets. Once you pick your travel dates, the service will quote you a price for round-trip airfare (or airfare with hotel and/or rental car). The service will find available flights, but while they won't be red-eye flights or require more than one connection each way, they might not be the most convenient flights, either.

Travel-Related Web Site	Web Site Address (URL)	Description
LastMinuteTravel	www.lastminutetravel.com	Enter your travel dates; then see available flights, their prices, and departure and arrival times displayed.
Orbitz	www.orbitz.com	This service allows you to enter your travel dates, then displays available flights, their prices, and departure and arrival times. One feature of Orbitz is that with one click of the mouse, you can check airfares for the day before and day after your ideal departure date to find the lowest possible airfare.
Priceline	www.priceline.com	"Name your own price" is this service's slogan. Ideally, if you shop around to get the best prices from other travel-related Web sites, you can bid 30 to 50 percent less and often save a bundle on round-trip airfares. The drawback is, you can only choose your travel dates, not your travel times or airline. You don't know what flights you'll be on until after you've purchased your nonchangeable and nonrefundable airfares. This is an excellent service for saving money, but make sure you understand exactly how it works before using it.

Travel-Related Web Site	Web Site Address (URL)	Description
SideStep	www.sidestep.com	This Web site automatically searches a handful of other travel-related Web sites and airline Web sites to find you the lowest airfares. You'll be required to first download a free program from the Web to use this service. One nice feature is that SideStep searches budget airlines, such as JetBlue and AirTran, along with more than 580 other major airlines.
Travelocity	www.travelocity.com	Enter your travel dates; then see available flights, their prices, and departure and arrival times displayed.
Yahoo! Travel	http://travel.yahoo.com	Enter your travel dates; then see available flights, their prices, and departure and arrival times displayed.

Travel Insurance to Protect Your Vacation Investment

Even if you purchase nonchangeable and nonrefundable airfares, if you or someone you're traveling with becomes ill or there's some type of emergency, having travel insurance will allow you to recoup your airfares and other expenses if you're unable to go on the trip. You will, however, have to prepurchase the optional travel insurance, plus obtain a note from a doctor indicating why you could not travel. Buying optional travel insurance is often a good investment, especially if you're traveling with children. Some travel insurance will also give you added financial coverage if your luggage is lost or stolen, or if you experience any type of emergency (medical or otherwise) during your trip.

Travel Guard (☎800-826-1300/✎*www.travelguard.com*) is one popular travel insurance company. Travel Guard International and its affiliate companies provide integrated travel insurance, assistance, and emergency travel services throughout the world. Travel Guard offers customer service, available twenty-four hours a day, seven days a week through its service center.

TripInsuranceStore.com (☎888-407-3854/✎*www.TripInsurance Store.com*) is a Web site that allows you to shop for travel insurance online and obtain price quotes from more than 100 insurance companies. Obtaining a free, no-obligation price quote takes just minutes.

Any travel agent can help you purchase travel insurance, plus many of the travel-related Web sites allow you to purchase it from a specific company when making your airline ticket purchase.

Airport Security Information

Security is extremely tight at all U.S. airports. Be sure to arrive at the airport at least sixty to ninety minutes prior to your scheduled departure time (for domestic flights) and have your driver's license, military ID, or passport ready to show multiple times at various security checkpoints, including the airline ticket counter.

TRAVEL ESSENTIAL

To save time getting through airport security, be sure to pack according to TSA guidelines. The Transportation and Security Administration has compiled a detailed list of items that can and can't be carried onto an airplane, plus a list of items that cannot be checked within your luggage. For a complete list of what you can and can't take with you on an airplane, point your Web browser to ✎*www.tsa.gov*.

There is a wide range of items, such as pocketknives, golf clubs, and scissors, that *cannot* be taken aboard any flight as part of a carry-on. For additional security information, point your Web browser to the Transportation Security Administration's Web site (✐www.tsa.gov).

Passing Through Airport Security

Keep available your airline boarding pass and government-issued photo ID for each adult traveler until you exit the airport's security checkpoint. Place the following items within your carry-on baggage prior to entering the screening checkpoint:

- Mobile phone
- Keys
- Loose change
- Money clips
- PDAs
- Lighters
- Large pieces of jewelry or metal you're wearing
- Metal hair accessories
- Large belt buckles

In addition:

- Take your laptop and video camera out of their cases.
- Take off any outer jackets (you do not have to remove your sport jacket).
- Remove your shoes, if they contain metal.

🧳 TRAVEL TIP

When going through airport security, keep a close eye on your children as well as your carry-ons, especially your laptop computer and electronics. If you're taken aside for further security screening, make sure the security personnel gather up all of your belongings and they remain in your line of sight at all times. Even at airport security checkpoints, theft is a concern.

If you're traveling with children, be sure to discuss the airport security procedures with them, in advance, so they don't get frightened. Remind your kids not to joke about threats, such as bombs or explosives. Advise your children that their bags (including their backpacks, portable video-game systems, dolls, etc.) will be put in the x-ray machine and will come out at the other end and be returned to them.

TRAVEL ESSENTIAL

Be sure to allow extra time to get through security if you're traveling with kids. If you're traveling with an infant, he must be removed from his stroller or infant carrier so that he can be individually screened. Do not attempt to hand your child to the TSA personnel. If your child can walk unassisted, it's best to have him walk through the airport's metal detector independently.

McCarran International Airport

The closest airport to Las Vegas and the Las Vegas Strip is McCarran International Airport. The airport itself is divided into two separate terminals. Terminal 1 is used mainly by domestic airlines and has four main gates (labeled A, B, C, and D). Terminal 2 is used primarily by international airlines and domestic charter services.

≡FAST FACT

For general information about McCarran International Airport, call ☎702-261-5211. For parking information, call ☎702-261-5121. For flight information (all airlines), call ☎702-261-INFO. To have someone paged within the airport, call ☎702-261-5733 and press 3. For lost and found, call ☎702-261-5134. You can also visit the airport's Web site at ✑www.mccarran.com.

The airlines listed in Table 2-5 fly to and from McCarran International Airport. (Airlines are subject to change.) Not all of these airlines will service your home city, so call the airline to inquire about flight availability.

TABLE 2-5
AIRLINE DIRECTORY

Airline	Toll-Free Phone Number	Web Site	Terminal Location Within McCarran Airport
AeroMexico	800-AERO-MEX	www.aeromexico.com	T2
Air Canada	800-776-3000	www.aircanada.ca	T2
AirTran Airways	800-247-8726	www.airtran.com	D
AirTransat	866-847-1112	www.airtransat.com	T2
Alaska Airlines	800-426-0333	www.alaskaair.com	A
Allegiant Air	877-202-6444	www.allegiant-air.com	D
Aloha Airlines	800-367-5250	www.alohaairlines.com	C
American Airlines	800-433-7300	www.aa.com	D
American Trans Air (ATA)	800-I-FLY-ATA	www.ata.com	T2
AmericaWest Airlines/British Airways	800-2-FLY-AWA	www.americawest.com	A, B
Aviacsa	188-85-28-42-27	www.aviacsa.com	T2
Belair	Contact your travel agent	www.belair-airlines.com	T2
Champion Air (CA)	800-387-6951	www.championair.com	A
Continental	800-525-0280	www.continental.com	A
Delta Airlines	800-221-1212	www.delta.com	D

Airline	Toll-Free Phone Number	Web Site	Terminal Location Within McCarran Airport
Frontier Airlines	800-432-1359	www.flyfrontier.com	D
Hawaiian Air	800-367-5320	www.hawaiianair.com	T2
HMY Airways	866-248-6789	www.hmyairways.com	T2
Japan Airlines (JAL)	800-JAL-FONE	www.jal.co.jp/en/	T2
JetBlue Airways	800-JET-BLUE	www.jetblue.com	A
Jetsgo	866-440-0441	www.jetsgo.net	T2
Mexicana	800-531-7921	www.mexicana.com	T2
Midwest Express	800-452-2022	www.midwest-express.com	D
My Travel	Call your travel agent	www.uk.mytravel.com	T2
Northwest Airlines	800-225-2525	www.nwa.com	D
NWA Northwest Airlines	800-225-2525	www.nwa.com	D
OmniAir International (OAI)	877-718-8901	www.omniairintl.com	T2
Philippine Airlines	800-435-9725	www.philippineair.com	T2
Ryan International Airlines	Call your travel agent	www.flyryan.com	T2
SkyService Airlines	877-485-6060	www.skyserviceairlines.com	T2
Skywest United Express	800-453-9417	www.united.com	D

Airline	Toll-Free Phone Number	Web Site	Terminal Location Within McCarran Airport
Song Airlines	800-359-7664	www.flysong.com	D
Southeast Airlines (Seal)	800-FLY-SEAL	www.flyseal.com	T2
Southwest	800-I-FLY-SWA	www.southwest.com	C
Spirit Airlines	800-772-7117	www.spiritair.com	D
Sun Country Airlines	800-FLY-N-SUN	www.suncountry airlines.com	D
Ted (United)	800-225-5833	www.flyted.com	D
Thomas Cook	Call your travel agent	www.thomas cook.com	T2
TransMeridian Airlines (TMA)	866-I-FLY-TMA	www.iflytma.com	T2
United/ Lufthansa	800-241-6522	www.united.com	D
US Airways	800-428-4322	www.usairways.com	D
Virgin Atlantic	800-862-8621	www.virgin-atlantic. com	T2
West Jet	888-WEST-JET	www.westjet.com	T2

A handful of other airlines also operate charter flights to and from McCarran International Airport and other major U.S. cities and foreign countries.

 TRAVEL TIP

Save money by using public transportation to get to the airport in your home city. It'll almost always be cheaper than parking your own car at the airport. The cheapest option is to have a friend or family member drop you off at the airport and pick you up when you return. Another option is to use a door-to-door shuttle bus service, which is almost always cheaper than a taxi, limo, or town car service.

Services available at McCarran International Airport include ticket counters for all airlines, shops, restaurants, full-service banks, ATM machines, a chapel, lockers and baggage-check room, a smoking lounge, information desks, foreign currency exchanges, slot machine gaming areas (for adults only), taxi and shuttle bus ground transportation desks, shoeshine stands, Internet-access kiosks, access to many rental car companies (Hertz, Avis, Budget, National, and others), parking, a post office, newsstands, a full-service fitness center, and airline clubs (membership required).

While there are shops, newsstands, and bookstores, for example, scattered throughout all of the airport's terminals, within the Esplanade area of the airport, located on Level 2 of Terminal 1, you'll find more than two dozen shops as well as several places to eat.

JUST FOR PARENTS

Work out while waiting for your flight. There's a full-service fitness center within McCarran International Airport. Located at Terminal 1, Level 2 (above the north Baggage Claim), it's the first of its kind fitness center located inside a major U.S. airport. The 24 Hour Fitness facility offers shower and locker room facilities, steam room and dry sauna, a cardiovascular workout area, and a full complement of exercise equipment. For more information, call ☎702-261-3971.

Getting from the Airport to the Strip

Once you arrive at McCarran International Airport, the Las Vegas Strip is just a short drive away by rental car, limousine, or taxi. Shuttle buses are also available that will take you directly to your hotel. From baggage claim, follow the appropriate signs to your desired ground transportation. Taxicabs are available on the east side of baggage claim, outside door exits one through five.

It is not necessary to preschedule a taxi from the airport to your hotel, since taxis will be waiting in the designated area. Airport personnel are available on the taxi curb to assist passengers.

Keep in mind that most taxicabs do not accept credit cards or checks. The average price for one to five passengers to travel by taxi from the airport to a Las Vegas–area hotel or resort is between $10 and $20, depending on the area of the Strip you're going to. (Tips and a $1.20 airport fee are not included in the price listed on the taxi meter.) Table 2-6 lists taxi companies that service the Las Vegas area.

TABLE 2-6
TAXI DIRECTORY

Taxi Company	Phone Number
Checker/Yellow/Star Taxicab	702-873-2000
ANLV/Ace/Union/Vegas-Western Taxicab	702-736-8383
Whittlesea/Henderson Taxi	702-384-6111
Western Cab Company	702-736-8000
Desert Cab Company	702-386-9102
Nellis Cab Company	702-248-1111
Lucky Cab Company	702-477-7555
Deluxe Taxicab Service	702-568-7700

Limousine Services

Limousine and town car or sedan service should be scheduled in advance. Check with your hotel's concierge for discounts and recommendations. These services offer door-to-door service throughout the Las Vegas area. Airport trips are often on a flat-fee basis, while other trips are charged by the hour. Major credit cards are typically accepted. The hourly fee for a limo is usually $35 to $60 an hour for an eight-passenger vehicle.

A flat-rate fare from the airport should run $35 to $40 (plus tip). Some of the limo services operating in the Las Vegas area are listed, in alphabetical order, in Table 2-7.

TABLE 2-7
LIMOUSINE DIRECTORY

Limousine Company	Phone Number
24 Hour Limo	702-384-9998
A Hook Up Entertainment	702-649-4328
A Limousine Service	702-739-6265
A-Humvee 4x4 Limo	702-275-4323
AKA Luxury Limo Service	702-257-7433
Ambassador Limousines	702-362-6200
Anytime Limo Service	702-641-8300
A-Star Limousine	702-275-4323
Bell Trans	702-739-7990
Fox Limousine	702-597-0400
Highroller Limousine	702-868-5600
Lucky Limousine	702-733-7300
LVL	702-736-1419
On Demand Sedan & Limousine	702-876-2222
Premier Luxury Coach	702-365-9999
Presidential Limousine	702-731-5577
Rent-A-Limo	702-791-5466
Silver Star Limousine	702-251-8105
Western Limousine Service	702-382-7100

Airport Shuttle Services

The following shuttle bus services are available to and from the airport and the Las Vegas Strip (and surrounding areas). All prices and hours of operation are subject to change. These shuttles can be met directly outside the airport's baggage claim area. Prices listed are one way, per person.

Airport Shuttle

☎702-798-5557 or ☎800-259-0515

✐*www.vegasride.com*

Contact the company for reservations and rates.

Bell Trans Shuttle Bus

✆702-739-7990

✉*www.bell-trans.com*

Hours: 7:45 A.M. to midnight

Strip hotels: $4.75

Downtown hotels: $6

Off-Strip hotels: $6

C.L.S.

✆702-740-4050

Hours: 24 hours

Strip hotels: $4.75 to $9

Downtown hotels: $6.50 to $12

Gray Line/Coach USA/Express Shuttle

✆702-739-5700

Hours: 7:00 A.M. to 1:30 A.M.

Strip hotels: $4.75

Downtown hotels: $6.50

Off-Strip hotels: $9 to $12

Las Vegas Limousine

✆702-736-1419

Hours: 7:00 A.M. to 2:00 A.M.

Strip hotels: $4.25

Downtown hotels: $5.50

Off-Strip hotels: $7 to $21

Showtime

✆702-261-6101

Hours: 7:00 A.M. to 11:30 P.M.

Strip hotels: $4.25

Downtown hotels: $6

Getting to Las Vegas by Train

Amtrak service to Las Vegas is available from most major U.S. cities. For travel schedules, rates, and other information, call ✆800-USA-RAIL or visit the Amtrak Web site at ✐*www.amtrak.com.*

Amtrak offers travel discounts to all students as well as to AAA members who present their membership card when purchasing a train ticket. Amtrak train tickets can be purchased from many travel agents, by visiting any Amtrak ticket office, or by calling Amtrak directly and using a major credit card.

Getting to Las Vegas by Bus

For information, schedules, and rates for Greyhound bus service to and from Las Vegas, call ✆800-229-9424, or visit the company's Web site at ✐*www.greyhound.com.* Discounted rates are available to students, military personnel, and senior citizens. No advance reservations are required, but to get the best rates and ensure a seat, they're recommended.

Greyhound operates more than 120 terminals nationwide where tickets are sold. Greyhound accepts cash and traveler's checks, as well as major credit cards issued in the United States. In addition to its major terminals, Greyhound offers ticket services at nearly 1,800 independent agents nationwide. Depending on where you purchase your bus ticket, you may be subject to a $15 service charge.

In Las Vegas, the Greyhound terminal is located at 200 South Main Street and can be reached by calling ✆702-384-9561. It's open twenty-four hours per day, seven days per week.

When You Get There . . .

This chapter offered some basic information about the Las Vegas area and suggested how to find and purchase airfares at the lowest available price. In the next two chapters, you'll determine whether renting a car while in Las Vegas is worthwhile for you, plus discover strategies for choosing the ideal hotel/resort accommodations (and save money in the process).

CHAPTER 3

Renting a Car

VIRTUALLY EVERYTHING THERE IS to see and do in Las Vegas (with the possible exception of taking a tour of the Grand Canyon and/or the Hoover Dam) can be found on or near the famous Las Vegas Strip. When it comes to getting around town, you have several options, including taxis, shuttle buses, free trams, the Las Vegas Monorail, walking, or renting a car.

Car Rental: A Worthwhile Convenience?

If your exploration and traveling around Las Vegas will be kept to a minimum, a rental car may be a nice convenience but not a necessity. On the other hand, if you want to explore all there is to see and do along the Strip (and neighboring areas), renting a car can be a worthwhile investment in terms of saving money, time, and patience, especially if you're traveling with kids or teens.

Each time you step into a taxi cab in Las Vegas, plan on spending between $6 and $15 each way. The money you spend on taxis will add up quickly as you travel between mega-resorts and nearby attractions. All of the mega-resorts offer free self-parking. All also offer valet parking, either for free or for a small fee.

TRAVEL ESSENTIAL

If you're planning to walk between destinations along the Strip, keep in mind that finding a taxi cab anywhere but in front of a resort property is extremely difficult. The taxi drivers are not allowed to stop in the middle of the street, as they do in New York City, for example. Thus, if you get tired of walking, you'll have to make your way to the nearest taxi stand at a resort or hotel.

The Pros and Cons of Renting a Car

If you're traveling with young kids, having a car is ideal, because you can have your car seat and stroller with you at all times, plus use your rental vehicle to store changes of clothes, for example, so you don't have to return to your hotel throughout the day. You'll also be able to come and go as you please and quickly travel between destinations in and around Las Vegas.

Keep in mind, however, that you may have to pay for nightly self- or valet parking at the resort/hotel where you'll be staying, although most resorts and hotels offer free self-parking. In addition, each time you drive to a different resort property for a visit, to dine, gamble, experience an attraction or see a show, you may have to pay valet parking fees if you want this added convenience.

TRAVEL TIP

The free self-parking structures connected with many of the mega-resorts along the Strip often require some walking to get to the main hotel lobby. If you're traveling with infants or kids, you'll probably want to utilize the valet parking for an additional fee. Be sure to calculate this into your travel budget.

Navigating around Las Vegas is relatively simple and there are several alternatives to car travel. There are free trams that connect certain mega-resort properties; the Las Vegas Monorail system, which travels up and down the Strip; the Las Vegas Strip Trolley; shuttle buses; and taxis.

Time and Money

Remember that the cost for a taxi ride in Las Vegas will be anywhere from $6 to $15, depending on the distance traveled. Traffic tends to build up along the Strip in the evenings, so you'll likely have to pay for waiting time in the taxi while you're stuck in traffic. Taking the Las Vegas Monorail ($3 per person) can also add up if you're traveling in a group, but you'll potentially save time as you travel along the Strip.

 TRAVEL ESSENTIAL

If you choose to walk between destinations along the Strip, allow at least twenty to thirty minutes per walk, even if the casino or resort property you're walking to is located "next door." Be sure to wear comfortable shoes and a hat, plus bring along a bottle of water if you walk outside.

The Las Vegas Strip Trolley buses are open-air buses that run up and down the Las Vegas Strip, approximately every fifteen minutes between 9:30 A.M. and 1:30 A.M. The fare is $1.75 per person, per ride. Exact change is required. The trolley has designated stops in front of the major hotels and attractions. (For additional information, call ☎702-382-1404.) The trolley is convenient and cost effective, but hardly a time saver.

Another benefit to renting a car is that you can easily travel to locations that are off the Strip or that public transportation doesn't readily travel to, such as the Wet 'n Wild theme park and stand-alone restaurants. If you're staying at a less-expensive hotel or motel, located off the Strip, having a rental car will make getting around much easier.

If you choose to rent a car to get around Las Vegas during your stay, take note of the following advice and money-saving strategies.

Choosing Your Car

There are many companies from which you can rent a car. Keep in mind, however, that the minimum age to rent a car from virtually all of these rental car companies is twenty-five. Also, a major credit card or debit card is needed (even if you ultimately plan to pay for the rental with cash, traveler's check, or a personal check). A valid driver's license for each driver is also required.

 TRAVEL TIP

Need driving directions? The Official Directions Street Guide (✐www.streetguide.com) allows you to get easy-to-follow, detailed driving directions to and from any location, using any computer or handheld wireless PDA device that's connected to the Internet. For more information, call ✆702-656-2161.

Most of the rental car companies will accept a U.S. driver's license or a license issued by a Canadian province. Most will also accept a license from a country that participated in the 1949 Geneva Convention on Road Traffic or the 1943 Convention on the Regulation of Inter-American Automobile Traffic, or that has a reciprocal agreement with the United States. If you have a driver's license issued outside the United States, check with the rental car company when you make your reservation to ensure that it will be accepted.

Convenient Locations

Several car rental companies have customer service counters right at the McCarran International Airport in Las Vegas (near the baggage claim area). Others offer complimentary shuttle service from the airport to the nearby car rental office. Several of these rental car companies also have rental desks at the various Las Vegas resorts and hotels. Contact the concierge at your hotel for details if you're interested in renting a car after you arrive at your hotel.

Table 3-1 lists rental car companies that have locations in the Las Vegas area.

TABLE 3-1
RENTAL CAR COMPANY DIRECTORY

Rental Car Company	Phone Number	Web Site
Airport Rent-A-Car	800-785-8578	
Aladdin Rent-A-Car	702-891-0807	
Alamo*	800-354-2322/ 702-261-5391	www.alamo.com
Allstate	800-634-6186	
Avis*	800-331-1212/ 702-261-5591	www.avis.com
Budget*	800-527-0700/ 702-736-1212	www.budgetvegas.com
Dollar*	800-800-4000/ 702-739-9507	http://lasvegas.dollar.com
Enterprise*	800-RENT-A-CAR/ 702-261-4435	www.enterprise.com
E-Z Rent-A-Car	888-755-4555	
Hertz*	800-654-3131/ 702-736-4900	www.hertz.com
Hertz Gold Club Reservations*	800-CAR-GOLD	
National*	800-227-7368/ 702-261-5391	www.nationalcar.com
Payless Car Rental	800-PAY-LESS	
Practical Rent-A-Car	877-401-7368	
PriceLess*	800-TOO-SAVE/ 702-736-6147	www.paylesscarrental.com
Rent-A-Wreck	800-227-0292	
Sav-more*	702-736-1234/ 702-736-1234	www.savmorerac.com
Savon Rent-A-Car	702-432-6627	
Sunbelt Car Rental	877-808-6117	
Thrifty*	800-367-2277/ 702-896-7600	www.thrifty.com
X-Press Rent A Car	702-795-4007/ 702-736-2663	

These rental car companies have counters or offices at McCarran International Airport. You'll find the customer service counters for each rental car company located in the center of the baggage claim area.

For those companies that don't have customer service counters at the airport, you'll find a bank of free telephones for contacting the company upon your arrival, also located in the baggage claim area. Each rental car company operates its own complimentary shuttle buses to transport customers from the baggage claim area to the rental car pickup area.

▼ TRAVEL ESSENTIAL

If you're worried about getting lost, Hertz offers an optional feature in some of its rental cars called NeverLost. Using the Global Positioning System (GPS), the unit identifies exactly where you are at any time and shows and tells you how to get wherever you want to go. You can add NeverLost to most midsize or larger Hertz rental cars for an additional $9 per day. Contact Hertz at ✆800-654-3131 for details.

Cruise the Strip in a Luxury Vehicle

If you want to enjoy the luxury and novelty of renting a flashy or exotic vehicle (such as a Jaguar, Hummer, BMW, Bentley, Porsche, Mercedes, Viper, Rolls Royce, Ferrari, Lamborghini, Range Rover, or Aston Martin), call Rent-A-Vette at ✆702-736-2592 or ✆800-372-1981, or visit the company's Web site at ✎*www.exoticcarrentalslasvegas.com*.

Rentals from Rent-A-Vette are available by the hour, day, week, or month. A Ferrari 360 Spider, for example, rents for $1,499 per day, which includes 100 free miles. Renters must be at least twenty-five years old and a cash deposit may be required.

You can also contact Dream Car Rentals (✎*www.dreamcarrentals. com*) at ✆877-373-2601, ✆702-731-6452, or ✆702-895-6661. This company, located at two locations along the Strip, also offers dozens of exotic and luxury cars, including Hummer H2s, which rent for $289 per day.

Money-Saving Strategies for Renting a Car

Just as when making airline reservations, there are several tricks to use when reserving a rental car that will help ensure that you get the lowest rate possible. First, if you're calling the rental car company directly, reserve your rental car as far in advance as possible (seven days in advance, minimum). If you can, try to get the weekly rental rate instead of the daily rate offered by the car rental company. Most rental car companies will apply their weekly rates to five- to seven-day rentals.

In tourist areas such as Las Vegas, rental car companies are always running special promotions. Be sure to ask about them, and look in your local newspaper and in your favorite magazines for ads promoting these specials.

Discount Options

Many of the rental car companies provide a discount to AAA members, so after getting the company's best rate, ask for a AAA member discount.

If you're a member of any airline's frequent-flier program, you can often receive a rental car discount from promotional partners of that airline. Check your monthly frequent-flier statement for information about special rental car offers.

 TRAVEL TIP

The Entertainment Book: Las Vegas Edition ($25, 888-231-SAVE/✐*www .entertainmentbook.com*) has discount coupons and special offers that apply to many of the popular rental car companies, including Avis, Hertz, Budget, National, and Alamo.

Some popular credit cards also have special promotional deals with the major rental car companies, so call the customer service phone number listed on your credit cards and inquire about what deals they offer for renting a car. While you're on the phone, also ask if your credit card automatically provides rental car insurance if you use that card to pay for the rental. American Express, Diners Club, and virtually all Visa and MasterCards (issued as part of an airline's frequent-flier program) automatically offer rental car insurance.

Other Considerations

If you think you've found an awesome rental car rate, reserve the car, but shop around. Call three or four other companies and see if they'll beat the deal you've been offered. Many travelers believe that the best-known rental car companies are always the most expensive, but this isn't always the case. You'll often be pleasantly surprised to discover that companies such as Hertz, Avis, and National offer highly competitive rates once you take advantage their special promotional deals, airline frequent-flier discounts, and AAA (or any auto club) member discount.

When making a reservation, find out whether unlimited mileage is included in the rental price. Some companies charge by the mile, in addition to the daily rental fee, so make sure you understand what's included in the price you're being quoted. Extremely low daily or weekly rental rates often do not include unlimited mileage, and once you travel more than the allowed miles, you're charged a hefty fee per mile.

The Insurance Question

No matter what hourly, daily, or weekly rate you're quoted, it will not include the insurance options offered or tax. In many cases, you'll also have to purchase gas. If you choose to pay for all of the different types of insurance options offered, the quoted rate for the rental car often more than doubles.

What most travelers don't know, however, is that they do not need *all* of the optional insurance offered by rental car companies. Their own auto and/or homeowner's insurance policies, as well as the travel insurance provided free of charge by some credit card companies or as part of the optional travel insurance they've purchased, may offer more than adequate protection. Prior to renting a car, check this by calling the customer service number for your auto insurance company, the travel insurance company, and your homeowner's (or renter's) insurance company.

 ## TRAVEL ESSENTIAL

Find out what insurance options make the most sense for your situation. You don't want to pay more than you have to, but making sure you're covered is important. Talk to your auto and homeowner's insurance companies, as well as to the travel insurance company, to find out what coverage you need.

Ask if rental car insurance is automatically offered under your existing insurance policy. If it is, you probably don't need any of the insurance offered by the rental car companies. If you rely on your existing insurance, however, and you're forced to make a claim due to an accident in the rental car, your regular insurance rates could go up in the future. One benefit of purchasing the optional insurance from the rental car companies is that your existing policies won't be affected if a claim has to be made (assuming any damage or injury claims are under the limit of the insurance you purchase).

The various rental car companies will offer several optional insurance plans that you can accept and pay for (per day) for the length of your rental agreement. The renter's financial responsibility for loss of or damage to the rental car varies by state. According to Hertz's literature, "the customer is responsible for loss of or damage to the car, up to its full value regardless of who is at fault, due to collision, rollover, and, in many instances, a limited number of other causes as specified in the rental agreement. The customer is generally not responsible for damage to the car resulting from acts of nature and accidental fire, provided the car is used in accordance with all terms and conditions of the rental agreement."

≡ FAST FACT

Insurance offers peace of mind and financial protection in case the unexpected happens. Whether or not you purchase the optional insurance from a rental car company should depend on how much added protection you desire, plus how much coverage you already have through your existing auto insurance, health insurance, home-owner's insurance, travel insurance, and umbrella insurance policies.

To sum up: Before purchasing the various insurance options offered by the rental car company, make sure you understand what's being offered and that you're not purchasing coverage you already have through your existing insurance policies.

Finding the Best Rental Car Deals Online

On the Web, visit any of the popular travel-related Web sites (includ-ing those described in Chapter 2) and select the rental car option. Using many of these Web sites, you can choose the class/size of vehi-cle you'd like, and save up to 60 percent off the rental car company's published rates. You can also visit the Web sites of the individual rental car companies, such as Hertz (✍*www.hertz.com*) or Avis (✍*www.avis.com*), for example.

After you've shopped around for the best rental car rates, con-sider visiting the Priceline Web site (✍*www.priceline.com*), which allows you to "name your own price" for the car rental. Enter a price that's between 25 and 50 percent lower than the lowest price you've been quoted either by the rental car companies or the other travel-related Web sites. While you won't always save this much, it's defi-nitely worth trying.

Make the Right Choice

When visiting any of the travel-related Web sites, such as Travelocity, Hotwire, Orbitz, etc., be sure to indicate that you'd like to pick up and drop off the rental car at McCarran International Airport in Las Vegas, then indicate the pickup date and time and the drop-off date and time. Next, you'll need to select the class or size of car you'd like to rent. Depending on the Web site you visit, possible options include:

- **Economy** (suitable for two people with luggage)
- **Compact** (suitable for two people with luggage)
- **Intermediate** (suitable for two to four people with luggage)
- **Standard** (suitable for two to four people with luggage)
- **Full-Size** (suitable for two to four people with luggage)
- **Luxury** (suitable for two to four people with luggage)
- **Convertible** (suitable for two people with minimal luggage)
- **Van** (suitable for four to six people with luggage)
- **Sport Utility Vehicle** (suitable for four to six people with luggage)

When choosing the type of vehicle you'll be renting, consider the number of passengers who will be riding at once in the vehicle and the amount of luggage you'll need to transport. A standard or full-size car will most likely be needed by a family of four traveling with two or three large suitcases, for example.

Special Services from Rental Car Companies

Most rental car companies will provide child safety seats, either free of charge or for a small daily fee, but these seats must be reserved in advance. This will save you the hassle of having to bring your own child safety seat(s) with you on your trip.

 **TRAVEL TIP**

If you're a nonsmoker, be sure to ask for a nonsmoking vehicle when you make your reservation.

When you pick up your rental car in Las Vegas, computer-generated driving directions and maps are often provided, free of charge, from the airport to virtually any location in the Las Vegas area, including all of the popular hotels and attractions.

Many rental car companies also offer cellular phone rentals; however, the rates are extremely high. If you have your own cellular phone that you can bring with you to Las Vegas, you're better off paying the roaming charges (if applicable) than the high daily rental and per-minute service fees associated with renting a cellular phone.

TRAVEL ESSENTIAL

If you plan to make many calls while on-the-go or even from your hotel room, it'll be more economical to bring your own cell phone from home or purchase a separate "pay-as-you-go" cell phone. Most hotels and resorts charge between $1 and $2 every time you make a local or toll-free call from the in-room phone. Much higher fees apply to long-distance calls.

Rental Policies

When you pick up the rental car, ask about the rental car company's policy for additional drivers. Typically, when you rent a car, only the person whose name appears on the rental agreement is legally permitted to drive the car, unless additional paperwork is completed. Some rental car companies charge to add names to the rental contract, allowing for multiple drivers. The following are often exempt from additional driver charges (but check with the rental car company): the renter's employer or regular fellow employee when on company business; the renter's spouse, mate, life companion, significant other, or live-in; and drivers for disabled renters who have completed a special form.

JUST FOR PARENTS

Many of the rental car companies now offer satellite radios, with programming from XM Radio or Sirius Satellite Radio. When driving with kids, consider listening to Radio Disney or XM Kids. For details, check out: ✏️*www.radiodisney.com*, ✏️*www.xmradio.com*, or ✏️*www.sirius.com* on the Web.

Questions to Ask

There are a number of questions to ask the rental car customer service agent that can help you save money and time when picking up and returning your vehicle. First, ask if you're required to return the car with a full tank of gas, or if you're paying for the gas in advance. If you're required to return the car with a full tank of gas and you fail to do so (which many people do), you'll be billed up to three times the going rate per gallon of gas needed to fill the tank. Before returning the car, find a low-priced gas station and fill the tank with basic unleaded gasoline. This will fulfill your obligation to return the car with a full tank of gas.

Know the Rules

When you pick up the car, ask what time the car must be returned by to ensure that you won't be billed overtime hours, and ask what the overtime rate is. If you pick up the car at 3:00 P.M., for example, you must return the car before 3:00 P.M. on the day your rental agreement ends, or you'll automatically be billed for additional hours at a high rate.

As soon as you pick up your car, before leaving the rental car company's parking lot, make sure there is nothing obviously wrong with the vehicle. If there's a problem, report it immediately. Once you leave the rental car company's parking lot, if you notice a problem, call the rental car company and report it. Likewise, if you get stuck on the road, call the rental car company and report your situation.

Free assistance, often including towing services, will be provided, and you'll often be given a replacement rental car.

When returning your car, plan on arriving at the airport at least ninety minutes to two hours prior to your flight time. You will most likely be returning your car away from the actual airport. Thus, you'll need to allow ample time to return the car, take the complimentary shuttle bus to your airline terminal, check in at the airline terminal, check your bags, go through security (which can take up to forty-five minutes), and get to the actual gate. It's a common problem for travelers to miss their flight because they didn't allow enough time to return their rental car, so plan accordingly.

Take Precautions

If you've had a long flight, you'll land in Las Vegas, pick up your rental car, and be driving in unfamiliar territory while you're tired. This provides an ideal condition to become involved in an auto accident, so before getting behind the wheel, make sure you're totally awake and alert and that you have detailed driving directions for reaching your destination. If you're too tired to be driving, take a taxi or shuttle bus to your hotel and pick up your rental car later in the day or the following day, but be sure to call the rental car company and mention your change of plans to avoid being charged.

TRAVEL ESSENTIAL

If this is your first time visiting Las Vegas, beware of the distractions when driving! If you're driving down the Strip, for example, it's very easy to get distracted looking at all there is to see, including the mega-resorts, the animated signs, the architecture, the shooting fountains, and the many pedestrians. Traffic accidents among tourists are common due to these many attention-grabbing attractions. Always be alert and pay attention to the road, not the many distractions.

CHAPTER 4

Choosing Accommodations and Dining

LAS VEGAS OFFERS A WIDE RANGE of accommodations, ranging from small, independent, no-frills motels (costing under $40 per night), to some of the most luxurious resort suites you'll find anywhere in the world (costing thousands of dollars per night). Most of the mega-resorts on or near the Strip offer comfortable guest rooms or suites suitable for families. The trick is to first define your needs, then find a resort or hotel that best meets those needs and that fits within your travel budget.

Evaluate Your Needs and Budget

Like any tourist destination in America, the Las Vegas area has an abundance of hotels, motels, and traditional resort properties, offered at a wide range of prices. What makes Las Vegas unique, however, are the dozens of mega-resorts located on or near the Strip.

A "mega-resort" is huge in terms of its size. Many of these resort properties offer everything you'd expect from traditional resorts, including multiple restaurants and lounges, a wide range of guest accommodation options, swimming pool, fitness center, spa, tennis, golf, and shops. However, each of these mega-resorts also has a distinctive theme, plus one or more large casinos. Many are home to one or more full production shows or Broadway productions, plus have multiple entertainment-oriented attractions and plenty of convention space.

Basically, the mega-resorts are entertainment-oriented cities unto themselves, each offering guests virtually everything that they could possibly want or need to relax and entertain themselves, whether they're on a tight budget or able to spend thousands of dollars per night for the most luxurious of accommodations.

Millions of people every year travel to Las Vegas to stay at one of the popular mega-resorts. While some of the resorts have youth-oriented themes—such as Circus, Circus, for example—many primarily cater to adults looking to have fun and gamble. However, nearly all of the mega-resorts also offer an abundance of activities, shows, attractions, dining options, shops, and accommodations that are suitable for the entire family.

This chapter will help you define your accommodation needs. You'll then be able to read the subsequent chapters of the book and learn about some of the most popular mega-resorts on or near the Strip that cater to families. This information will help you choose which of the mega-resorts you and your family would enjoy staying at the most.

Of course, you may choose to save money and avoid the hustle and bustle of the busy mega-resorts by staying at a nearby hotel or motel, then renting a car to visit some of the more popular mega-resorts in order to experience their attractions, shows, activities, restaurants, and shops.

 TRAVEL ESSENTIAL

If you'll be staying in Las Vegas for five or more days, to save on the amount of clothing you need to pack, plan on doing laundry at least once, if where you're staying offers self-service, coin-operated laundry facilities. Taking advantage of the full-service laundry or dry-cleaning services offered by the hotels, however, can get very expensive.

This chapter will also discuss some of the alternatives available to you, should you decide to stay at a hotel, motel, or resort that isn't located on the Strip and that isn't considered a mega-resort.

Before choosing where you want to stay, however, focus on your accommodation needs. Consider factors such as the following:

- How many adults will be traveling and staying with you?
- How many kids or teens will be traveling with you?
- How many beds and rooms will be needed? (Assume a basic hotel room has two queen-size beds per room.)
- If multiple bedrooms are needed (one for the parents and one for the kids), do you want or need connecting hotel rooms?
- If you're traveling with teenagers, would they be more comfortable having the privacy of their own room?
- Would your family be more comfortable staying in a multi-room suite?
- What special amenities do you and your family require, such as a refrigerator, a full kitchen, multiple bathrooms, multiple television sets, a high-speed Internet connection, extra space for a crib, in-room dining (a full room-service menu), or coin-operated (self-service) laundry facilities in the hotel/motel)?
- Do you want a smoking or nonsmoking room?
- Do you need a room that's handicap accessible?
- What is your nightly budget for accommodations?

Travel Companions

As you're planning your Las Vegas vacation, consider carefully whom you'll be traveling with and what your budget is. Also think about what types of activities your travel companions enjoy. Knowing these three pieces of information will help you choose the very best accommodations for your family, plus find what you're looking for at the lowest possible price.

Traveling with Kids or Teens

Depending on your kids' ages, chances are they'll have special needs and interests that you'll want to cater to in order to make their vacation more pleasant (and by default, your vacation less stressful).

For a family of four traveling with two kids, for example, there are a variety of accommodations options. One choice may be one room with two queen-size beds. You can usually request that an additional cot be placed in the room if you have two or more kids who can't or won't share a bed. You can also bring along or request a crib for the room, if necessary. The drawback to this basic type of accommodation is the lack of space. While this option will be the least expensive, when more than two people stay in a basic hotel room, things tend to get very crowded, especially if you're constantly stepping over luggage and can't agree on what TV shows to watch, and when several people need to use the bathroom at once.

Another option is to get two connecting rooms. One room could contain a single king-size bed for the parents, and the connecting room could have two queen-size beds for the kids. This option offers more living space and some added privacy, but allows the kids to have constant parental supervision. It also gives the kids their own television set and bathroom, plus extra space for luggage. This type of room is perfect for a family traveling with an infant or young child. At night, the parents can watch television or socialize in one room, while the child sleeps undisturbed by the noise in the adjoining room.

A multiroom suite may be the way to go. Available in all of the mega-resorts and many traditional hotels, a multiroom suite typically contains at least two bedrooms, a living room, and at least two bathrooms. Some also offer a separate dining area and/or a kitchenette. This option offers the parents and the kids some privacy, yet allows the family to stay together. A suite is also perfect for a family traveling with an infant or young child.

Yet another option might be apartment-like accommodations. If you're willing to pay a lot extra for it, all of the mega-resorts offer multiroom suites and apartment-like accommodations that are extremely luxurious. For much less money, however, some of the hotels located near the Strip offer apartment-style accommodations, containing multiple bedrooms, a living room, a dining area, a full kitchen, and several bathrooms. For a family, this type of accommodation has several advantages. For example, you'll save a lot of money using the kitchen to prepare breakfasts or lunches for the family as opposed to dining out.

Traveling with Senior Citizens

Perhaps you're traveling with your parents or in-laws. You'll definitely want multiple bedrooms to give everyone some privacy, especially if you're also traveling with kids or teens. In this situation, connecting rooms aren't as important as having two nearby rooms (on the same floor of the hotel, for example).

Some of the things you'll need to consider when traveling with senior citizens include:

- Do you need a room that requires minimal walking to get to?
- Do you require a room that's handicap accessible?
- Will you need a refrigerator in the room to store medications?
- Does the restaurant in the hotel need to cater to special dietary needs?
- What hotel amenities and activities will the senior citizens want or need? For example, are they interested in a having access to a golf course, slot machines, and/or a swimming pool? Would they prefer a mega-resort that features world-renowned art galleries as opposed to roller coasters and nightclubs?

Why Room Rates Fluctuate Dramatically

Room rates in Las Vegas fluctuate dramatically (especially along the Strip) depending on a variety of factors, including how close to capacity the hotel/resort is, the time of year, and what conventions or special events are going on. During an off-peak travel time, a room at one of the mega-resorts may go for under $100 per night. However, during a peak travel time or when a special event is happening in Las Vegas, that same room could go for $500 or more per night.

Understanding the Room Rates

Since room rates at the various Las Vegas mega-resorts and hotels vary greatly, based on season and demand, the room rates listed in this book are provided as a general reference only. Under each hotel or resort's description, you'll see the heading "Room and Suite Rates" followed by dollar signs ($). Use the following key to better understand the average room rate for each mega-resort, hotel, or motel.

$ = Under $50 per night
$$ = $51 to $100 per night
$$$ = $101 to $250 per night
$$$$ = $251 and up per night

Finding the Best Room Rates and Deals

Once you know what type of accommodations you're looking for and you've narrowed down the list of places you'd like to stay, your best bet is to shop around for the best deals in order to save money.

There are a number of ways you can try to find the lowest room rates. Call the hotel, motel, or resort directly. Tell them when you'll be visiting Las Vegas and ask for the room rate. Be sure to ask for any special discounts you may be entitled to, such as an AAA or AARP member discount. Don't be surprised if you're quoted different rates for different nights during your stay. For example, if you're staying in the same room over a Thursday, Friday, and Saturday night (checking out on Sunday morning), you may be quoted a higher rate for Friday and Saturday night. You may also want to visit the hotel or resort's Web site to see if any special "online only" rates or special promotions are being offered during the dates you'll be in Las Vegas.

Another strategy is to check the travel section of your newspaper and look for ads in magazines that promote specials and discounted package deals. Also, call a travel agent and ask them to find you the best room rates and provide you with multiple options, based on your specific needs. In summer 2004, the Las Vegas Convention and Visitors Authority launched a new program for travel agents, called "Vegas Certified." It enables travel agents to become experts on the destination and its myriad entertainment options and amenities. Approximately 27,000 travel agencies in the United States and Canada received related materials that contain everything they need to know to become a certified Vegas expert. As a traveler looking to work with a knowledgeable travel agent, you should find one who is "Vegas Certified."

TRAVEL TIP

When traveling to Las Vegas, you'll often save the most money if you purchase a package deal (including airfare and hotel) as far in advance as possible. If you're booking your travel with short notice, you'll almost always find the best "last-minute" deals on the travel-related Web sites.

Visit the Vegas.com (*www.vegas.com*) Web site and search for accommodations based on your needs, paying special attention to any package deals and promotions being offered. Visit several travel-related Web sites and shop for the best deals online. While many of these Web sites, such as Hotwire.com, Travelocity.com, Orbitz.com, Expedia.com, and Priceline.com, may look the same, they often offer different rates for the same type of room, at the same hotels or resorts, for the specific dates you're looking for. These Web sites also offer special package deals if you book your airfare and hotel/resort reservations at the same time. Some travel-related Web sites, such as Hotels.com, focus exclusively on finding the lowest hotel rates possible. All of these travel-related Web sites allow you to make hotel reservations at any of the popular mega-resorts or nearby hotels or motels in Las Vegas.

Your Accommodation Options

Now that you know the type of accommodations that would be ideal for your family, the following section offers a summary of the types of mega-resorts, resorts, hotels, and motels you'll find in the Las Vegas area.

When it comes to finding accommodations, your options are plentiful. In 2005, with existing hotels and resorts undergoing expansion, plus new properties such as the Wynn Las Vegas being built, more than 5,400 new hotel rooms will be made available, boosting the total number of available rooms in the Las Vegas area to well over 139,000.

Mega-Resorts on or near the Strip

Most people travel to Las Vegas specifically to experience the special ambiance offered by the mega-resorts located on or near the Strip. Each of these mega-resort properties offers a unique theme along with an overall experience you won't find anywhere else.

For example, you'll truly feel as if you've traveled to Italy once you step foot within The Venetian and see actual gondolas floating along canals that wind around and through the property, which is filled with authentic artwork and offers an incredible décor. Likewise, the Luxor, which is housed in a giant pyramid, allows guests to feel as if they've been transported to ancient Egypt, while New York–New York captures the atmosphere of New York City.

The ultra-trendy twenty- and thirty-something crowd tends to congregate and party at the Palms, the Hard Rock Hotel & Casino, and the Rio, while people looking for the ultimate in luxury accommodations might choose the Bellagio, Mandalay Bay, or The Venetian.

TRAVEL ESSENTIAL

As you're searching for the best deals, don't get frightened off by a mega-resort's listed room rates. While these rates are typically in effect during peak travel periods, you can often find special deals and promotions that make these world-class resort properties much more affordable to everyone.

Some of the mega-resorts offer midpriced accommodations in addition to more luxurious rooms and suites. However, some of the mega-resorts are rated among the best and most luxurious resorts in

America. Thus, you can expect to pay rates equivalent to a five-star resort when you stay at places such as The Venetian, Mandalay Bay, the Bellagio, or the new Wynn Las Vegas, for example.

Another thing that sets the mega-resorts apart from traditional resorts, hotels, and motels is the wide range of accommodations offered. Within a single mega-resort, you'll typically find a wide selection of basic rooms (offering one king-size bed or two queen-size beds) as well as connecting rooms, deluxe rooms, suites, multiroom suites, and accommodations that can only be called the ultimate in luxurious (where high rollers, celebrities, and royalty from around the world come to stay).

In addition to various types of accommodations, the mega-resorts also offer several levels of service and amenities. Many of the mega-resorts offer "concierge suites," which might include anything from a private elevator to an unpacking service for your luggage to an in-room butler, plus added or upgraded amenities within the room to make your stay more comfortable.

TRAVEL TIP

The Las Vegas mega-resorts are all-inclusive cities unto themselves, featuring restaurants, shows, activities, attractions, casinos, bars, lounges, spas, and a wide range of things to see and do. The basic guest rooms, however, are designed to offer comfort, but at the same time, encourage you to spend your time (when you're not sleeping) outside the room.

Off-Strip Accommodations

In addition to the mega-resorts, located a short distance from the Strip (often less than a five-minute drive) are a wide range of smaller resorts, as well as more traditional hotels and motels. In fact, almost every major hotel and motel chain offers at least one location in the Las Vegas area.

By staying at an off-Strip property or a more traditional hotel or motel, you'll often save money. However, you'll most likely want to rent a car so you can easily travel to the Strip without racking up taxi bills or spending hours dealing with public transportation or shuttle buses.

These off-Strip properties are much smaller than the mega-resorts and don't offer anywhere near the number of amenities. For families, however, you're more apt to find comfortable places to stay that don't force you to walk through huge casinos and past multiple lounges, nightclubs, and bars, for example, in order to get to your room.

TRAVEL ESSENTIAL

The main reason most people travel to Las Vegas, as opposed to other resort destinations, is to experience the exciting and luxurious mega-resorts and all they have to offer. The main reason some people opt to find lodging *away* from the Strip, however, is to save money and/or avoid the casinos' noise and crowds as much as possible.

Traditional Resorts and Time-Shares

Located a short distance from the Strip, you'll find a large selection of more traditional resort properties, offering several levels of accommodations. What sets a traditional resort apart from a hotel, for example, might be that the resort features its own golf course, swimming pool, day spa, tennis courts, camplike programs for kids, and/or has multiple restaurants. These properties tend to be more expensive to stay in than a regular hotel, but they offer a lot more to do on-site.

In addition to the traditional resorts, in recent years Las Vegas has become home to many time-share resort properties. You can purchase a membership or ownership in one of these properties, or if you own a time-share elsewhere through a company that also has properties in Las Vegas, you may be able to do an exchange that allows you to visit a Vegas property. Also, when these time-share properties aren't at capacity, some operate like normal resorts and open up their facilities to non-members/owners.

Hotels and Motels

Las Vegas is also the home of countless more traditional hotels and less expensive motels, most located only a short distance from the Strip. These hotels and motels typically don't offer a casino, but some have a swimming pool and/or other amenities. Some of the name-brand hotels and motels you'll find in the Las Vegas area are shown in Table 4-1.

 TRAVEL TIP

To learn more about hotels and motels located in the Las Vegas area, visit the Hotel Locators Web site at *www.hotellocators.com*, or call 800-423-7846. Also visit the Las Vegas Convention and Visitors Authority Web site at *www.lasvegas24hours.com*.

▲ Located in the Lake Las Vegas area, The Hyatt Regency is a family-friendly resort.

TABLE 4-1
LAS VEGAS AREA HOTELS AND MOTELS

Hotel or Motel	Phone Number	Web Site
Amerisuites	877-280-3434	www.amerisuites.com
Best Western	800-626-7575	www.bestwestern.com
Budget Suites of America	866-877-2000	www.budgetsuites.com
Comfort Inn	877-424-6423	www.comfortinn.com
Courtyard By Marriott	888-236-2427	www.marriott.com
Crowne Plaza	888-303-1746	www.ichotelsgroup.com
Days Inn	800-329-7466	www.daysinn.com
Double Tree	800-222-TREE	www.doubletree.com
EconoLodge	877-424-6423	www.econolodge.com
Embassy Suites	800-EMBASSY	www.embassysuites.com
Emerald Suites	866-847-2002	www.emeraldsuites.com
ExtendedStay	800-804-3724	www.extendedstay.com
Fairfield Inn	888-236-2427	www.marriott.com
Hampton Inn	800-HAMPTON	www.hamptoninn.com
Hilton	800-HILTONS	www.hilton.com
Holiday Inn Express	866-655-4669	www.holiday-inn.com
Howard Johnson	800-446-4656	www.hojo.com
Hyatt Regency	888-964-9288	www.hyatt.com
La Quinta Inn	866-725-1661	www.lq.com
Marriott	888-236-2427	www.marriott.com
Quality Inn	877-424-6423	www.qualityinn.com
Ramada Inn	800-272-6232	www.ramada.com
Rodeway Inn	877-424-6423	www.rodeway.com
Super 8	800-800-8000	www.super8.com
Travelodge	800-578-7878	www.travelodge.com
Westin (Sheraton)	888-625-5144	www.starwood.com

Apartment-Style Accommodations

Some of the best family-oriented accommodations in the Las Vegas area are suites, which include two or more bedrooms, multiple bathrooms, a living room, dining area, and either a kitchen or kitchenette. While not all of these types of properties would be considered luxurious, they're highly functional and spacious for families consisting of four or more people, including infants, kids, and/or teens.

For the same price as (or less than) a single room at a nearby mega-resort, apartment-style or multiroom suite accommodations are available at more traditional hotels. Some off-Strip properties that offer this type of apartment-style accommodations are shown in Table 4-2.

TABLE 4-2
APARTMENT-STYLE ACCOMMODATIONS

Hotel/Resort	Phone Number	Web Site
Amerisuites	877-280-3434	www.amerisuites.com
Budget Suites of America	866-877-2000	www.budgetsuites.com
Embassy Suites	800-EMBASSY	www.embassysuites.com
Emerald Suites	866-847-2002	www.emeraldsuites.com
ExtendedStay	800-804-3724	www.extendedstay.com
Tuscany Suites & Casino	877-887-2261	www.tuscanylasvegas.com

 **TRAVEL TIP**

To find vacation properties that offer apartment- or condominium-style accommodations and multiroom suites at discounted prices in the Las Vegas area, contact CondoSaver at ☎800-469-9757 (✉www.condosaver. com), or CondoDirect at ☎800-597-2681 (✉www.condodirect.com).

The Lake Las Vegas Area

Located about a twenty-minute drive (seventeen miles) away from the Las Vegas Strip is the Lake Las Vegas area. Here you'll find some incredibly luxurious resorts that are family-friendly and that offer a wide range of activities that are nothing like what you'll find at the mega-resorts along the Strip. Targeted to more affluent travelers, outdoor activities and world-class accommodations are their specialties.

In addition to its 496 extremely comfortable and spacious guest rooms and suites, the Hyatt Regency Lake Las Vegas Resort (✆800-55-Hyatt/✐*www.lakelasvegas.hyatt.com*) offers its own Jack Nicklaus signature golf course (several other courses are located nearby), a small casino, a world-class day spa, two swimming pools, various outdoor activities on the lake (including fishing, kayaking, sailing, and canoeing), several fine restaurants, and the top-notch service you'd expect from an award-winning Hyatt Regency Resort.

Other available activities on or near the Hyatt Regency property include biking, bird watching, hiking, swimming, tennis, volleyball, jogging, shopping, rafting, touring the nearby Grand Canyon and Hoover Dam, horseback riding, hot-air ballooning, Hummer tours, miniature golf, rock climbing, and skydiving.

TRAVEL ESSENTIAL

Like many Hyatt properties, this one offers "Camp Hyatt" specifically for kids. Your kids can participate in supervised, camplike activities throughout the day and/or evening. Two- to four-hour activity sessions are available and are priced between $27 and $40 per child. Camp Hyatt is open to kids between the ages of three and twelve who are toilet trained. For an additional fee, special field trips are often arranged.

A shuttle service to and from the Strip is provided; however, it's more convenient to rent a car if you'll be staying in the Lake Las Vegas area and want to explore the Strip at your leisure.

One of the nicest things about the Lake Las Vegas area and the Hyatt Regency is that the atmosphere is much more relaxed, less commercial, and nowhere near as focused on the casinos. This is a somewhat remote and beautiful area where many of the guest rooms have a stunning view of the lake or immaculately landscaped property.

HYATT REGENCY OVERALL FAMILY-FRIENDLINESS RATING

Ages Up to 5	Ages 6–15	Ages 16–20	Ages 21 & Up	Senior Citizens
☆☆☆	☆☆☆	☆☆☆	☆☆☆	☆☆☆

Located near the Hyatt Regency in the Lake Las Vegas area are several other world-class resorts, including the Lake Las Vegas Resort (✆800-654-1603/✎*www.lakelasvegas.com*), the Ritz-Carlton (✆702-567-4700/✎*www.ritzcarlton.com*), and Montelago Village (866-564-4799/✎*www.montelagovillage.com*).

Dining Guidelines

To help you choose the best places to eat, based on your budget, each restaurant featured within this book is categorized based on the average price per person. You'll find between one and three dollar signs ($) next to each restaurant's name and description.

$ = Entrées are priced under $10 each.

$$ = Entrées are priced under $20 each.

$$$ = Entrées are priced over $20 each. At these restaurants, plan on spending between $50 to $100 (or more) per person for a fine-dining experience for dinner.

At any full-service restaurant, you're expected to leave a tip for your server. The customary amount to leave is 15 percent of the total bill; however, you may choose to leave slightly more or less depending on the quality of service you receive. Many restaurants automatically add a gratuity to the bill for groups, so be sure to determine whether a gratuity has already been added to your meal bill if you're dining with a group of people. (A 15-percent tip is almost always automatically added to your room service bill, so be sure to check this before adding an additional tip.)

If you're traveling with kids, be sure to ask for a children's menu at the various restaurants. Many of the fine-dining restaurants in particular will go out of their way to accommodate special requests or dietary needs, so consult with your waiter.

Dining Options in and Around Las Vegas

For decades, Las Vegas has been famous for those all-you-can-eat buffets, located in the various mega-resorts and casinos. While this remains a viable dining option, in recent years some of the world's most renowned chefs have opened fine-dining restaurants in the Las Vegas area. In addition, you'll find plenty of casual-dining options, theme restaurants, and virtually every chain fast-food restaurant in existence. Many of the hotels and resorts offer in-room dining (room service), too.

Whether you're looking to spend $10 per person, per meal or $100 per person, per meal, your choices are plentiful. In Las Vegas, you'll find every type of food, often within walking distance or a short cab ride from where you're staying. Many of the mid- to higher-priced restaurants will also cater to specific dietary needs and restrictions, so be sure to speak with your waiter prior to ordering your meals.

Fine-Dining Restaurants

Virtually every mega-resort on or near the Strip offers at least one or two fine-dining restaurants that are typically open for dinner. In addition, there are dozens of world-famous stand-alone restaurants located on or near the Strip.

These restaurants tend to be costly ($35 to $100 or more per person), but they offer a complete multicourse meal with top-notch service. For example, if you're in the mood for some of the best seafood you've ever tasted, either for lunch or dinner, McCormick & Schmick's Seafood Restaurant (335 Hughes Center Drive, ☎702-836-9000) offers dozens of extremely fresh seafood dishes, featuring fish flown in daily from around the world, at under $40 per person ($25 per person for lunch). There's also an inexpensive kid's menu available.

Located in the heart of the Excalibur is the Steakhouse at Camelot (✆702-597-7777), a perfect example of a fine-dining restaurant located within a mega-resort. This restaurant offers some of the best steak dinners you'll find anywhere in Las Vegas. Make sure you leave plenty of room for the restaurant's unusual and incredibly delicious desserts. The service is impeccable and the atmosphere is formal, yet romantic!

TRAVEL TIP

To avoid long waits (especially on Friday and Saturday nights) and to ensure that you'll get into your first restaurant choice, it's always a good idea to make advance reservations at the fine-dining restaurants. At some of these restaurants, proper attire is required, while others have a more relaxed dress code. When making your reservation, inquire about the dress code.

Some fine-dining establishments, such as McCormick & Schmick's Seafood Restaurant, focus on a specific type of food, while others, such as the Steakhouse at Camelot, offer a broader menu. The majority of these restaurants cater to adult vacationers and business travelers. Most offer romantic settings and provide the perfect atmosphere for celebrating a special occasion. These restaurants focus on offering a relaxing meal, which can take two or more hours as you enjoy numerous courses.

While these fine-dining restaurants won't necessarily appeal to kids (who would prefer a McDonald's hamburger over a filet mignon steak prepared by an award-winning chef), many of these restaurants offer special children's menus.

Ask your hotel's concierge for specific fine-dining recommendations offered at or near the hotel. If you're looking to spend at least

$35 per adult for a formal, multicourse dinner, you'll find a few fine-dining suggestions in Table 4-3.

TABLE 4-3
FINE-DINING RESTAURANT RECOMMENDATIONS

Restaurant	Location	Phone	Type of Cuisine
808	Caesars Palace	702-731-7731	Seafood
AJ's Steakhouse	Hard Rock Hotel & Casino	702-693-5500	Steak
Crustacean Las Vegas	The Aladdin	702-650-0507	EuroAsian
Del Frisco's Double Eagle Steakhouse	3925 Paradise Road	702-796-0063	Steak, seafood
Eiffel Tower Restaurant	Paris Las Vegas	702-948-6937	French
Fiamma Trattoria	MGM Grand	702-891-1111	Italian
Gallagher's Steakhouse	New York–New York Hotel & Casino	702-740-6450	Steak
La Cirque	Bellagio	702-693-7223	French
Lawry's The Prime Rib	4043 Howard Hughes Parkway	702-893-2223	Prime rib
Mikado	The Mirage	702-791-7223	Japanese
Morton's of Chicago	400 East Flamingo Road	702-893-0703	Steak, seafood
Nobu	Hard Rock Hotel & Casino	702-693-5090	Japanese, sushi
Picasso	Bellagio	702-693-7223	French, Mediterranean
Ruth's Chris Steak House	3900 West Paradise Road	702-791-7011	Steak, seafood
The Steakhouse at Camelot	Excalibur	702-597-7777	Steak, seafood
Zeffirino	The Venetian	702-414-3500	Italian

TRAVEL ESSENTIAL

Need more fine-dining recommendations? Be sure to pick up a free copy of *What's On: The Las Vegas Guide*. It's a biweekly, full-color magazine available from virtually every resort, hotel, and motel on or near the Strip. You can also visit the magazine's Web site at *www.ilovevegas.com*.

Casual-Dining (Full-Service) Restaurants

The casual-dining restaurants within each of the mega-resorts offer full waiter/waitress service and some of the most extensive menus you'll find anywhere. While not at all fancy, the food is usually good, offering a great alternative to fast food. Most are open late or even twenty-four hours per day, and are reasonably priced (under $15 per person) for breakfast, lunch, or dinner. These casual-dining restaurants are family-friendly, although many of them are located directly adjacent to casinos.

FAST FACT

If you're dining at a full-service restaurant, leaving a 15- to 20-percent tip for your server (calculated based on the total of your bill) is custom-ary. When you're dining at a buffet, however, it's customary to leave just a $1 per-person tip for the server who gets your drink orders.

All-You-Can-Eat Buffets

For somewhere between $6 and $15 per adult for lunch and $7 and $25 per adult for dinner, the all-you-can-eat buffets within the various mega-resorts offer large menus, which almost always include steak, chicken, seafood, salads, soups, desserts, and a wide range of other tasty treats.

What you won't find at these buffets is full waiter/waitress service. Plus, the hours of operation tend to be limited, and vary based on whether it's a weekday or weekend. Most of the buffets also offer a Sunday brunch and special pricing for children. The buffets tend to open for breakfast, again for lunch, and then for dinner. Sorry, you can't stay all day.

Food Courts/Fast Food

Located within many of the mega-resorts, as well as various places along the Strip, you'll find many food courts and familiar fast-food restaurants. Many are open twenty-four hours per day and offer relatively inexpensive meals. The prices do, however, tend to be a bit higher than what you might pay in your home city for the same food at the popular fast-food chains. All of these fast-food establishments and food courts are family-friendly. Plan on spending between $6 and $10 per person for breakfast, lunch, or dinner.

 TRAVEL TIP

A healthier alternative to fast food are the many casual-dining restaurants and coffee shops located in the various mega-resorts. You'll spend a bit more per person, but the food is better and the menus are far more extensive. Besides, you didn't travel all the way to Las Vegas for a Big Mac, did you?

Theme Restaurants

Imagine dining in the middle of a tropical rain forest or aboard the DS9 space station from the *Star Trek: Deep Space Nine* television series. If you're a movie buff, you can surround yourself with props and costumes from Hollywood's biggest blockbuster movies as you eat. This is just some of what the various theme restaurants in Las Vegas have to offer.

When it comes to dining with your kids and teens, what's better than transforming a typical lunch or dinner meal into a fun-filled, entertaining experience? Within Las Vegas, you'll find a handful of theme restaurants that make dining fun and memorable (see Table 4-4). Sure, you'll pay a premium to dine at these places, but they're generally worth it. These theme restaurants are excellent places to celebrate a child's birthday or special event, or just to enjoy a quality meal with the entire family.

TABLE 4-4
TOP PICKS FOR FAMILY-ORIENTED THEME RESTAURANTS IN LAS VEGAS

Restaurant	Theme	Address	Phone	Web Site
Benihana Village	Japanese demonstration-style cooking	Las Vegas Hilton	702-732-5755	www.benihana.com
ESPN Zone	Sports	New York–New York Hotel & Casino	702-933-ESPN	www.espnzone.com
Hard Rock Café	Rock music	4475 Paradise Road	702-733-7625	www.hardrock.com
Harley Davidson Café	Motorcycles	3725 Las Vegas Boulevard South	702-740-4555	www.harley-davidsoncafé.com
NASCAR Café	Auto racing (NASCAR)	Sahara Hotel & Casino	702-734-7223	www.nascarcafé.com
Planet Hollywood	Hollywood movies	The Forum Shops at Caesars	702-791-7827	www.planethollywood.com
Quark's Café	Star Trek	The Las Vegas Hilton	702-697-8725	www.startrekexp.com
Rainforest Café	Wild animals/tropical rainforest ambiance	MGM Grand Hotel & Casino	702-891-8580	www.rainforestcafé.com

TRAVEL ESSENTIAL

To save money when dining in Las Vegas, be sure to pick up a copy of *The Entertainment Book: Las Vegas* ($25, 888-231-SAVE/⌨*www. entertainmentbook.com*). Within it, you'll find dozens of buy-one-entrée, get-one-free and other coupon offers from more than 200 Las Vegas-area restaurants.

Plan on spending between $12 and $25 per person. Lunch and dinner are served daily. Reservations aren't required, but during peak travel times, they're certainly recommended. Special souvenir glasses and T-shirts are among the items sold within each restaurant's adjoining gift shop.

In-Room Dining and Delivery Options

If you're staying at one of the Las Vegas-area mega-resorts or hotels, most offer in-room dining (room service). From room service, you can typically order anything that's served within the hotel's in-house restaurants, twenty-four hours per day. The drawback is that there's always a significant surcharge and delivery charge for in-room dining, and the server's tip is always automatically added to the bill.

An alternative to ordering room service from your hotel is to call a local restaurant that delivers, such as Domino's Pizza (☎702-644-3030).

CHAPTER 5

The Las Vegas Strip at a Glance

YOU'RE ABOUT TO GET A QUICK overview of every mega-resort located on or near the Las Vegas Strip. This mega-resort listing is divided into two primary categories: those that are more suitable for families and those that cater almost exclusively to adult travelers, business people, and gamblers. (Even in these mega-resorts, however, you will find some amenities for younger people.) This chapter also lists all of the major shows offered in the Las Vegas area. This listing provides you with a quick glance at what's available; detailed information follows later in the book.

Age-Appropriateness Ratings

Some resorts, hotels, shows, rides, attractions, and activities within Las Vegas are suitable for the entire family. Others are more suitable for just teenagers (not kids), or adults over the age of twenty-one. This rating system will help you determine whether something is appropriate for someone in a specific age group. The rating system is broken down into five distinct age groups. Within each age group, a particular resort, hotel, show, ride, attraction, or activity, for example, will receive between one and three stars or a Not Suitable rating.

Look to the age-appropriateness ratings to help you determine whether something is suitable for:

- Young children (up to five years old)
- Children (ages six to fifteen)
- Teenagers (ages sixteen to twenty)
- Adults (ages twenty-one and up)
- Senior citizens

Within the chart will be one to three stars for each category (or the words "Not Suitable"— meaning that the resort, hotel show, ride, attraction, or activity isn't suitable for a specific age group):

($\star$) = Fair value/interest level
($\star\star$) = Good value/interest level
($\star\star\star$) = Excellent value/interest level

Sample Overall Rating for Value and Age-Appropriateness

According to the sample chart in Table 5-1, this resort, show, attraction, ride, or activity would not necessarily be suitable for young children and only mildly suitable for kids under the age of fifteen (hence it received only one star in this category). Based on the chart, the featured resort, show, attraction, ride, or activity, however, would appeal to anyone over the age of sixteen, including adults and senior citizens.

TABLE 5-1
SAMPLE OVERALL RATING

Ages Up to 5	Ages 6–15	Ages 16–20	Ages 21 & Up	Senior Citizens
Not Suitable	$\star$	$\star\star\star$	$\star\star\star$	$\star\star\star$

In this chapter, only basic information is provided about each mega-resort property and show. From here, you can get a quick overview of what's in Las Vegas and what mega-resorts and shows are suitable for your family.

Within Chapters 6 through 18, detailed information will be provided about each mega-resort located on or near the Strip, with additional focus on and coverage of the properties that are the most family-friendly.

The More Family-Oriented Mega-Resorts

The following is an overview of the mega-resorts that offer the most amenities, activities, and services suitable for the entire family. Additional information about each of these properties can be found within Chapters 6 through 18.

You can use the phone numbers listed in this chapter to:

- Contact guests staying at any of the properties listed.
- Make your reservation, confirm your reservation, or inquire about room rates.
- Make dining reservations at any of the restaurants located within the resort.
- Get transferred to the property's box office to make show reservations and purchase tickets.

The Bellagio (See Chapter 6)
✉3600 Las Vegas Boulevard South
☏888-987-6667
☏702-693-7111
✎*www.bellagio.com*

THE BELLAGIO OVERALL RATING

Ages Up to 5	Ages 6–15	Ages 16–20	Ages 21 & Up	Senior Citizens
☆	☆☆	☆☆☆	☆☆☆	☆☆☆

Caesars Palace (See Chapter 7)

✉3570 Las Vegas Boulevard South

✆800-634-6661

✆702-731-7110

✎*www.caesarspalace.com*

CAESARS PALACE OVERALL RATING

Ages Up to 5	Ages 6–15	Ages 16–20	Ages 21 & Up	Senior Citizens
☆☆	☆☆	☆☆☆	☆☆☆	☆☆☆

Circus, Circus Hotel, Casino, and Theme Park (See Chapter 8)

✉2880 Las Vegas Boulevard South

✆800-634-3450

✆702-734-0410

✎*www.circuscircus.com*

CIRCUS, CIRCUS OVERALL RATING

Ages Up to 5	Ages 6–15	Ages 16–20	Ages 21 & Up	Senior Citizens
☆☆☆	☆☆☆	☆☆☆	☆☆	☆☆

The Excalibur Hotel & Casino (See Chapter 9)

✉3850 Las Vegas Boulevard South

✆800-937-7777

✆702-597-7777

✎*www.excalibur-casino.com*

THE EXCALIBUR OVERALL RATING

Ages Up to 5	Ages 6–15	Ages 16–20	Ages 21 & Up	Senior Citizens
☆☆	☆☆☆	☆☆☆	☆☆	☆☆

The Four Seasons (See Chapter 10)

✉3960 Las Vegas Boulevard South

☎877-632-5000

☎702-632-5000

✍*www.fourseasons.com*

THE FOUR SEASONS OVERALL RATING

Ages Up to 5	Ages 6–15	Ages 16–20	Ages 21 & Up	Senior Citizens
★★	★★★	★★★	★★★	★★★

The Luxor Hotel and Casino (See Chapter 11)

✉3900 Las Vegas Boulevard South

☎800-288-1000

☎702-262-4000

✍*www.luxor.com*

THE LUXOR HOTEL AND CASINO OVERALL RATING

Ages Up to 5	Ages 6–15	Ages 16–20	Ages 21 & Up	Senior Citizens
★★	★★	★★★	★★★	★★★

Mandalay Bay (See Chapter 12)

✉3950 Las Vegas Boulevard South

☎877-632-7000

☎702-632-7777

✍*www.mandalaybay.com*

MANDALAY BAY OVERALL RATING

Ages Up to 5	Ages 6–15	Ages 16–20	Ages 21 & Up	Senior Citizens
★★	★★	★★★	★★★	★★★

The MGM Grand (See Chapter 13)

✉3799 Las Vegas Boulevard South

✆800-929-1111

✆702-891-1111

✍*www.mgmgrand.com*

THE MGM GRAND OVERALL RATING

Ages Up to 5	Ages 6–15	Ages 16–20	Ages 21 & Up	Senior Citizens
☆☆	☆☆	☆☆	☆☆☆	☆☆☆

The Mirage (See Chapter 14)

✉3400 Las Vegas Boulevard South

✆800-627-6667

✆702-791-7111

✍*www.mirage.com*

THE MIRAGE OVERALL RATING

Ages Up to 5	Ages 6–15	Ages 16–20	Ages 21 & Up	Senior Citizens
☆☆	☆☆☆	☆☆☆	☆☆☆	☆☆☆

New York–New York Hotel & Casino (See Chapter 15)

✉3790 Las Vegas Boulevard

✆800-693-6763

✆702-740-6969

✍*www.nynyhotelcasino.com*

NEW YORK–NEW YORK HOTEL & CASINO OVERALL RATING

Ages Up to 5	Ages 6–15	Ages 16–20	Ages 21 & Up	Senior Citizens
☆	☆☆	☆☆	☆☆☆	☆☆☆

Treasure Island (TI) Las Vegas (See Chapter 16)

✉3300 Las Vegas Boulevard South

☎800-944-7444

☎702-894-7111

🖮*www.treasureisland.com*

TREASURE ISLAND OVERALL RATING

Ages Up to 5	Ages 6–15	Ages 16–20	Ages 21 & Up	Senior Citizens
★★	★★★	★★★	★★★	★★★

The Venetian Resort (See Chapter 17)

✉3355 Las Vegas Boulevard South

☎888-283-6423

☎702-414-1000

🖮*www.venetian.com*

THE VENETIAN RESORT OVERALL RATING

Ages Up to 5	Ages 6–15	Ages 16–20	Ages 21 & Up	Senior Citizens
★	★★	★★	★★★	★★★

The More Adult-Oriented Mega-Resorts

The mega-resorts listed here have been given less coverage within this book, either because they don't cater to families or they're located off the Strip (in the downtown area, for example). More detailed information about some of these properties can be found in Chapter 18.

Aladdin Resort & Casino

(Note: In the future, this property is scheduled to be transformed into the Planet Hollywood Resort & Casino, based upon the popular theme restaurants.)

✉3667 Las Vegas Boulevard South
📞877-333-9474
📞702-785-5555
🖢*www.aladdincasino.com*

ALADDIN RESORT & CASINO OVERALL RATING

Ages Up to 5	Ages 6–15	Ages 16–20	Ages 21 & Up	Senior Citizens
☆	☆	☆☆	☆☆	☆☆

Bally's Las Vegas

✉3645 Las Vegas Boulevard South
📞800-634-3434
📞702-739-4111
🖢*www.ballyslasvegas.com*

BALLY'S LAS VEGAS OVERALL RATING

Ages Up to 5	Ages 6–15	Ages 16–20	Ages 21 & Up	Senior Citizens
☆	☆	☆☆	☆☆	☆☆☆

Boardwalk Hotel & Casino

✉3750 Las Vegas Boulevard South
📞800-635-4581
📞702-735-2400
🖢*www.boardwalklv.com*

BOARDWALK HOTEL & CASINO OVERALL RATING

Ages Up to 5	Ages 6–15	Ages 16–20	Ages 21 & Up	Senior Citizens
☆	☆	☆	☆	☆

The Flamingo Las Vegas

✉3555 Las Vegas Boulevard South

✆800-732-2111

✆702-733-3111

✎*www.flamingolasvegas.com*

THE FLAMINGO LAS VEGAS OVERALL RATING

Ages Up to 5	Ages 6–15	Ages 16–20	Ages 21 & Up	Senior Citizens
☆	☆	☆	☆☆	☆☆

The Golden Nugget

✉129 Fremont Street

✆800-634-3454

✆702-385-7111

✎*www.goldennugget.com*

THE GOLDEN NUGGET OVERALL RATING

Ages Up to 5	Ages 6–15	Ages 16–20	Ages 21 & Up	Senior Citizens
☆	☆	☆	☆☆	☆☆

The Hard Rock Hotel & Casino

✉4455 Paradise Road

✆800-473-7625

✆702-693-5000

✎*www.hardrockhotel.com*

THE HARD ROCK HOTEL & CASINO OVERALL RATING

Ages Up to 5	Ages 6–15	Ages 16–20	Ages 21 & Up	Senior Citizens
☆	☆	☆	☆☆☆	☆

Harrah's Las Vegas
✉3475 Las Vegas Boulevard South
✆800-427-7247
✆702-369-5000
☞*www.harrahs.com*

HARRAH'S LAS VEGAS OVERALL RATING

Ages Up to 5	Ages 6–15	Ages 16–20	Ages 21 & Up	Senior Citizens
☆	☆	☆	☆☆	☆☆

Imperial Palace
✉3535 Las Vegas Boulevard South
✆800-634-6441
✆702-731-3311
☞*www.imperialpalace.com*

IMPERIAL PALACE OVERALL RATING

Ages Up to 5	Ages 6–15	Ages 16–20	Ages 21 & Up	Senior Citizens
☆	☆	☆	☆☆	☆☆

The Las Vegas Hilton
✉3000 Paradise Road
✆800-732-7117
✆702-732-5111
☞*www.lvhilton.com*

THE LAS VEGAS HILTON OVERALL RATING

Ages Up to 5	Ages 6–15	Ages 16–20	Ages 21 & Up	Senior Citizens
☆	☆☆	☆☆	☆☆☆	☆☆☆

The Monte Carlo

✉3770 Las Vegas Boulevard South

✆800-311-8999

✆702-730-7777

✍*www.montecarlo.com*

THE MONTE CARLO OVERALL RATING

Ages Up to 5	Ages 6–15	Ages 16–20	Ages 21 & Up	Senior Citizens
☆	☆	☆	☆☆	☆☆

Palms Casino Resort

✉4321 West Flamingo Road

✆866-725-6773

✆702-942-7777

✍*www.palms.com*

PALMS CASINO RESORT OVERALL RATING

Ages Up to 5	Ages 6–15	Ages 16–20	Ages 21 & Up	Senior Citizens
☆	☆	☆	☆☆☆	☆☆

Paris Las Vegas

✉3655 Las Vegas Boulevard South

✆888-266-5687

✆702-946-7000

✍*www.parislasvegas.com*

PARIS LAS VEGAS OVERALL RATING

Ages Up to 5	Ages 6–15	Ages 16–20	Ages 21 & Up	Senior Citizens
☆	☆	☆	☆☆☆	☆☆☆

The Rio All-Suite Hotel & Casino
✉3700 West Flamingo Road
☎800-752-9746
☎702-777-7777
🖱www.playrio.com

THE RIO ALL-SUITE HOTEL & CASINO OVERALL RATING

Ages Up to 5	Ages 6–15	Ages 16–20	Ages 21 & Up	Senior Citizens
☆	☆	☆☆	☆☆☆	☆☆

Riviera
✉2901 Las Vegas Boulevard South
☎800-634-6753
☎702-734-5110
🖱www.rivierahotel.com

RIVIERA OVERALL RATING

Ages Up to 5	Ages 6–15	Ages 16–20	Ages 21 & Up	Senior Citizens
☆	☆	☆	☆☆	☆☆

Sahara Hotel & Casino
✉2535 Las Vegas Boulevard South
☎888-696-2121
☎702-737-2111
🖱www.saharavegas.com

SAHARA HOTEL & CASINO OVERALL RATING

Ages Up to 5	Ages 6–15	Ages 16–20	Ages 21 & Up	Senior Citizens
☆	☆	☆	☆☆	☆☆

The Stardust

✉3000 Las Vegas Boulevard South

✆800-634-6757

✆702-732-6111

✑*www.stardustlv.com*

THE STARDUST OVERALL RATING

Ages Up to 5	Ages 6–15	Ages 16–20	Ages 21 & Up	Senior Citizens
☆	☆	☆	☆☆	☆☆

The Stratosphere Las Vegas Hotel & Casino

✉2000 Las Vegas Boulevard South

✆800-998-6937

✆702-380-7777

✑*www.stratospherehotel.com*

THE STRATOSPHERE LAS VEGAS HOTEL & CASINO OVERALL RATING

Ages Up to 5	Ages 6–15	Ages 16–20	Ages 21 & Up	Senior Citizens
☆	☆	☆☆	☆☆	☆☆

Tropicana

✉3801 Las Vegas Boulevard South

✆800-634-4000

✆702-739-2222

✑*www.tropicanalv.com*

TROPICANA OVERALL RATING

Ages Up to 5	Ages 6–15	Ages 16–20	Ages 21 & Up	Senior Citizens
☆	☆	☆	☆☆	☆☆

Wynn Las Vegas (Opening Spring 2005)

✉3131 Las Vegas Boulevard South

☏877-770-7077

☏702-733-4300

✎*www.wynnlasvegas.com*

WYNN LAS VEGAS OVERALL RATING

Ages Up to 5	Ages 6–15	Ages 16–20	Ages 21 & Up	Senior Citizens
☆	☆☆	☆☆	☆☆☆	☆☆☆

The Las Vegas Shows

Las Vegas is famous for its glitzy production shows, but more recently, some of Broadway's biggest shows, such as *Mamma Mia!*, *Blue Man Group*, and *Phantom of the Opera*, have also found a home in Las Vegas.

While Elvis has left the building, these days you'll also find big-name recording artists, such as Celine Dion, Elton John, and Gladys Knight appearing regularly, plus an assortment of comedy and magic shows that are thoroughly entertaining.

═FAST FACT

Many of the shows in Las Vegas have had their theaters custom-designed specifically for the multimillion-dollar productions that'll be presented. In 2006, for example, when *Phantom of the Opera* opens at The Venetian, it will be a $35 million production, with an additional $25 million being spent to custom-build the theater.

The following is a list of the major shows in the Las Vegas area. This list does not include special events or limited engagements. For more information about specific events, such as concerts, sporting events, or limited engagements, contact the appropriate resort, theater, arena, or venue directly.

You can also visit the Vegas.com (*www.vegas.com*) Web site for event listings and to purchase tickets, or contact Ticketmaster (702-474-4000, *www.ticketmaster.com*). When purchasing tickets outside of the venue's own box office, you will most likely have to pay a surcharge for each ticket.

TRAVEL ESSENTIAL

Save 50 percent off the ticket price for some of Las Vegas's shows when you visit one of the Tix4Tonight (877-849-4868/*www.tix4tonight.com*) box offices located along the Strip. All credit cards and cash, but no personal checks, are accepted.

Shows are listed here in alphabetical order and are subject to change, as are the ticket prices.

American Superstars, at the Stratosphere
702-380-7777

www.stratospherehotel.com

This celebrity-impersonator tribute show featuring a cast of talented performers is suitable for the whole family. Ticket prices are $38.75 (children $27.75). A $44 package, including a show ticket, dinner buffet, and two drinks, is also available for adults.

Blue Man Group Live, at the Luxor
702-262-4400

www.blueman.com

Musical entertainment featuring a troupe of "blue men." It's utterly unique and suitable for the whole family. Kids in particular will enjoy sitting in the first five rows of the theater. Audience members are provided with waterproof ponchos to protect them from the mess created on stage. This show is all about music, visual art, and creativity. Special lighting and sound effects are used to enhance the crazy and colorful stunts performed by the cast. Ticket prices are $93.50.

Celine Dion: A New Day . . . , at Caesars Palace

✆702-474-4000

✐www.celinedion.com

Music superstar Celine Dion puts on an incredible concert featuring many of her biggest hits. She's accompanied by sixty dancers and performs live in front of the world's largest LCD screen. This is a must-see show for everyone! (When Celine isn't performing, Elton John takes her place for an equally amazing show.) Ticket prices range from $87.50 to $225.

Circus Acts, at Circus, Circus

Ongoing circus acts are performed throughout the day and into the night. Performances take place under the indoor big top and are perfect for kids. Tickets are free.

Danny Gans, at The Mirage

✆702-796-9999

✐www.dannygans.com

He's called "The man of many voices." He's a singer, comedian, and impressionist. It's a show suitable for the entire family. Expect to hear sixty to a hundred celebrity impressions during this thoroughly entertaining show. Tickets are $100.

═FAST FACT

In 2006, the theater where Danny Gans currently performs will become the new home to a $100 million production of a new Cirque du Soleil show. The new show is currently in development in conjunction with the original living members of the Beatles (and the deceased members' widows). When the show opens, it'll surely become one of the hottest tickets on the Strip.

Elton John: *The Red Piano*, at Caesars Palace

☎702-866-1400 (also available from Ticketmaster)

🖰*www.eltonjohn.com*

The music legend performs a concert you won't soon forget! It's suitable for the entire family. Songs featured include: "Benny and the Jets," "Philadelphia Freedom," "Believe," "Daniel," "Rocket Man," "I Guess That's Why They Call It the Blues," "Tiny Dancer," "Don't Let the Sun Go Down on Me," "I Want Love," "Candle in the Wind," "Pinball Wizard," "The Bitch Is Back," "I'm Still Standing," "Saturday Night's Alright for Fighting," and "Your Song." This show is presented on many dates when Celine Dion isn't performing. Contact the box office for specific dates, and reserve your tickets as far in advance as possible. Ticket prices range from $100 to $250.

An Evening at La Cage, at the Riviera

☎702-794-9433

Female impersonators (guys performing as girls) perform music and comedy. It's suitable for teens and adults. Ticket prices are $39.95 each.

Folies Bergere, at the Tropicana

☎702-739-2411

This is one of the longest-running production shows on the Strip. It features singing, dancing, juggling, and comedy. The early show is suitable for everyone, but the late show is for adults only. Tickets are $18.95.

Gladys Knight, at the Flamingo

☎702-733-3333

One of the greatest soul singers of all time performs nightly. Tickets are $60 and $70.

Imperial Hawaiian Luau!
at the Imperial Palace

☎702-794-3114

Experience the magic and entertainment of a real-life Hawaiian luau while enjoying a seafood buffet dinner. It's definitely suitable for the whole family. Tickets are $31.95.

Jubilee! at Bally's
☎702-946-4567

This is one of Las Vegas's longest-running production shows. It features music, dance, acrobatics, and several production numbers. This show is for the eighteen-and-over crowd. Ticket prices are $55 and $74.

"KA" (Cirque du Soleil), at The Mirage
☎800-929-1111

A unique Cirque du Soleil performance with an Asian twist. Ticket prices are $99, $125, and $150.

The King in Concert, at Elvis-A-Rama Museum
☎702-309-7200

An Elvis impersonator performs. Tickets are $14.95.

Lance Burton: Master Magician, at the Monte Carlo
☎702-730-7160

✎www.lanceburton.com

The famous illusionist and magician offers an extremely impressive show. It's suitable for the entire family. Lance invites kids from the audience to be his assistants. Ticket prices are $60.45 and $65.95.

Legends in Concert, at Imperial Palace
☎702-794-3261

Celebrity impersonators perform in this amazing show. Tickets are $24.95.

The Mac King Comedy Magic Show, at Harrah's
☎702-369-5111

Enjoy a family-oriented magic show featuring Mac King, who was recently awarded the title "Magician of the Year" by Magic Castle. Shows are presented in the afternoon, at 1:00 P.M. and 3:00 P.M. Tickets are $16.95.

TRAVEL TIP

Several of the family-oriented shows in Las Vegas feature matinee performances. If you're looking for afternoon entertainment, also consider experiencing some of the many family-oriented attractions located along the Strip.

The Magic of Rick Thomas, at the Tropicana

✆702-739-2411

A family-oriented magic show. Shows are presented in the afternoon, at 2:00 P.M. and 4:00 P.M. Tickets are $18.95.

Mamma Mia! at Mandalay Bay

✆702-632-7580

✍*www.mamma-mia.com*

Straight from the Broadway stage, this award-winning musical features the music of Abba intermixed with a funny and outrageous story line. It's a must-see show for the entire family. Ticket prices are $45, $75, and $100.

Mystère: Cirque du Soleil, at Treasure Island

✆702-796-9999

✍*www.cirquedusoleil.com*

The Cirque du Soleil circus troupe offers an incredible show for the entire family. It features one amazing acrobatic, dance, and musical act after the next. It's definitely a must-see show and one of the best in Las Vegas! Tickets are $95.

 **TRAVEL TIP**

For adults only, Las Vegas also features a handful of music, dance, and variety shows. But without a doubt, the most amazing and visually stunning shows along the Strip are the four Cirque du Soleil shows: *Mystère, "O," Zumanity*, and *KA*.

"O" Cirque du Soleil, at the Bellagio

✆702-769-9999

✐*www.cirquedusoleil.com*

The world-famous Cirque du Soleil French circus troupe performs an incredible show that takes place mainly in 1.5 million gallons of water. It's a show that's not to be missed! Ticket prices range from $93.50 to $150 each.

Outlaws, Cowboys & Men in Black, at Gold Coast

✆702-251-3574

A salute to some of America's best known country artists. Tickets are $31.95.

Penn & Teller, at the Rio

✆702-777-7776

✐*www.pennandteller.com*

The famous comedic magicians perform their own special brand of magic. Suitable for teens and adults, not young kids. Tickets are $70.

Phantom of the Opera (Opening Spring 2006), at The Venetian

✆702-414-1000

✐*www.thephantomoftheopera.com*

The Broadway show comes to Las Vegas in a ninety-minute, $35 million production that shouldn't be missed. Ticket prices are not yet available.

Rita Rudner, at New York–New York

✆702-740-6815

The comedienne performs nightly in a cabaret-style theater. It's a family-friendly show. Ticket prices are $49 and $55.

Saturday Night Fever, at the Sahara

✆702-737-2515

A former Broadway musical based on the hit motion picture. Suitable for the entire family. Features music from the Bee Gees and plenty of dancing. Tickets are $39, $52, and $69.

The Second City, at the Flamingo

✆702-733-3333

✐*www.secondcity.com*

Get ready for sketch comedy at its best. Suitable for children and teens. Tickets are $29.95.

Spirit of the Dance, at the Golden Nugget

✆702-386-8100

✐*www.spiritofthedance.com*

The Irish dance troupe performs. It's a family-oriented show featuring stunning costumes and high-energy, perfectly choreographed dance numbers. Ticket prices are $45 for adults and $35 for children.

Spotlight, at Bourbon Street

✆702-737-7200

A magic and comedy show featuring acts that rotate weekly. One child is admitted free with each paid adult. Tickets are $39.95.

Tony 'n' Tina's Wedding, at Rio

✆702-777-7776

✐*www.tonylovestina.com*

Attend an Italian-style wedding filled with comedy mishaps. Suitable and fun for teens and adults alike. Tickets are $39.95.

Tournament of Kings, at Excalibur

☎702-597-7600

✍www.excalibur.com

A fun-filled, family-oriented show featuring knights, real-life horses, and plenty of jousting. This is a dinner show during which you'll enjoy a medieval feast. Tickets are $43.95.

The Tropicana Bird Show, at the Tropicana

☎702-739-2222

Bird trainer Tiana Carroll performs with her feathered friends in a family-oriented show. Tickets are free.

"V" The Ultimate Variety Show, at Desert Passage at the Aladdin

☎702-932-1818

✍www.vtheshow.com

This is a variety show for the whole family. Ticket prices are $59 and $69 per adult (children are half price).

We Will Rock You, at Paris Las Vegas

☎877-ROCK-SHOW/702-946-4567

A musical featuring twenty of Queen's most popular songs, including "We Are the Champions" and "Another One Bites the Dust." The show offers singing, dancing, special effects, complex laser lights, rock-and-roll fashions, and a talented cast. This is a family-friendly show, suitable for anyone over the age of sixteen. Tickets are $80.50, $97, and $113.50.

Start Exploring the Mega-Resorts

Starting in the next chapter, you'll discover detailed information about each of the popular mega-resorts located on or near the Strip, with extra emphasis on those properties that are most suitable for families. With each property offering a distinctive theme, multiple attractions, shows, a variety of dining options, plenty of shopping, world-class day spas, and so much more, you'll easily find many exciting places to stay in and visit during your trip to Las Vegas.

CHAPTER 6

The Bellagio Las Vegas

ELEGANCE, BEAUTY, magnificent architecture, visually appealing artwork, stunning décor, and top-notch service are just some of what you can expect when you step through the grand entrance of the Bellagio. Created for upscale vacationers and high rollers, the Bellagio is one of the higher-priced mega-resorts on the Strip, but it's definitely worth every penny. This resort is conveniently located in the middle of the Las Vegas Strip, which makes getting to neighboring resorts easy—that is, if you decide to leave the comfort of the Bellagio.

Mega-Resort Overview

✉3600 Las Vegas Boulevard South, Las Vegas, NV 89177
✆888-987-6667
✆702-693-7111
✐*www.bellagio.com*
Room and Suite Rates: $$$$

Built at a cost of over $1.6 billion, this resort also offers world-class restaurants, a luxurious day spa, upscale shops, plus all of the amenities you'd expect from this type of vacation destination. While the focus of the Bellagio is to create a glamorous and lavish environment for guests, you can be as thrifty as your travel budget requires when you stay here and still be able to enjoy the amenities offered by this resort.

▲The Bellagio offers an amazing fountain show. Photo © The Las Vegas News Bureau.

Basic guest rooms start at just $159 and go up to about $800 per night. Thus, the Bellagio is affordable to most vacationers. Yet if you're looking for the ultimate in luxury, you can stay in one of the more elegant and spacious suites, which start at $375 per night and go up considerably to more than $6,000 per night.

The Bellagio is the perfect place for adults, senior citizens, honeymooners, and anyone looking for a romantic getaway. The Bellagio offers many amenities within the guest rooms and suites that help to make this resort ideal for business travelers and conventioners as well.

═FAST FACT

The Bellagio consists of 928 rooms and suites in the Spa Tower, plus 3,005 newly remodeled rooms and suites in the Bellagio Tower. It takes more than 8,000 employees to keep the Bellagio operational.

There's only one drawback to this resort: It's so beautiful and popular that it has become a tourist attraction unto itself. At any given time, day or night, the resort's main lobby, casino, shops, and garden areas are open to the general public and are typically packed with exploring tourists. To limit the crowds, certain areas of the resort are accessible only to guests.

BELLAGIO OVERALL FAMILY-FRIENDLINESS RATING

Ages Up to 5	Ages 6–15	Ages 16–20	Ages 21 & Up	Senior Citizens
☆	☆☆	☆☆☆	☆☆☆	☆☆☆

Guest Room Accommodations

Extreme elegance is a term often used to describe the Bellagio. Looking out the window of virtually any deluxe guest room, you can expect to see an excellent view of the resort's lake, the surrounding mountains, or the beautiful Las Vegas skyline. Each guest room is equipped with virtually every amenity a guest could want or need. Rooms are decorated with European-style furnishings and art.

Standard guest rooms feature an armoire, which houses a remote-controlled cable television, stereo, electronic in-room safe, and a lighted wardrobe section (large enough for hanging full-length gowns or other formal attire). There's also a writing desk (equipped with a two-line telephone and computer/fax-accessible data ports), high-speed Internet access, and a small table with two chairs. Guests are offered a choice of one king-size or two queen-size beds, all triple-sheeted. Electronic drapes, a stocked mini bar, iron and ironing board, and well-equipped bathrooms (which include robes) are among the other standard amenities.

The larger and more elaborate guest suites offer even more luxurious surroundings. Additional amenities include a marble foyer, a separate living room and bedroom(s), an entertainment center (containing a remote-controlled cable television, VCR, and stereo), powder room, wet bar (with refrigerator and icemaker), private fax machine, high-speed Internet access, separate climate control in the bedroom, two master bathrooms (one with a steam shower and the other equipped with a whirlpool tub), a second cable television set, a telephone in the bathroom, robes, slippers, and an assortment of spa products.

Featured Attractions and Activities

The Bellagio features a prestigious art gallery plus indoor gardens as its primary attractions. The overall atmosphere is upscale and sophisticated, appealing mainly to an adult crowd.

The Bellagio Gallery of Fine Art

✆877-957-9777

✆702-693-7871

✐www.bgfa.biz

Until recently, the last thing you'd expect to find in Las Vegas was an art museum showcasing some of the greatest works of art in the world. Well, in recent years, several such museums have opened right on the Strip, including the Bellagio Gallery of Fine Art. Displayed here are collections that feature works from artists such as Matisse, Miró, Monet, Picasso, Renoir, and van Gogh.

═FAST FACT

During much of 1993 and 1994, the main exhibit at the Bellagio Gallery of Fine Art was *Monet: Masterworks from the Museum of Fine Arts, Boston.* This exhibit presents works spanning fifty years of Claude Monet's career and features some of his most recognizable and important paintings.

Housing one of the most comprehensive art collections in America, the gallery is open daily between 9:00 A.M. and 9:00 P.M. A taped audio tour (available in four languages) that explains each painting and piece of artwork is provided.

Understandably, this gallery has become an extremely popular attraction, so tickets should be purchased in advance. Tickets can be purchased up to seven days in advance. Ticket prices are $15 per person ($12 for Nevada residents) and $12 for students and senior citizens.

THE BELLAGIO GALLERY OF FINE ART

Ages Up to 5	Ages 6–15	Ages 16–20	Ages 21 & Up	Senior Citizens
Not Suitable	Not Suitable	★★	★★★	★★★

The Conservatory and Botanical Gardens

Travelers from around the world continue to visit the Bellagio to see the artwork that's on display at the Bellagio Gallery of Fine Art, but what you'll find across the resort's front lobby is one of the prettiest attractions in all of Las Vegas: the Conservatory and Botanical Gardens.

Admission is free and though it's open twenty-four hours a day, this attraction is usually crowded. Hotel guests and visitors alike can stroll through this area and enjoy the colors and fragrances of more than 10,000 flowering plants, arranged to create living art. The floral displays change regularly with the seasons.

This attraction was created and is maintained by a team of 100 horticulturists. It's the perfect place to snap a photo, propose marriage, or enjoy a romantic walk.

THE CONSERVATORY AND BOTANICAL GARDENS

Ages Up to 5	Ages 6–15	Ages 16–20	Ages 21 & Up	Senior Citizens
★	★★★	★★★	★★★	★★★

The Fountains of Bellagio

Over fifty years ago, Walt Disney discovered that people are fascinated and entertained by fountains that shoot water high into the air. Thus, at the Disneyland Hotel in Anaheim, California, he created a colorful, musical, and visually stunning dancing-waters show. Here in Las Vegas, a bigger, more modern, and more exciting show has been created.

This is an impressive show that's presented on a man-made lake spanning more than 8.5 acres. You can witness this presentation every afternoon and evening in front of the Bellagio (weather permitting). This free show features more than 1,000 shooting fountains that are synchronized with colored lights and music.

TRAVEL TIP

The Fountains of Bellagio show can be seen from anywhere in front of the mega-resort's property on the sidewalk along Las Vegas Boulevard (the Strip). If you visit the top of the Eiffel Tower at Paris Las Vegas (located across the street), you'll be treated to an awesome view of the Fountains of Bellagio show.

The Fountains of Bellagio is definitely suitable for all ages. The accompanying music ranges from Copland, Strauss, Pavarotti, and Sinatra to contemporary music and popular Broadway show tunes. The show is more impressive after dark.

THE FOUNTAINS OF BELLAGIO

Ages Up to 5	Ages 6–15	Ages 16–20	Ages 21 & Up	Senior Citizens
☆☆	☆☆☆	☆☆☆	☆☆☆	☆☆☆

It's Showtime at the Bellagio

In addition to the mega-resort's unique attractions, the Bellagio is also the home to one of Las Vegas's most amazing and entertaining shows: Cirque du Soleil "O."

Cirque du Soleil's "O"

☎888-488-7111

☎702-693-7722

✉*www.cirquedusoleil.com*

The world-renowned French circus troupe, Cirque du Soleil, has a large and ever-growing presence along the Strip. It all started with a show called *Mystère* over a decade ago. Later, on October 19, 1998, Cirque du Soleil's "O" premiered, offering a totally new form of entertainment.

Today, in addition to these two innovative and highly entertaining shows, you'll also find three other Cirque du Soleil extravaganzas presented nightly at the MGM Grand, New York–New York, and The Mirage.

Of all the shows and attractions in Las Vegas, only a handful can boast of being sold out virtually every night. "O" is one such show . . . and with very good reason! "O" introduces audiences to a totally new form of original live entertainment, which Cirque du Soleil has become so famous for creating.

This ninety-minute performance stars a cast of seventy-four circus performers, acrobats, clowns, and artists from around the world. "O" incorporates all of the elements that have made Cirque du Soleil a worldwide phenomenon. You'll see lavish costumes, original music, special effects, and incredible circus talent featured throughout the performance. Yet what makes "O" so extraordinary is that it adds another component to Cirque du Soleil's unusual form of entertainment: water.

The entire performance takes place in the air, on a traditional stage, *and* under water. Cirque du Soleil's "O" is truly original, breathtaking, absolutely entertaining! "O" marks Cirque du Soleil's first venture into aquatic theater. Acrobats, trapeze artists, clowns, high-wire artists, and other performers coexist with synchronized swimmers and other water-based acts. The state-of-the-art, custom-built theater includes a 1.5-million-gallon pool. For much of the show, the pool acts as the stage.

═ FAST FACT

The show's name was inspired by the concept of infinity and the circle of life. "O" is elegance in its purest form. Phonetically speaking, "O" (spelled *eau*) is the French word for water.

This show is one of the most elaborate productions in Las Vegas. As a result, ticket prices are steep—$93.50, $99, $125, and $150—but well worth every penny. If you're planning to stay at any of The Mirage resorts, tickets can be purchased up to ninety days in advance. (Nonguests can purchase tickets up to twenty-eight days in advance.) This is definitely one of the hottest-selling shows in Las Vegas, so ordering your tickets as far in advance as possible is an absolute must.

Two performances are held Friday through Tuesday nights at 7:30 P.M. and 10:30 P.M. There are no performances Wednesday or Thursday nights. If you can't purchase tickets well in advance, unclaimed tickets go on sale shortly before each performance; however, people start lining up to buy these tickets several hours before showtime.

Anyone who appreciates ballet and synchronized swimming will truly love "O," which is very different than Cirque du Soleil's *Mystère* (presented at Treasure Island), Cirque du Soleil's *Zumanity* (presented at New York–New York), or any of the troupe's touring performances. Like *Zumanity*, "O" is definitely more suitable for an adult crowd. In this case, with its water-ballet element, some of the show may be too sophisticated for children and teens to truly appreciate and enjoy. If you're traveling with younger people, Cirque du Soleil *Mystère* is probably more suitable.

Fans of the Beatles' music will definitely want to experience the latest Cirque du Soleil show slated to open in 2006 at The Mirage. This new show is being developed with the help of the remaining living members of the Beatles, as well as the widows of the deceased members.

CIRQUE DU SOLEIL'S "O"

Ages Up to 5	Ages 6–15	Ages 16–20	Ages 21 & Up	Senior Citizens
Not Suitable	Not Suitable	★★★	★★★	★★★

Shopping

The Las Vegas area features several upscale malls and shopping areas, such as the Forum Shops at Caesars Palace. Within many of the resorts along the Strip, you'll also find a few fine shops and exclusive boutiques. At the Bellagio, however, you'll find a collection of upscale shops, the likes of which you won't find anywhere else on the Strip.

Whether you have a wallet full of cash to spend or you just want to spend several hours browsing, the shopping experience at the Bellagio is memorable.

An Old World porte-cochère leads the way to the elegant Via Bellagio promenade, where you'll find the following upscale designer shops and boutiques:

- **Chanel**: A fashion and fine jewelry boutique, this shop offers the complete range of Chanel apparel and accessories from the current collection, such as handbags, accessories, shoes, and fragrances. The Chanel Fine Jewelry Boutique houses the complete collection of fine jewelry by this designer.
- **Giorgio Armani**: This boutique carries the Giorgio Armani "black label" collection for men and women that includes tailored clothes, dresses, sportswear, evening wear, and accessories.
- **Prada**: Shoppers can choose from ready-to-wear accessories and footwear as well as the line of Prada sports clothes offered at this boutique.
- **Tiffany & Co.**: Modeled after Tiffany & Co.'s famous Fifth Avenue (New York) store, this boutique features a full selection of Tiffany's classic merchandise, including fine jewelry, watches, clocks, china, crystal, sterling silver flatware, writing instruments, fragrances, and personal accessories.
- **Fred Leighton**: The fine jewelry at this boutique includes a rare collection of diamonds, rubies, emeralds, and sapphires, plus estate and antique jewelry.

- **Hermés**: This boutique features sportswear and leather goods from the popular French designer.
- **Gucci**: Here you'll find Gucci's trademark handbags, luggage, small leather goods, shoes, ties and scarves, women's and men's clothing, watches, household items, jewelry, eyeglasses, and perfumes.
- **Yves Saint Laurent**: Designer fashions are offered here.

In addition to the boutiques and shops you'll find along the Via Bellagio promenade, other shops within the resort include:

- **The Lobby Shop**: Here you'll find a selection of designer gifts and accessories, cosmetics, home decorations, and more. (Open daily, between 9:00 A.M. and midnight.)
- **D. Fine**: This shop offers men's designer clothing. (Open daily, between 9:00 A.M. and midnight.)
- **Tutto**: Bellagio merchandise, gifts, cosmetics, and sundries are sold here. (Open twenty-four hours per day.)
- **The Cirque du Soleil Store**: A wide selection of souvenirs from one of Las Vegas's most popular shows is available here, including the soundtrack from "*O*," clothing items, and other unusual gifts for both adults and kids. (Open daily, between 10:00 A.M. and 1:00 A.M.)
- **Capri**: A selection of swimwear and activewear is offered at this shop. (Open daily, between 9:00 A.M. and midnight.)
- **Tesorini**: This is a fine jewelry and watch boutique. (Open daily, between 9:00 A.M. and midnight.)
- **Origins**: Cosmetics and body care products from the popular Origins line are available here. This store is located within Capri. (Open daily, between 9:00 A.M. and midnight.)
- **The Botanical Garden Store**: This is a lovely home and garden accessories store. (Open daily, between 9:00 A.M. and midnight.)

 **TRAVEL TIP**

Many of the upscale beauty and salon products used at Salon Bellagio and Spa Bellagio are available for purchase, including a wide range of body care, beauty, and hair care products. Be sure to drop into the boutique area of Salon Bellagio and/or Spa Bellagio after your appointment.

Day Spa, Salon, and Fitness Facilities

If you're looking to relax and truly pamper yourself, be sure to book appointments at Spa Bellagio and/or Salon Bellagio early. These are among the most upscale and lovely spa facilities on the Strip. If you can't get yourself an appointment here, an excellent alternative is the world-famous Canyon Ranch SpaClub at The Venetian.

Spa Bellagio

✆702-693-7472

Spa Bellagio, located in the Conservatory and Botanical Gardens, offers a full complement of therapeutic and rejuvenating body care treatments. Spa visitors are pampered while surrounded by the tranquil beauty of the gardens.

Choose from a variety of treatments, including aromatherapy, various types of massages, hydrotherapy treatments, facials, and body treatments, or experience the day spa's famous Vichy showers. For all of the treatments, Spa Bellagio uses its own, top-of-the-line, private-label products.

Separate men's and women's locker room facilities provide the maximum in comfort, complete with steam rooms, saunas, whirlpools, and deluxe lounges. While the price of individual treatments varies, you can utilize just the facilities themselves for a daily fee of $25. The fee includes the use of the redwood sauna, eucalyptus steam room, heated whirlpools, cold plunge, relaxation lounge, shower facility, fitness room, and vanity amenities. Spa attire, including robes, sandals, shorts, and T-shirts, are provided. Use of these facilities is included with all spa treatments. The spa is open daily between 6:00 A.M. and 8:00 P.M. Reservations can be made up to three months in advance.

TRAVEL ESSENTIAL

Between March and December 2004, the main Bellagio spa was closed for renovation. The new 65,000-square-foot facility has reopened and now offers guests a truly memorable, relaxing, and rejuvenating experience in a world-class day spa facility.

The Fitness Center

Spa Bellagio also offers a coed exercise facility. It features a complete line of Cybex weight machines and free weights, state-of-the-art cardiovascular equipment, and a staff of attendants to assist you. For an additional fee, personalized one-on-one training sessions are available.

There is a $25 daily fee to use this facility. The fee includes the use of the redwood sauna, eucalyptus steam room, heated whirlpools, cold plunge, relaxation lounge, shower facility, exercise room, and vanity amenities. Spa attire, including robes, sandals, shorts, and T-shirts, are provided.

FAST FACT

Visitors to Spa Bellagio must be over age eighteen. The fitness center is open to guests over the age sixteen with adult supervision of minors required.

Salon Bellagio

✆702-693-8080

The Bellagio offers a full-service, upscale salon for male and female clientele. The salon is open daily from 9:00 A.M. to 7:00 P.M.

Appointments should be booked as far in advance as possible, especially if you're visiting the salon in preparation for a special occasion. Contact the salon directly (or visit the Bellagio's Web site) for a menu of available services and pricing.

Family-Oriented Amenities

While the Bellagio isn't the ideal family-oriented resort for those traveling with kids or teens, it does offer a handful of amenities that cater to families, including several casual-dining options, multiple swimming pools, and multiroom suites.

The swimming pool area at the Bellagio is divided into six courtyard settings. Six swimming pools, plus spas and private cabanas (available for a fee), are available to guests. The landscaping around the pool area, like everything else at the Bellagio, conveys pure elegance and beauty. The pools are heated year-round, but hours of operation vary by season. Contact the hotel's concierge for details.

Dining Options

Whether you choose one of the formal restaurants within the Bellagio or a more casual dining experience, this mega-resort offers a wonderful selection of restaurants and lounges, staffed by world-class chefs.

Fine Dining

Careful attention to detail has obviously been paid to every menu item served within these fine-dining establishments. Award-winning chefs have been brought in and offer a wide range of cuisine types to cater to guests' diverse tastes.

Whether you're planning a romantic dinner for two, a business dinner for a small group, or an outing with friends, when you dine at one of the Bellagio's restaurants, you can be certain that the food and service will be top-notch and the atmosphere will be elegant, even extravagant.

To make an advance reservation at any of the Bellagio's fine-dining restaurants, call ✆702-693-7223.

Le Cirque ($$$)

Open seven nights a week, between 5:30 P.M. and 10:30 P.M., this restaurant serves contemporary French cuisine in an elegant setting that overlooks the resort's lake. There's an à la carte menu; however, the restaurant specializes in serving complete multicourse meals, priced starting at $85 per person.

The dress code is formal (a jacket and tie is required for men). This restaurant is rather small (it seats eighty people), so reservations are an absolute must.

Circo ($$$)

✆702-693-8150

Open Wednesdays through Sundays for lunch (11:30 A.M. to 2:30 P.M.) and dinner nightly (between 5:30 P.M. and 11:00 P.M.), this restaurant serves home-style Tuscan food, inspired by Egidiana Maccioni. Complete multicourse dinners start at $95 per person; there's also an à la carte menu available. The wine list offered at Circo includes more than 400 selections. The dining room has seating for 175 guests, and two private dining rooms are available. The restaurant is located along the lake, next to Le Cirque. The dress code is described by the management as "casual elegance." Reservations are recommended.

Picasso ($$$)

Picasso overlooks the Bellagio's lake and is open every evening for dinner (except Tuesdays) between 6:00 P.M. and 9:30 P.M. The restaurant offers elegant French cuisine with a menu that changes with the seasons. Entrées typically feature a Spanish influence and can be accompanied by American or European wine. Dinner costs $65 to $75 per person. The dress code is casual elegance. Reservations are recommended.

Aqua ($$$)

Michael Mina and Charles Condy's world-renowned San Francisco–based seafood restaurant now has a second location. You'll find this restaurant near the Bellagio Gallery of Fine Art. Open daily for dinner between 5:30 P.M. and 10:00 P.M., the menu offers a selection of contemporary seafood dishes that are prepared using French-influenced cooking techniques that incorporate ingredients imported from California and the Mediterranean. A four-course and a five-course dinner are offered, priced at $85 and $95, respectively. (A vegetarian five-course meal is also available.) The dress is casual elegance. Reservations are recommended.

Olives ($$/$$$)

Modeled after the Olives restaurant in Boston, Chef Todd English offers a casual Mediterranean café atmosphere located in the heart of the Via Bellagio shopping area. From a lively open kitchen, lunch is served from 11:00 A.M. to 2:30 P.M., and dinner is served from 5:00 P.M. until 10:30 P.M. daily.

Olives described its style of food as "interpretive Mediterranean," with lunch main courses priced from $15 to $22, and dinner main courses priced between $20 and $38. The dress code is casual. Food is served in the main dining area as well as on an outside patio.

Prime Steakhouse ($$$)

If you're in the mood for a hearty steak, chops, or seafood dinner, Prime Steakhouse offers everything you'd find on the menu of a 1930s chophouse, complete with an extensive wine list. Dinner is served nightly between 5:30 P.M. and 10:00 P.M. Main entrées are priced between $25 and $48. Men are asked to wear jackets at this lakeside restaurant. Reservations are recommended.

Jasmine ($$$)

The décor of this restaurant features subtle European influences, but the food selection is contemporary Chinese and traditional Hong Kong Cantonese. Dinner is served nightly from 5:30 P.M. to 10:00 P.M.

Main courses range in price from $22 to $39. The restaurant itself is located alongside the resort's lake, which offers a stunning view of the fountains. Reservations are recommended.

Shintaro ($$$)

Authentically prepared Teppanyaki, sushi, and multicourse California-inspired tasting menus are what you'll find offered at this midpriced restaurant. The bar offers a selection of Japanese beers and sakes, plus a large selection of American and French wines. Shintaro is open nightly from 5:30 P.M. to 10:30 P.M. Entrées range in price from $24 to $50. The Kaiseki menu is priced between $35 and $85 per entrée. The dress code is casual elegance. Reservations are recommended.

Noodles ($$)

The chefs here prepare traditional noodle dishes from Thailand, Japan, China, and Vietnam. Also offered are authentic Hong Kong–style barbecue dishes. Traditional Chinese dim sum is also served daily. Noodles is a casual restaurant open daily for lunch and dinner. Sunday through Thursday, hours are between 11:00 A.M. and midnight. Fridays and Saturdays, hours are from 11:00 A.M. until 2:00 A.M. Dim sum is served Friday through Sunday, between 11:00 A.M. and 3:00 P.M. Dinner entrées range in price from $12 to $30. Reservations are not required.

Casual Dining

The Bellagio also offers the following casual-dining options for light meals and snacks throughout the day and evening:

- Café Bellagio
- The Breads of La Brea Bakery
- The Buffet at Bellagio
- Café Gelato ice cream and sweets
- The Pool Café (open seasonally)
- Palio Espresso Bar
- Fix Restaurant and Bar

 **TRAVEL TIP**

The Buffet at Bellagio offers an elegant, all-you-can-eat meal. Hours vary, so make sure you call ahead.

Lounges and Bars

The Bellagio offers a number of lounges and bars that cater to adult guests. If you're looking to sit and enjoy a drink and some good entertainment, consider some of the following places.

Fontana Bar

Located in the heart of the Bellagio's casino, live entertainment and full bar service are available. Open daily until 1:00 A.M. or 2:00 A.M.

Allegro Bar

This full-service bar is located within the Bellagio's casino and offers everything from Bordeaux to cognacs. Open twenty-four hours a day, with live entertainment presented every afternoon and evening.

Petrossian Bar

Offering afternoon tea (between 2:00 P.M. and 5:00 P.M.) along with the finest champagnes, plus caviar and smoked salmon, this bar is an elegant place to meet and enjoy a drink with friends or loved ones. The bar is located in the lobby and is open twenty-four hours. Live piano music is played throughout the day and evening.

Baccarat Bar

Located next to the Baccarat Salon, this bar offers a selection of cocktails, including martinis, fruit-blended wine drinks, and Italian Bellinis. Live piano music is presented every afternoon and evening. The bar is open twenty-four hours a day.

Pool Bar

Located on the pool promenade; full bar service is offered.

Caramel Bar & Lounge

A disc jockey plays music nightly between 5:00 P.M. and 5:00 A.M. Dance, drink, and socialize virtually all night.

The Race & Sports Book Bar

Enjoy a drink while watching your favorite sporting events. This bar overlooks the Bellagio's Poker Room and Race & Sports Book.

 TRAVEL TIP

In addition to offering a handful of upscale bars and lounges, the Bellagio has a premiere nightclub called Light. It features a sexy yet refined atmosphere with an emphasis on comfort. Tables are available within the club by reservation only. Open Thursdays through Sundays, between 10:30 P.M. and 4:00 A.M.

Bellagio's Casino

Catering to the discriminating gambler, the 100,000-square-foot casino and gaming area at the Bellagio offers a wide range of table games, including blackjack, Big Six, craps, Let It Ride, roulette, Pai Gow, Caribbean Stud poker, and baccarat. There's also a poker room, a keno lounge, and a race and sports book, plus thousands of slot and video poker machines. At the table games, the minimum bets tend to be higher than at most of the other casinos.

When it comes to gaming, the Bellagio offers its exclusive Poker Room. With nonstop action and high and low limits, you're bound to find a perfectly suited hand. Popular games include Texas Hold 'em and Seven Card Stud. The Bellagio Poker Room is a smoke-free environment. Regular events held within the Poker Room include:

- A $500 + $40 buy-in No Limit Hold 'em tournament every Wednesday at 1:15 P.M.
- A $1,000 + $60 buy-in No Limit Hold 'em tournament every Friday at 5:00 P.M.

This casino is affiliated with the MGM Mirage Player's Club, which offers slot and table-game players opportunities to earn points redeemable for cash, complimentary rooms, and show tickets at several mega-resorts located along the Strip, including The Mirage, Treasure Island, MGM Grand, and New York–New York.

Useful Information for Guests

While the Bellagio isn't the ideal hotel if you're traveling with kids or teens, it will provide for an extremely comfortable, memorable, and fun vacation if you're traveling with other adults, including senior citizens.

Between the multiple outdoor swimming pools, the attractions (such as the Conservatory and Botanical Gardens and the Bellagio Gallery of Fine Art), the fine restaurants, Cirque du Soleil's "O," the Spa Bellagio, and the Salon Bellagio, you'll easily find many ways to relax, entertain, and pamper yourself.

 JUST FOR PARENTS

Thinking about getting married or renewing your wedding vows? The Bellagio offers two luxurious wedding chapels as well as the Terrace of Dreams. For more information, call the Wedding Chapels at Bellagio at 888-464-4436. The chapels and terrace can accommodate between thirty and more than a hundred guests.

The Bellagio is located near the center of the Strip, which makes getting around the area extremely convenient. In February 2005, however, the Tram will open and make getting to and from the Bellagio and the Monte Carlo resort even more convenient.

From the moment you step into the Bellagio's breathtaking lobby, you'll discover why this is an award-winning resort, rivaled in Las Vegas only by The Venetian, the Four Seasons, and the Wynn Las Vegas. To save some money, be sure to shop for the best room rates online, and contact the MGM Mirage Vacation Planning department at ☎800-360-7111 (✉*www.mgmmiragevacations.com*) to learn about discounted vacation packages.

Bellagio Information on Your Wireless Web Device

If you have a handheld wireless Web surfing device, a Palm OS-compatible PDA, or a cell phone that allows you to surf the Internet—you can obtain a wide range of information about the Bellagio anytime and from anywhere.

To access this special "mobile-optimized" Web site from your handheld wireless Internet device, wireless PDA, or Smartphone:

1. Launch your device's mini-browser.
2. Choose "Go To . . ." link.
3. Key in *mobile.bellagio.com* as the "mobile-optimized" Web site address and select "OK."

CHAPTER 7

Caesars Palace

WHAT DOES IT TAKE to build an empire? Well, Julius Caesar managed to do it in ancient Rome using military force. Today, another empire based on Caesar's legacy has been built and continues to expand. But it's an army of construction workers, architects, and resort operators who are responsible for this empire.

Mega-Resort Overview

✉3570 Las Vegas Boulevard, Las Vegas, NV 89109
✆877-427-7243
✆702-731-7110
✍*www.caesars.com*
Room and Suite Rates: $$$/$$$$

Caesars Palace is an extremely popular resort that continues to undergo massive expansion and renovation. It's become one of the largest yet most fairly priced of the mega-resorts in Las Vegas, as well as a classic Las Vegas landmark (having been open since August 1966).

This resort caters to just about everyone. It offers the finest of casinos, shopping at one of the most successful and classiest malls in the world, tennis, swimming, plenty of dining options, a luxurious full-service spa, plenty of entertainment-oriented activities, plus comfortable rooms and suites.

Caesars Palace provides all of the amenities and services you could ask for. Yet the room rates aren't overpriced. This is definitely one of the most popular mega-resort properties on the Strip. If you haven't visited this resort in a few years, though, chances are you'll barely recognize it.

▲Celine Dion performs at Caesars Palace.   Photo ©The Las Vegas News Bureau.

Over $376 million has already been spent to expand and modernize this mega-resort property. Expansion includes an all-new, 949-room, twenty-six-story luxury hotel tower. With this addition, Caesars Palace now contains 3,370 guest rooms and suites. Even with all of these rooms, be sure to book your reservations early. For the past five years, the resort has averaged over a 94 percent occupancy rate.

Connected to this new tower is the Colosseum, a state-of-the-art, 4,100-seat theater, which is now home to Celine Dion's show, *Celine Dion: A New Day . . .*, as well as Sir Elton John's *The Red Piano* show.

There's also a new open-air Roman plaza, a recently completed three-level expansion to the world-famous Forum Shops, a lavish new casino entrance, plus a handful of new restaurants. In summer 2004, celebrity chef Bobby Flay opened the Mesa Grill. In the past several years, other fine-dining restaurants to open in this mega-resort include 808 (a seafood and Pan Pacific–inspired restaurant) and Café Lago (a twenty-four-hour café).

TRAVEL ESSENTIAL

Caesars Palace has its own stop along the new Las Vegas Monorail system. Utilizing the monorail (as opposed to shuttle buses or taxis) makes it easier and cheaper to travel up and down the Strip to visit other mega-resorts and attractions.

More recently, several new casual-dining options opened in conjunction with the Cypress Street Marketplace, which is a casual-dining destination/food court area within Caesars Palace. Featuring a variety of dining options, it's open daily, between 11:00 A.M. and 11:00 P.M. (and until midnight on Fridays and Saturdays).

Since 2003, Caesars Palace also renovated more than 600 of its existing guest rooms, plus has added a new high-limit slot salon, several pool villa suites, and the Palace Court (a high-limit table game salon). This ongoing expansion and renovation continues to make Caesars Palace a fun place to stay, whether you're traveling with kids, teens, adults, or senior citizens.

CAESARS PALACE OVERALL FAMILY-FRIENDLINESS RATING

Ages Up to 5	Ages 6–15	Ages 16–20	Ages 21 & Up	Senior Citizens
☆☆	☆☆	☆☆☆	☆☆☆	☆☆☆

Guest Room Accommodations

When it comes to guest room accommodations, Caesars Palace has several room and suite configurations that are suitable for almost anyone, and that can fit almost any vacation budget. Caesars Palace is a midpriced mega-resort; however, the more luxurious suites are definitely comparable to other lavish, upscale resorts on or near the Strip.

Caesars Palace offers basic rooms located in one of the resort's three original towers. Standard Deluxe Rooms offer about 325 square feet of living space. These rooms include a wardrobe closet, a small sitting area, and a bathroom with a vanity that is elegantly done in marble and brass. The rooms are ideal for two people.

You can upgrade from the Standard Deluxe Room to a Spa Deluxe Room (featuring an oversized marble Jacuzzi bathtub) or a Superior Deluxe Room, which offers considerably more space and additional amenities. If you're traveling with one or two children and can't afford a suite, a Superior Deluxe Room is an excellent option.

Superior Deluxe Rooms offer 500 square feet of living space in the Palace Tower. Amenities include a small entrance hall, a writing desk that is fax accessible, a marble dry bar, a lighted wardrobe closet, climate control, and a marble and brass bathroom that features a split vanity and an oversized Jacuzzi tub, along with its own telephone. Within a Superior Deluxe Room, you'll also find a 27-inch television, iron and ironing board, one king-size bed or two queen-size beds, an in-room safe, and high-speed Internet access.

 TRAVEL TIP

When shopping for a package deal to stay at any of the mega-resorts, be sure to check the various travel-related Web sites, such as Travelocity.com, Hotwire.com, Priceline.com, and Vegas.com. You can often save money by booking your airfares and hotel accommodations together as a package or take advantage of other special promotions offered online only.

For a more extravagant experience during your stay at Caesars Palace, consider a more expensive Petite Suite (also ideal for families needing extra space), a Royal Suite (offering a separate bedroom, dining area, and living room area), a Double Bay Suite (a one-bedroom, apartment-style suite that can be connected to an adjoining room to offer the convenience of a two-bedroom suite), or a Duplex Suite in the Forum Tower (which offers two bedrooms, a spacious living room, multiple bathrooms, a dining table that seats six, and many other amenities).

More extravagant and expensive multiroom suites are also available. Contact the resort's reservations department for details. Throughout the year, Caesars Palace offers special promotions and package deals, some of which include two or three nights' accommodations, two show tickets (for Celine Dion, Elton John, or another headliner), a $100 food and beverage credit, transportation to and from the McCarran International Airport, and two admissions to the spa and fitness center. Packages range in price from $350 to $2,500 for double occupancy.

Featured Attractions and Activities

Caesars Palace doesn't offer a lot in the way of kid-oriented attractions. It does, however, offer an excellent location on the Strip, several lovely outdoor swimming pools, fairly priced room accommodations, and many affordable and family-friendly dining options. The resort is attached to the Forum Shops, which offer some of the best shopping in Las Vegas. Kids will love exploring the FAO Schwartz superstore, which recently reopened in the Forum Shops.

This mega-resort offers a lot in the way of adult-oriented attractions, activities, and dining options. Caesars Palace even has its own golf course, located a short distance from the Strip.

Cascata Golf Club

✆877-222-2455

✆702-294-2000

✍*www.cascatagolf.com*

Designed by golf course architect Rees Jones, Cascata opened in 2000. It's since been described as having one of the finest original course designs in the world. Cascata offers the ultimate in privacy, luxury, and service. It's located less than thirty minutes from the Strip. Rates are $350 on Mondays, Wednesdays, and Thursdays, and $500 on Fridays, Saturdays, and Sundays.

 TRAVEL ESSENTIAL

In Italian, the word *Cascata* means "waterfall." Thus, Cascata Golf Club is suitably named. A stunning, 418-foot waterfall flows from the nearby mountainside and cascades into a river that flows directly through the luxurious clubhouse.

This golf course was created exclusively for the customers of Caesars Entertainment's various resort properties, including Caesars Palace. Here, you'll find mountains, waterfalls, rivers, perfect landscaping, and incredible views that add to the ambiance of this award-winning golf course. Within the clubhouse, you'll find a pro shop staffed by knowledgeable experts.

CASCATA GOLF CLUB

Ages Up to 5	Ages 6–15	Ages 16–20	Ages 21 & Up	Senior Citizens
Not Suitable	Not Suitable	☆☆	☆☆☆	☆☆☆

It's Showtime at Caesars Palace

Some mega-resorts offer magic shows. Others offer full-production shows, featuring showgirls and/or comedy acts. You'll also find a handful of mega-resorts offering Broadway shows. Caesars Palace's approach to in-house entertainment is to have some of the best-known recording artists in the world headline at the Colosseum theater.

Recording superstar Celine Dion is the resident headliner. However, on dates when she's not performing Sir Elton John takes center stage at the Colosseum, offering an equally incredible and memorable concert.

Celine Dion: A New Day . . .

☎702-474-4000

☎877-4-CELINE

🖋*www.celinedion.com*

You're about to discover what happens when you take a state-of-the-art theater, which houses the largest LCD video screen in the world, invite one of the world's most successful recording artists to perform, then throw into the mix live musicians and sixty talented dancers. Next, add over 4,000 fans to watch the performance and you wind up with *Celine Dion: A New Day . . .*

This show is so much more than a traditional live concert. It's a full-scale, multimillion-dollar production that is suitable for the entire family and is absolutely amazing.

Celine Dion: A New Day . . . is presented 200 nights per year (on Wednesdays through Sundays). Each nightly performance begins at 8:30 P.M. Since its opening, *Celine Dion: A New Day . . .* has become one of the most popular shows in Las Vegas, typically selling out weeks or months in advance. Tickets prices range from $87.50 to $225.

During the memorable performance, Celine chats with the audience and performs twenty-one of her greatest hits, including "The Power of Love," "Because You Loved Me," "To Love You More," "Fever," "I Drove All Night," and "My Heart Will Go On."

≡FAST FACT

Born in Charlemagne (a small town near Montreal, Quebec, Canada), Celine is the youngest of fourteen children. At age five, Celine began singing and performing with her siblings. At age twelve, together with her mother and one of her brothers, Celine composed her first song. René Angélil, a well-respected personal manager, heard the tape and became determined to make her a star.

Throughout the concert, visually stunning images and animations are shown on the massive video wall. These images seamlessly mesh with the sets, the dancers' perfect choreography, the live musicians, and, of course, Celine's amazing vocal performance. You're in for an incredible treat when you watch this family-oriented show.

CELINE DION: A NEW DAY . . .

Ages Up to 5	Ages 6–15	Ages 16–20	Ages 21 & Up	Senior Citizens
Not Suitable	☆☆	☆☆☆	☆☆☆	☆☆☆

Sir Elton John: *The Red Piano*

☏702-866-1400

✐*www.eltonjohn.com*

The musical living-legend known as Sir Elton John performs a concert you won't soon forget! His personality, outfits, and talent combine to create an incredible show that showcases many of the hit songs from his illustrious career.

Songs featured (in the order they're performed) include: "Benny and the Jets," "Philadelphia Freedom," "Believe," "Daniel," "Rocket Man," "I Guess That's Why They Call It the Blues," "Tiny Dancer," "Don't Let the Sun Go Down on Me," "I Want Love," "Candle in the Wind," "Pinball Wizard," "The Bitch Is Back," "I'm Still Standing," "Saturday Night's Alright for Fighting," and "Your Song."

This show is presented on many dates when Celine Dion isn't performing. Contact the box office for specific dates, and reserve your tickets as far in advance as possible. Ticket prices range from $100 to $250.

Like *Celine Dion: A New Day . . .*, Elton John's *The Red Piano* is much more than just a concert. It's a musical event that the entire family will absolutely love.

SIR ELTON JOHN: *THE RED PIANO*

Ages Up to 5	Ages 6–15	Ages 16–20	Ages 21 & Up	Senior Citizens
Not Suitable	☆☆	☆☆☆	☆☆☆	☆☆☆

Shopping

If you enjoy shopping, Caesars Palace is home to the newly expanded Forum Shops, one of the most popular, beautiful, and fun-filled malls in the entire world. In addition, there's also a smaller shopping area within this mega-resort, known as the Appian Way.

Not only is it easy to spend at least an entire day doing nothing but shopping within the Forum Shops, it's also a great place to find incredible deals on designer clothing and name-brand merchandise, especially between seasons when older merchandise and fashions are being phased out to make room for new items.

The Appian Way

Within the Caesars Palace resort is a shopping promenade, known as the Appian Way. This area is distinctive for its corridors of imported fine marble, as well as its giant statue of David, which is an exact replica of Michelangelo's masterpiece. The Appian Way is open from 10:00 A.M. to 11:00 P.M. Sunday through Thursday, and from 10:00 A.M. to midnight on Friday and Saturday.

Here you'll find the following upscale shops, boutiques, and restaurants:

- **Ancient Creations**: Rare coins and unique jewelry
- **Art in Crystal**: Fine-art glass and crystal from America and Europe
- **Bernini Couture**: Fine apparel
- **Brittany & Company**: Fine jewelry
- **Caesars Exclusively!**: Merchandise featuring the Caesars Palace logo
- **Carina**: Women's designer apparel
- **Cartier**: Jewelry and accessories
- **Ciro**: Jewelry and accessories
- **Colosseum Cigars**: Handmade cigars, lighters, cutters, and humidors

- **Cuzzens**: Men's apparel
- **Emperors Essentials**: Sundries
- **Galerie Michelangelo**: Fine art
- **Godiva Chocolatier**: Gourmet chocolates
- **Jane Carrol**: Florist
- **La Paradis**: Jewelry and accessories
- **Oculus**: Fine opticians, designer eyewear
- **Paradiso**: Designer swimwear and lingerie boutique
- **Paul & Shark Yachting**: Men's and women's sportswear and cruise clothing
- **Sun Gods**: Sun care products and poolside apparel

The Forum Shops
✆702-893-4800
✐*www.caesars.com/Caesars*

Even if you hate shopping, this is one of the most unusual indoor malls in the world—and also one of the most popular, so don't miss it! Sundays through Thursdays, the Forum Shops are open from 10:00 A.M. to 11:00 P.M. On Fridays and Saturdays, the hours are extended to midnight. (Some establishments are open later.) It features more than 110 shops and restaurants, plus several indoor attractions, including the free *Fountain of the Gods* show (shown throughout the day).

The Fountain of the Gods show features animatronic characters (the Roman Gods) along with dancing fountains and special effects. The show lasts under fifteen minutes and is presented every hour, on the hour, between 10:00 A.M. and 11:00 P.M. (midnight on Fridays and Saturdays). Near this attraction is a 50,000-gallon saltwater aquarium. The fish are fed at 3:15 P.M. and 7:15 P.M. daily, which is also an event kids enjoy watching.

THE FOUNTAIN OF THE GODS

Ages Up to 5	Ages 6–15	Ages 16–20	Ages 21 & Up	Senior Citizens
Not Suitable	☆☆☆	☆☆	☆☆	☆☆

Just some of the popular shops within the Forum Shops include:

- A/X—Armani Exchange
- Abercrombie & Fitch
- Ann Taylor
- Banana Republic
- Bebe
- Burberry
- Christian Dior
- Diesel
- Dolce & Gabbana
- Escada
- Estée Lauder
- Express Men
- FAO Schwartz
- Fendi
- Gianni Versace
- Gucci
- Guess
- Hugo Boss
- Kenneth Cole
- Lacoste
- Louis Vuitton
- Niketown
- The Coach Store
- The Polo Store
- Victoria's Secret
- Virgin Megastore

You'll also find world-class and family-oriented restaurants here, including Spago, the Palm, the Stage Deli, Planet Hollywood, and the Cheesecake Factory.

≡FAST FACT

In October 2004, three levels of new designer shops opened as part of a major expansion to this incredible, one-of-a-kind mall.

Some 50,000 to 70,000 people per day visit this mall, which offers a wonderful shopping experience for the whole family. Plan on spending between several hours and an entire day exploring and shopping here. The mall is completely indoors and fully air-conditioned. It's also very large, so plan on doing a lot of walking. (Comfortable shoes are a must.) If you're traveling with young kids, bring along a stroller.

Day Spa, Salon, and Fitness Facilities

If you're looking to relax, rejuvenate, and pamper yourself, Caesars Palace is just one of the mega-resorts offering a world-class day spa. Prices for treatments vary; however, all include access to the spa and fitness facilities.

The Spa at Caesars
✆702-731-7776

Caesars Palace's spa and fitness center features treatment rooms that offer a full selection of services, such as massages, body treatments, wraps, salt glows, baths, Vichy showers, a coed relaxation room, and a juice bar with outdoor terrace seating. It's open daily from 6:00 A.M. to 8:00 P.M.

The facility includes men's and women's whirlpools, steam rooms, saunas, tanning booths, a fully equipped coed fitness facility with cardiovascular and strength-training equipment, a rock-climbing wall, and an aerobic/yoga studio. Private personal trainers are available (for an additional fee and by reservation only).

Book your treatments early, especially during peak travel times. A full menu of available treatments and prices can be found at the Caesars Palace Web site.

Venus the Salon at Caesars
✆702-731-7791

This full-service salon will have you looking your absolute best in no time. Facials, manicures, pedicures, aromatherapy treatments, and therapeutic scalp treatments are just some of what's offered here. Venus also offers waxing, nail, and hair treatments by highly trained stylists and technicians. Makeup application and lessons are available. Appointments are required. The salon is open daily from 8:00 A.M. to 8:00 P.M.

Family-Oriented Amenities

Within the mega-resort complex, Caesars Palace offers the Garden of the Gods Pool Oasis, containing three large swimming pools and two outdoor whirlpool spas. The resort also offers its own golf course, six tennis courts, and shopping that's unparalleled.

For added convenience, Caesars Palace has its own Las Vegas Monorail stop, making it easy to travel up and down the Las Vegas Strip in order to visit other resorts and attractions.

Dining Options

Advance reservations for any of Caesar Palace's fine-dining restaurants are definitely recommended (and in some cases required). Call ✆877-346-4642 to make a reservation.

Special dinner and show packages for *Celine Dion: A New Day . . .* and Elton John: *The Red Piano* are available. Additional fine-dining restaurants, as well as casual-dining options, are available within the Forum Shops, which are connected to Caesars Palace. Of course, twenty-four-hour room service is also available to registered guests.

Fine Dining

Whether you're looking to celebrate a special occasion or simply to enjoy a fancy, multicourse meal prepared by an award-winning chef, Caesars Palace offers several fine-dining restaurants to choose from. Kids and teens are welcome at any of these restaurants (when accompanied by an adult). The younger crowd, however, will find a wider selection of kid-friendly lunch and dinner entrées at the Cypress Street Marketplace.

808 ($$$)

Acclaimed chef Jean-Marie Josselin offers a taste of Hawaii and Euro-Pacific cuisine. The restaurant offers an exotic menu, featuring the chef's signature cuisine, which incorporates Thai, Indian, Japanese, Chinese, Italian, and French cooking techniques and ingredients.

808's eclectic menu offers a variety of seafood appetizers and main courses, as well as veal, beef, chicken, and lamb entrées. The dessert offerings include seasonal fruits, ice cream, and other sweets.

Bradley Ogden ($$$)

At this restaurant, famed chef Bradley Ogden, who is from the San Francisco Bay area, offers his own take on classic "farm-fresh" American cuisine that has earned him national acclaim.

Ogden rose to national prominence as the executive chef at San Francisco's famous Campton Place Hotel. Later, he opened his signature restaurant, the Lark Creek Inn in Marin County (north of San Francisco), which has been ranked as one of the top restaurants in the nation. Now Bradley Ogden's talents are showcased at this award-winning restaurant in Las Vegas.

Empress Court ($$$)

You'll enjoy the spectacular view from this restaurant's dining room as you savor your meal and gaze upon the resort's famous Garden of the Gods swimming pools and nicely landscaped gardens. The Empress Court was inspired by restaurants in Hong Kong. Order à la carte, or select one of two multicourse meals.

The menu spotlights varied Asian fare, including Malay, Thai, and Indonesian delicacies. Giant freshwater and saltwater aquariums hold daily seafood shipments that often include live rock cod, Dungeness crab, and lobster.

Jackets are suggested for gentlemen. Empress Court is open for dinner only, Thursday through Monday nights. As with all of the fine-dining restaurants in Caesars Palace, reservations are recommended.

Hyakumi ($$$)

In English, Hyakumi means *one hundred tastes*, which is exactly what you can expect when you dine at this Japanese restaurant. On the menu, you'll find both traditional and contemporary favorites.

Within the Teppanyaki section of the restaurant, a chef will prepare your dinner at a tableside grill. In the regular dining room, an à la carte menu is offered. There's also a full sushi bar that overlooks the casino.

The restaurant is open for dinner only, Tuesday through Saturday nights. Jackets are considered optional but preferred for gentlemen. Reservations are recommended. Kids and teens will really enjoy the entertainment offered by the chefs as meals are created right before their eyes in the Teppanyaki dining room.

Mesa Grill ($$$)

Award-winning chef, best-selling cookbook author, and television personality Bobby Flay now offers in Las Vegas the same Southwestern cuisine that made him famous in New York.

"My goal with Mesa Grill has always been to create boldly flavored food in a high-energy environment," said Flay. Menu selections include shrimp and roasted corn tamale, New Mexican spice-rubbed pork tenderloin with bourbon-ancho chile sauce, and sweet potato tamale with crushed pecan butter.

Neros ($$$)

An à la carte selection of prime steaks (aged to perfection), fresh seafood (flown in daily), lamb, chicken, and veal all spotlight the talents of Neros' master chef, Mario Capone, and his culinary team. Neros serves dinner only. The suggested attire is "country club casual."

Terrazza ($$$)

Terrazza (pronounced "tear-ahtz-ah") is the name of this 220-seat restaurant and lounge located in the Garden of the Gods pool area. Italian for *terrace*, Terrazza is located on the pool level, at the juncture of the Roman Tower and the Palace Tower. The dining room features country rustic Italian cuisine.

The dining facility features an exhibition kitchen, plus a wood-burning brick pizza oven and both interior dining and dining alfresco on a poolside terrace. Terrazza is open for dinner only. Terrazza's lounge features live jazz trios performing Wednesday through Sunday evenings.

Casual Dining

For more family-friendly dining options, be sure to visit these casual-dining restaurants located within Caesars Palace. Within the Forum Shops, however, you'll find several additional family-friendly restaurants, including Planet Hollywood and the Cheesecake Factory.

Viale ($$)

Located in the new open-air Roman Plaza, Viale features patio seating, which allows you to witness firsthand the sights and sounds of the Strip. The menu celebrates modern Roman cooking, with pasta, pizza, panini, focaccete, and salads being among the popular options. The restaurant also offers an extensive wine list.

Finish your meal with a sweet dessert, such as fresh gelato, an Italian pastry, or an espresso. To start your day, enjoy a selection of breakfast items available at the take-out window. Breakfast, lunch, and dinner are served daily.

Café Lago ($$)

Café Lago features a diverse international à la carte menu, as well as complete breakfast and lunch buffets daily. There's also a popular dinner buffet on Friday and Saturday nights and a weekend brunch buffet.

Open twenty-four hours, the extensive menu offers multinational and American favorites for breakfast, lunch, dinner, and late-night dining. Five buffet stations are a favorite among guests who enjoy having the chefs prepare requests to order as part of the weekend brunch.

More upscale than your typical casino coffee shop, Café Lago features live entertainment on the Frank Sinatra Steinway, at which pianists play seven days a week.

Cypress Street Marketplace ($/$$)

This dining area is ideal for families. It's affordable and offers plenty of options available at nine different food court–style stations. Prices range from $2.25 to $12.95 per entrée. Beneath a canopy of cypress trees, this innovative "Napa-Style Picnic in the Park" is the latest concept in casual dining.

Here you'll find a wide range of affordable dining options, including hand-carved sandwiches, wraps, barbecue dinners, seafood dishes, pizza, and burgers. Specialty coffees, freshly baked pastries, and Häagen-Dazs ice cream are also available. Cypress Street Marketplace is open daily from 11:00 A.M. to 11:00 P.M. (midnight on Fridays and Saturdays).

Lounges and Bars

Caesars Palace offers a handful of bars and lounges throughout the mega-resort property, several of which have live music and are open twenty-four hours per day. Each has its own unique atmosphere.

Terrazza Lounge

This lounge offers a place to meet friends or enjoy a nightcap. A martini bar, appetizer menu, and live entertainment (from 6:00 P.M. to midnight) set this lounge apart.

Spanish Steps

Kick back . . . relax . . . and within this outdoor lounge, feel free to enjoy a large selection of frozen fruit cocktail drinks and a full liquor bar.

Seahorse Lounge

Bringing what Caesars Palace calls "tranquilly hip" nightlife to the resort, this lounge was inspired by the underwater world of mermaids and seahorses. A towering 1,700-gallon aquarium is surrounded by guest seating. This lounge offers a full cocktail menu, specialty martinis, and more than twenty different champagnes served in half-bottles and individual "pops." Complementing the beverage menu is an assortment of fresh seafood appetizers. Specialty coffees and espressos are available every morning. In the afternoons, tea is served.

Galleria Lounge

Just steps away from the Palace Casino, you can relax in this comfortable lounge that's open twenty-four hours. Galleria Lounge serves morning coffee and offers full bar service.

Cleopatra's Barge

For the over-twenty-one crowd, Cleopatra's Barge is housed within a replica of the massive ship that transported the royalty of Egypt along the Nile River in the times of Julius Caesar. You'll find live music and disc jockeys spinning the latest pop hits here, along with a dance floor. Cocktail "goddesses" dressed as Cleopatra's handmaidens serve up the drinks.

Shadow

Featuring contemporary designs and eclectic furnishings, the atmosphere of this lively lounge is enhanced by "shadow dancers." Their silhouetted performances bring the drinking and socializing experience offered here to a new level. You'll find a wide selection of cocktails and exotic drinks. Bartenders entertain guests by juggling bottles, twirling glasses, and even doing gymnastics as they prepare beverages. A menu of appetizers are offered in the evening, including sushi platters, smoked salmon, fresh oysters, crab cakes, fresh fruits, a variety of imported cheeses, and beluga caviar. Shadow offers a more trendy, nightclub-like atmosphere than a bar or lounge. It's a great place to stop for a drink after a show or after dinner.

Caesars Palace's Casino

At the Caesars Palace Casino, you'll find more than 129,000 square feet of casino gaming. Gamblers will find everything from high-limit slots to their favorite table games within this casino. Blackjack, craps, roulette, baccarat, Spanish twenty-one, mini-baccarat, Pai Gow, and Pai Gow poker are among the table games offered.

 TRAVEL ESSENTIAL

Of all the casinos in the world, Caesars Palace boasts awarding the most million-dollar (or more) slot machine jackpots.

Caesars Palace offers a wide variety of slot machines in a variety of denominations. You can wager anything from a nickel to $500 with each pull of the slot handle. Play a reel-type slot machine, video slot machine, poker, twenty-one, or keno. The Race and Sports Book features live satellite horse racing and broadcasts of exciting sporting events.

 TRAVEL TIP

Looking for the ultimate Caesars Palace theme gift or souvenir? You can purchase a wide range of Caesars Palace logo merchandise throughout the resort, or by pointing your Web browser to *www.shopcaesars.com*. You can also purchase Caesars Palace Gift Certificates, which make an excellent gift if you know someone who will be staying at this resort.

CHAPTER 8

Circus, Circus

CLOWNS, ANIMALS, EXCITING ACTS, and acrobats . . . Everyone loves the circus! Well, instead of waiting for the circus to come to your town or city, you can visit the circus . . . literally! Circus, Circus is perhaps the most family-friendly resort on the Strip. Plus, it's ideal for travelers on a tight budget.

Mega-Resort Overview

✉2880 Las Vegas Boulevard South, Las Vegas, NV 89109
✆800-634-3450
✆702-734-0410
✐*www.circuscircus.com*
Room and Suite Rates: $$/$$$

This resort offers guest rooms starting at under $50 per night and features the world's largest indoor theme park as its primary attraction. Thanks to the selection of family-friendly activities offered here, Circus, Circus continues to be an ideal place to stay if you're visiting Las Vegas with kids or teens.

Since it opened on October 18, 1968, Circus, Circus has been catering to families traveling with young children and teens—not just to business travelers, adult vacationers, and gamblers, which is unlike most of the other mega-resorts along the Strip.

▲Circus, Circus is family fun.   Photo provided by PR Newswire Photo Service.

Thanks to its popularity among family vacationers, Circus, Circus continues to expand. The West Tower houses more than 1,000 rooms, and a shopping promenade containing a dozen retail shops and boutiques is among the resort's newest additions. Even Adventuredome, the world's largest indoor theme park, has expanded recently, with several new "thrill rides" suitable more for adults than kids.

≡FAST FACT

Circus, Circus has its own RV park, offering extremely affordable accommodations for those traveling to Las Vegas in their recreational vehicles. This is the only RV park located directly on the Las Vegas Strip.

Circus, Circus continues to be one of the least expensive resorts along the Strip and is ideal for budget travelers or those looking for a casino and resort that offers a fun-filled atmosphere for the young at heart.

CIRCUS, CIRCUS OVERALL FAMILY-FRIENDLINESS RATING

Ages Up to 5	Ages 6–15	Ages 16–20	Ages 21 & Up	Senior Citizens
☆☆☆	☆☆☆	☆☆☆	☆☆	☆☆

Guest Room Accommodations

Circus, Circus is divided into multiple towers and contains a total of 3,638 guest rooms and 135 suites. The Casino Tower is a fifteen-story building with 776 guest rooms. This tower is located in the center of the Circus, Circus property and features two casinos, a race and sports book, the famous indoor "big top" arena, a carnival midway, a video game arcade, multiple dining facilities, a wedding chapel, and retail shops.

Located above the main casino in this tower is the Midway Stage, which houses the largest permanent circus big top in the world. The twenty-nine-story Skyrise Tower contains 1,188 guest rooms, its own casino and pool, and an indoor connection to the resort's shopping promenade.

The West Tower is a thirty-five-story tower containing an additional 1,000 guest rooms. Circus, Circus Manor is a set of five three-story buildings with 810 guest rooms, a pool, and its own parking lot. The Manor is considered the resort's "budget area," with room rates under $50 per night.

The basic guest rooms at Circus, Circus are about 460 square feet and offer air conditioning, a color television (with cable TV and pay channels), telephones, and twenty-four-hour room service. Two people will be comfortable in each basic room. Parents and kids can share a room that has two double beds, though two adjoining rooms will provide more space and comfort.

Nonsmoking and wheelchair-accessible rooms are available upon request. As mentioned earlier, Circus, Circus is one of the Strip's more affordable resorts. The rooms don't offer many of the luxuries of other resorts located along the Strip, but the rooms are comfortable, clean, and available with one king-size or two double beds.

All of the tower rooms have European-style furniture. The Manor rooms are decorated in bright circus colors. All rooms have a bathtub/shower combination (with the exception of wheelchair-accessible rooms, which offer roll-in showers).

Featured Attractions and Activities

Circus, Circus has three swimming pools, one located within the RV park and two at the Skyrise Tower. All swimming pools are outside and also have Jacuzzis. The pools are heated to eighty degrees.

 TRAVEL TIP

The Circusland RV Park contains 399 spaces with full-service utility hook-ups. Within the RV park's grounds, there are a convenience store, an arcade, a Laundromat, a playground, pet runs, disposal stations, and a handful of other amenities. For reservations, call ☏800-562-7270 or book online by pointing your Web browser to ✎www.koa.com.

Sure, swimming is fun for kids, teens, and adults alike, but the highlight of staying at Circus, Circus is definitely the rides and attractions within the Adventuredome theme park.

▲Adventuredome has rides for all ages. Photo ©The Las Vegas News Bureau

The Adventuredome Theme Park

☎702-794-3939

✐*www.adventuredome.com*

This $90 million indoor theme park opened back in 1993 and has since ranked among the top twenty-five most popular theme parks in North America. When driving along the Strip, it's impossible to miss seeing the Adventuredome's dome structure. Its five-acre glass dome is almost 200 feet high, so there's plenty of room for the park's thrill rides inside.

Set in a Grand Canyon–inspired motif, the theme park is open every day of the year, though hours vary by season. Since it's indoors, weather has no impact on a guest's ability to enjoy a fun-filled day or night on the rides. It's always a comfortable seventy-two degrees. All-day ride passes are $21.95 for adults and $13.95 for kids. Individual rides are between $4 and $6 each.

ADVENTUREDOME

Ages Up to 5	Ages 6–15	Ages 16–20	Ages 21 & Up	Senior Citizens
☆☆	☆☆☆	☆☆☆	☆☆☆	☆

≡FAST FACT

At the indoor Adventuredome theme park, the busiest day ever was back on November 23, 2001, when 36,353 people crossed through the gates to enjoy the rides and attractions.

The Adventuredome features the following thrill-ride attractions, suitable for teens and adults (or kids who meet the height requirements and are accompanied by an adult). Without an all-day ride pass, the price per ride is $6.

═FAST FACT

The highest "mountain peak" within Adventuredome is 140 feet. The dome that houses this theme park is 200 feet high and is fully enclosed with 8,615 panes of glass. Since it opened in 1993 with only four rides, this theme park has hosted more than 20 million visitors. Today, Adventuredome features seventeen attractions and rides, spread over five acres.

The Canyon Blaster

The world's largest indoor double-loop, double-corkscrew roller coaster awaits you in the Adventuredome! Travel at speeds up to fifty-five miles per hour and experience both positive and negative G-forces before the one minute and forty-five second ride comes to an end.

THE CANYON BLASTER

Ages Up to 5	Ages 6–15	Ages 16–20	Ages 21 & Up	Senior Citizens
Not Suitable	☆☆	☆☆☆	☆☆☆	☆

Must be over 48" tall

The Rim Runner

Enjoy this wet and wild boat ride (water flume) that ends with a giant splash as you drop down a 60-foot waterfall while traveling at over 40 feet per second. This is one of the most exciting rides in Adventuredome.

THE RIM RUNNER

Ages Up to 5	Ages 6–15	Ages 16–20	Ages 21 & Up	Senior Citizens
Not Suitable	☆☆	☆☆☆	☆☆☆	☆

Must be over 48" tall

Sling Shot

Get ready for a free-fall drop. This tower ride proves that what goes up, must come down . . . fast! You'll experience four Gs during the 100-foot drop. It's the newest thrill ride on the Strip.

SLING SHOT

Ages Up to 5	Ages 6–15	Ages 16–20	Ages 21 & Up	Senior Citizens
Not Suitable	☆	☆☆☆	☆☆☆	☆

Must be over 48" tall

Chaos

If you're looking for a thrill ride that features tilts and spinning, Chaos is right up your alley. It's not recommended if you've just eaten.

CHAOS

Ages Up to 5	Ages 6–15	Ages 16–20	Ages 21 & Up	Senior Citizens
Not Suitable	☆	☆☆☆	☆☆☆	☆

Must be over 48" tall

Inverter

This thrill ride will take you on a high-speed spin, as you rotate 360 degrees and experience constant G forces.

INVERTER

Ages Up to 5	Ages 6–15	Ages 16–20	Ages 21 & Up	Senior Citizens
Not Suitable	☆	☆☆☆	☆☆☆	☆

Must be over 48" tall

SimEX Theater

All aboard the Fun House Express! This is a state-of-the-art motion-simulator ride. As you watch a movie, you'll feel as if you're racing through a spooky world. The technology is somewhat similar to *Star Tours* at Disneyworld or Disneyland, for example.

SimEX THEATER

Ages Up to 5	Ages 6–15	Ages 16–20	Ages 21 & Up	Senior Citizens
Not Suitable	☆☆	☆☆☆	☆☆☆	☆☆

Must be over 42" tall

Lazer Blast Laser Tag Arena

This 7,500-square-foot black-lit arena is where people go head-to-head in laser tag battles. Participants gear up with specially designed vests and laser guns. Once a competition begins, people are divided into two groups and the "red team" and "green team" battle each other for the highest individual and team score.

Each game is five minutes long. The arena is filled with physical obstacles that provide hiding places and opportunities to launch surprise attacks or ambushes against opponents.

LAZER BLAST LASER TAG ARENA

Ages Up to 5	Ages 6–15	Ages 16–20	Ages 21 & Up	Senior Citizens
Not Suitable	☆☆☆	☆☆☆	☆☆	☆

Must be over 42" tall

Reboot: The Ride

At this attraction, based on the popular TV series, prepare yourself for a high-speed four-minute journey through a futuristic cyber city.

REBOOT: THE RIDE

Ages Up to 5	Ages 6–15	Ages 16–20	Ages 21 & Up	Senior Citizens
Not Suitable	☆☆☆	☆☆☆	☆☆	☆

Must be over 42" tall

Dino Island 1 and 2

It's your job to help save the T-Rex from extinction when you experience these exciting thrill rides.

DINO ISLAND 1 AND 2

Ages Up to 5	Ages 6–15	Ages 16–20	Ages 21 & Up	Senior Citizens
Not Suitable	☆☆	☆☆☆	☆☆	☆

Must be over 42" tall

TRAVEL TIP

If the indoor thrill rides at Circus, Circus aren't enough, step outside and experience AJ Hackett Bungee, a bungee-jumping attraction (✆702-385-4321/810 Circus, Circus Drive). Here you can leap off a 52-meter-high tower. No reservations are required. This location (and seven others located around the world) have a 100 percent safety record after over 1.5 million successful jumps. The first jump costs $59. Open 11:00 A.M. to 8:30 P.M. (weekdays) and until 10:00 P.M. on Saturdays.

Junior Rides

To experience these rides, guests must be between 36 and 58-inches tall. These are "kiddy" rides, not suitable for adults. Without an all-day ride pass, these rides cost $4 each.

- Frog Hopper: A "tower" ride for young people
- Miner Mike: A mini roller coaster
- Thunderbirds: An airplane ride
- Cliffhangers: An interactive play area

Family Rides

To experience these rides, visitors must be at least 42 inches tall, unless accompanied by an adult. Without an all-day ride pass, the rides cost $4 each. They are designed for young people but suitable for visitors of all ages.

- **Road Runner**: A mini Himalayan ride
- **BC Bus**: A giant school bus that moves up, down, and around in circles
- **Circus Carousel**: A classic carousel ride
- **Drifters**: A traditional ferris-wheel ride with cars shaped like hot-air balloons

Other Adventuredome Attractions

Adventuredome offers a handful of other attractions, including Xtreme Zone, where guests can experience rock-wall climbing and indoor bungee jumping. The wall climb is suitable for beginners or advanced climbers. There's also Pikes Pass Miniature Golf Course. This eighteen-hole indoor miniature golf course offers a fun-filled activity for the entire family.

 TRAVEL ESSENTIAL

Located within a five-minute walk from Circus, Circus is the Guinness World Records Museum (☎702-792-0640/✉*www.guinnessmuseum.com/2780* Las Vegas Boulevard South), a family-oriented, self-paced, indoor attraction. Admission is $6.50 per adult and $4.50 per child; however, a two-for-one coupon can be obtained from the museum's Web site. It's a fun and unusual place to spend between one and three hours.

The Midway

The carnival-like atmosphere of Circus, Circus comes alive in the Midway area, which contains more than 200 games and a state-of-the-art arcade. Along the Midway, test your skills and try to win a prize at one of the many carnival games that cost $.50 to $2 each. (Some of the games offer small prizes to all kids who play.) Classic arcade games, such as Ms. Pac-Man, are mixed with state-of-the-art arcade games.

If you get hungry while exploring the Midway, you'll find a McDonald's (look for those famous golden arches) near the circus stage area. Another option is the Horse-A-Round Bar, which looks like a carousel with booth seating.

It's Showtime at Circus, Circus

Twice every hour, throughout the day and night (11:00 A.M. until midnight), live circus acts perform under the indoor big top. The performers are from around the globe and include aerialists, trapeze artists, jugglers, and clowns. All circus shows are free of charge and suitable for the entire family. Many of the clowns and performers interact with guests in between performances.

CIRCUS ACTS

Ages Up to 5	Ages 6–15	Ages 16–20	Ages 21 & Up	Senior Citizens
☆	☆☆☆	☆☆☆	☆☆	☆☆

Shopping

Keeping the carnival atmosphere alive, the shopping promenade at Circus, Circus offers a fun-filled shopping experience that allows you to take some of the circus fun home with you in the form of souvenirs.

The retail shops within Circus, Circus include:

- **Exclusively Circus, Circus**: Here you'll find mugs, glasses, postcards, and other souvenirs as well as adults' and children's clothing imprinted with the famous Circus, Circus logo.
- **Circus Spirits**: This is Circus, Circus's in-house liquor store, featuring a large selection of mini-liquor bottles, soft drinks, bottled water, milk, juices, snack food items, sundries, film, and tobacco products.

- **Circus Gifts**: If you're looking for souvenirs that scream "Las Vegas," you'll find them here. This shop is located in the Main Tower and offers Circus, Circus items and other Las Vegas memorabilia.
- **Market Express**: Find snack foods, newspapers, sundries, film, candy, soda, and bottled water at this convenience store, located in the Main Tower.
- **Under $10**: For shoppers on a budget, check out this Under $10 store where everything is priced at $10 or less. Las Vegas souvenirs and other keepsakes are offered.
- **Houdini's**: Located along the promenade, this magic shop features hundreds of tricks that anyone can perform. Plan to spend some time watching the ongoing magic demonstrations by professional magicians—they're entertaining and absolutely free, and all tricks performed during the demonstrations can be purchased.
- **LYCNSPL8**: All kinds of merchandise based on licensed cartoon characters is available here.
- **Gold Castle**: This jewelry store, located in the Main Tower, specializes in fine gold jewelry.
- **Sweet Tooth**: Ice cream and candy are the specialty of this shop, located along the promenade. Ten different ice cream flavors are served, along with popcorn, bulk candies, and cotton candy.
- **Headliners**: This newspaper and convenience store is located along the promenade. Film, sundries, candy, soda, and inexpensive souvenirs are sold here.
- **Marshall-Rousso**: Casual and dress clothing for men and women, including shoes, is available here.
- **Circus Kids**: Children's clothing, toys, and other items for kids are available from this shop, located along the promenade.
- **Nothing But Clowns**: This shop, located in the Main Tower, offers clowns in every shape and size. It's a fun place to visit if you're looking for gifts or souvenirs for the kids, or more valuable collectibles.

- **Sweet Stuff**: Located on the main level, here you'll find a wide assortment of candy and treats.
- **Time Tunnel**: Watches, in a wide range of styles and at various price points, are this store's specialty.
- **Trading Post**: Find T-shirts and souvenirs from Adventuredome at this shop, located within the indoor theme park.

Salon Facilities

The full-service Annee of Paris Beauty Salon (☎702-731-3201) is open seven days per week and offers massages, hairstyling, manicures, pedicures, facials, and a range of other services. While it's not exactly a world-class day spa, it does offer a chance to relax and pamper yourself.

Dining Options

Circus, Circus features a few fine-dining restaurants, such as the Steak House and Stivali Italian Ristorante; however, the majority of the eating establishments at this resort offer casual and affordable dining experiences suitable for the entire family.

In addition to the restaurants, Circus, Circus has several bars and lounges that cater to adult guests.

Fine Dining

The whole family will enjoy the fine-dining options available at Circus, Circus. Most of the dining at this resort is casual, but you won't want to miss the chance to indulge in the establishments that do offer a fine-dining experience.

The Steak House ($$/$$$)

☎702-794-3767

Ranked as one of the top steakhouses in Las Vegas, this restaurant serves top-quality Midwestern beef that's been aged to perfection in a glass-enclosed aging room (which is available for all to see from within the main dining room). All meat entrées are then prepared over an exhibition-style, open-hearth mesquite charcoal broiler. The portions are plentiful.

The Steak House is open daily for dinner from 5:00 P.M. to midnight. On Sundays, a champagne brunch is served during three separate seatings (9:30 A.M., 11:30 A.M., and 12:30 P.M.). Reservations for dinner or brunch are required. The dress code is casual, and the average meal cost is about $25 per person.

Stivali Italian Ristorante ($$/$$$)
☎702-691-5820

In 1997, Circus, Circus opened this fine Italian restaurant, which rivals the Steak House in terms of food quality and top-notch service. During the restaurant's first year in operation, it won the *Las Vegas Review-Journal* reader's poll for "Best Italian Restaurant."

The menu includes many classic Italian dishes, plus some of the chef's personal favorites, such as stuffed portobello mushrooms filled with bay shrimp, imported cheeses, and seasoned bread crumbs. There is also a large selection of pizzas, including the restaurant's specialty, called Pizzette, which is a pizza appetizer.

Stivali Italian Ristorante is open Sundays through Thursdays from 5:00 P.M. to 11:00 P.M., and Saturdays and Sundays from 5:00 P.M. to midnight. Reservations for dinner are strongly recommended. The dress code is casual.

Casual Dining

In addition to these casual-dining options located throughout the mega-resort, in-room dining is available twenty-four hours per day.

Blue Iguana ($/$$)
Enjoy mouthwatering Mexican cuisine with a margarita, or try a selection from more than thirty varieties of tequila in the Cantina. Open for dinner and located on the promenade.

Circus Buffet ($)
With a dining room that seats over a thousand people, the Circus

Buffet serves more than 10,000 customers daily. Enjoy this inexpensive, all-you-can-eat extravaganza, which recently underwent a $9.5 million renovation.

A large selection of entrées is offered during every meal period. The buffet is open Mondays through Fridays for breakfast (6:00 A.M. to 11:30 A.M.), lunch (noon to 4:00 P.M.), and dinner (4:30 P.M. to 11:00 P.M.). On weekends, a brunch is served from 6:00 A.M. to 4:00 P.M.

Seating is on a first-come basis. This is one of the best deals around. The breakfast buffet is priced at $7.99 per person. Lunch or brunch is priced at $8.99 per person, and dinner is only $9.99 per person, for an all-you-can-eat meal.

Promenade Café ($/$$)

Enjoy a large selection of American dishes at this twenty-four-hour restaurant.

The Pink Pony ($/$$)

This café, located near the main casino and under the big top, is open twenty-four hours a day. Sundays through Thursdays between 3:00 P.M. and 11:00 P.M., a complete prime rib dinner (12-ounce prime rib, potato, vegetable, roll, and soup or salad) is priced at $9.99. Between 11:00 P.M. and 5:00 A.M., try the Graveyard Special (two eggs, hash browns, bacon or sausage, and coffee) for only $3.99.

Pizzeria ($)

Freshly baked pizzas, calzones, and salads are the specialties of this casual restaurant. Open every day from 11:00 A.M. to midnight, this is a great (and affordable) place to bring the entire family for lunch or dinner.

Snack Bars ($)

For a light snack or a quick meal, check out the various fast-food establishments in the Circus, Circus complex, including the Westside Deli, McDonald's, and the Adventuredome Snack Bar. These places are inexpensive and offer table service or nearby seating.

Lounges and Bars

Circus, Circus has several bars and lounges. Some offer live entertainment, while others feature TV screens for watching sporting events. Several of these bars and lounges simply offer a friendly atmosphere to enjoy a drink with friends, relatives, business associates, or loved ones. Your choices include the Sports Bar, West Casino Bar, Steak House Bar, Stivali Bar, Skyrise Lounge, and the Horse-A-Round Bar.

Circus, Circus's Casino

Adults can try their luck in the casinos at Circus, Circus. The resort offers three separate casinos containing a total of 2,220 slot machines, fifty-two blackjack tables, four craps tables, seven roulette tables, one Big Six game, four Pai Gow poker tables, one Caribbean Stud poker table, two Let It Ride games, one casino war game, and ten poker tables. There's also a 160-seat keno lounge (on the main level of the Casino Tower), and a race and sports book.

 TRAVEL TIP

Check out the Las Vegas-area tourist publications (such as *What's On: The Las Vegas Guide*) for a $4-off coupon good toward the purchase of an all-day ride pass at Adventuredome. Each coupon can be used to purchase up to four discounted passes.

The casino's race and sports book offers wagering on horse and greyhound racing as well as major sporting events. All races eligible for wagering are simulcast live from the tracks and shown on big-screen televisions. Sports fans can watch their favorite teams on one of the fourteen television monitors. Fans can also keep up with sports results throughout the country via the sports book's electronic display board.

CHAPTER 9

Excalibur

LAS VEGAS ALLOWS VISITORS of all ages to tap into their imaginations and immerse themselves in a fantasy. What type of fantasy you live out is entirely up to you. If you'd like to step back in time, to the days of medieval knights, then the Excalibur Resort is the ideal place to stay. The main building of this resort resembles a giant medieval castle, but that's only the beginning of how the popular medieval theme is expressed throughout the resort.

Mega-Resort Overview

✉3850 Las Vegas Boulevard South, Las Vegas, NV 89109
☎800-937-7777
☎702-597-7777
✍*www.excalibur-casino.com*
Room and Suite Rates: $$/$$$

Excalibur is located on the southwest corner of the Strip, about one mile from McCarran International Airport and diagonally across from the MGM Grand. With its medieval theme, it is one of the few mega-resorts that truly caters to kids, teens, and families, with a wide range of accommodations, activities, dining options, and attractions. It's important for parents to understand, however, that while Excalibur is family-friendly, it's primarily a resort casino, like all of the other mega-resorts on or near the Strip.

When this opened in 1990, it was the largest hotel and casino in the world, with its two twenty-eight-story towers containing almost 4,000 guest rooms. Although other larger resorts have since opened, Excalibur remains a favorite destination for families, because of the ingenious ways the medieval theme is interwoven with virtually every aspect of each guest's visit.

It's not just the mega-resort's castle exterior that makes Excalibur so appealing to kids and teens. What's housed within the giant castle (and throughout the mega-resort) makes Excalibur a fun and exciting place to visit and explore.

The entire 117-acre resort complex features décor from medieval times. To add to the fantasy, expect to see actors dressed as knights, kings, and other members of the royal court roaming throughout the property. There's also the popular *Tournament of Kings* dinner show, which further immerses guests in the medieval fantasy.

The Fantasy Faire Midway, containing motion-simulator rides, an assortment of carnival-style games, and a variety of other attractions, helps to make this property particularly suitable for young people.

▲ Excalibur's architecture is unique.   Photo provided by PR Newswire Photo Service.

TRAVEL ESSENTIAL

When you book your room reservations at the Excalibur Web site, you can save $10 per night off the published rate. Prior to doing this, determine whether you can get an even lower nightly rate by visiting the various travel-related Web sites, such as Hotels.com, Travelocity. com, or Hotwire.com.

For adults, the casino is large and well equipped to handle almost anyone's gaming pleasures, and there are plenty of shops designed to help you part with your winnings. With all that it has to offer, vacationers traveling with kids and teens should definitely consider staying at Excalibur while visiting Las Vegas. It's a well-equipped, midpriced resort complex.

EXCALIBUR OVERALL FAMILY-FRIENDLINESS RATING

Ages Up to 5	Ages 6–15	Ages 16–20	Ages 21 & Up	Senior Citizens
☆☆	☆☆☆	☆☆☆	☆☆	☆☆

Guest Room Accommodations

All rooms at Excalibur offer air conditioning, color television (with pay-per-view movies), high-speed Internet access, and telephones. The Standard King or the Jacuzzi King rooms are ideal for a couple traveling without kids. These rooms offer one king-size bed and a handful of amenities to provide convenience and comfort for guests.

For families, the Standard Queen rooms are perfect, because they offer two queen-size beds, along with a wide range of amenities you'd expect to find at a midpriced resort. Rates for these rooms range in price from $39.95 to $199.95 per night, depending on the dates of your stay.

If your travel budget permits, connecting rooms are available, allowing parents to relax in the spacious comfort of a Standard King room while the kids or teens enjoy a Standard Queen room with a door that connects the two rooms.

If you want additional space, more privacy, added luxury, and more amenities, Excalibur offers several different types of suites. The Parlor Suites offer both elegance and style. They contain a full living room, dining area, mini-kitchen, guest restroom, and pass-though doorway into the master sleeping area. The sleeping area is equipped with a color TV with cable, marble Jacuzzi and shower, full-size vanity, and dressing area.

The Parlor Suites are available with one king-size bed only. However, adjoining rooms with two queen-size beds are available for an additional charge, so you can create perfect family-oriented accommodations, whether you're traveling with kids, teens, or in-laws. For a small nightly fee, cots can also be placed in the rooms or suites to accommodate additional guests.

JUST FOR PARENTS

If you're celebrating a special occasion at Excalibur, you can arrange to have balloons, champagne, or a gift basket delivered to any guest room by calling ☎702-597-7777. Twenty-four-hour room service is also available.

Nonsmoking rooms are available and should be requested when making your reservation. When making your room reservation, discuss all of your room needs with the representative to ensure that you receive the proper accommodations on your arrival.

While Excalibur doesn't offer the same luxurious accommodations or amenities as a mega-resort such as the Bellagio, The Venetian, the Four Seasons, or Mandalay Bay, for example, it's an excellent mid-priced resort that offers comfort, cleanliness, and the basic in-room amenities you'll need.

Featured Attractions and Activities

Throughout the entire mega-resort, the medieval theme is prominent but isn't at all tacky. Many of the resort's activities, attractions, and entertainments also encompass this theme, which adds to the fun and excitement, especially for kids.

The Swimming Pool

The Excalibur's outdoor swimming pool area offers the perfect place to relax and enjoy a swim. Hours of operation vary by season. The resort offers two heated pools, a sixteen-seat spa, waterfalls, water slides, and a shaded dining area nearby. The snack bar and cocktail bar in the pool area are open daily.

The Fantasy Faire Midway

This is the perfect place to spend time with your kids. If you're traveling with teens, you can let them loose in this area to enjoy the two "Magic Motion Film Rides" and numerous midway-style games (prizes can be won, just like at a carnival), and guests can challenge themselves at the state-of-the-art video game arcade.

The Fantasy Faire Midway is connected to the popular Medieval Village area, where you'll find dozens of fun shops, four restaurants, two wedding chapels, a food court, and ongoing live entertainment (in the form of costumed performers who roam around interacting with guests, plus perform throughout the day and evening on the Jester's Stage).

These areas are located away from Excalibur's casinos and lounges (located on the lower level), so they're more family-friendly.

FANTASY FAIRE MIDWAY

Ages Up to 5	Ages 6–15	Ages 16–20	Ages 21 & Up	Senior Citizens
☆☆	☆☆☆	☆☆☆	☆☆	☆☆

It's Showtime at Excalibur

You'll definitely be treated like royalty when it comes to experiencing the entertainment at Excalibur. *The Tournament of Kings* is a fun-filled and exciting dinner show suitable for the entire family. For women ages eighteen and up, *Thunder from Down Under* offers a fun-filled and equally exciting evening, but of a very different nature.

Tournament of Kings

☎702-597-7600

If you're expecting to see a typical Las Vegas–style show at Excalibur, you're in for a shock. There are no showgirls in this show, no big dance numbers, and no master illusionists or comedians. Instead, you'll be getting your hands a bit dirty as you participate in *Tournament of Kings* interactive dinner show, which is presented twice nightly (at 6:00 P.M. and 8:30 P.M.). Tickets are $47.50 per person, and include dinner.

═FAST FACT

While you'll definitely want to take pictures during your vacation, keep in mind that cameras are prohibited at all of the shows along the Strip.

Medieval jousting, scary dragons, fire-throwing wizards, invading armies, and brave knights on horses will all entertain you and your family as you dine on a traditional medieval-style dinner. There's no silverware provided for this feast. You'll be using your hands to eat this meal. (It's an added touch of realism that kids love.) Special effects, pyrotechnics, and highly detailed costumes all add to the ambiance.

Tournament of Kings is a lavish, $1 million production that takes place in a custom-designed, 900-seat dinner theater/arena. The main star of the show (aside from the knights, acrobats, and horses) is the audience. You'll be led through choruses of cheers and sing-alongs as the action unfolds.

This show offers an evening's worth of exciting entertainment for people of all ages, but it will particularly appeal to kids. A multicourse dinner, which includes soup, Cornish hen, potato wedges, steamed broccoli, a dinner roll, a drink (soda, tea or coffee), and dessert, is included.

Since this show features real-life horses, the best seating is actually several rows away from the main stage/arena area. This will help avoid having sand from the arena kicked up by the horses into your food.

TOURNAMENT OF KINGS

Ages Up to 5	Ages 6–15	Ages 16–20	Ages 21 & Up	Senior Citizens
☆	☆☆☆	☆☆☆	☆☆	☆☆

The Glockenspiel Fairy Tale

This free show involves a large clock with audio-animatronic characters. It is presented over the giant clock at the rear entrance of Excalibur every hour, between 10:00 A.M. and 10:00 P.M.

THE GLOCKENSPIEL FAIRY TALE

Ages Up to 5	Ages 6–15	Ages 16–20	Ages 21 & Up	Senior Citizens
☆☆	☆☆	☆	☆	☆

The Court Jester's Stage

Starting at 11:00 A.M. daily, bring your kids to enjoy free entertainment on the Court Jester's Stage. Singers, jugglers, magicians, and puppeteers rotate throughout the day, presenting ten-minute shows every forty-five minutes.

THE COURT JESTER'S STAGE

Ages Up to 5	Ages 6–15	Ages 16–20	Ages 21 & Up	Senior Citizens
☆☆☆	☆☆☆	☆	☆	☆

Australia's Thunder from Down Under (For Women, Age 18+ Only)

☎702-597-7600

✍www.thunderfromdownunder.com

Just about everyone has heard of *Chippendales*, the male "strip show" that's been around for decades. Well, *Australia's Thunder from Down Under* puts a fun but very classy twist on the all-male strip show concept. While the costumes are certainly skimpy, there's no full nudity. What you can expect, however, is plenty of lighthearted fun.

Every night, there are at least several bachelorette parties that come to enjoy the show. This adds to the energy in the theater. *Australia's Thunder from Down Under* features a handful of gorgeous men from Australia who clearly enjoy what they do, but don't take themselves too seriously. Women are invited to kick back and enjoy the loud music, cheer on their favorite dancer, and have a few drinks. There's absolutely no tipping, however, so everyone gets to enjoy the same entertaining show.

Australia's Thunder from Down Under was conceived back in 1989 and has toured to more than fifteen countries and been seen by over 14 million women. Now this group of guys has a home in Las Vegas and dances up a storm twice nightly (at 8:30 P.M. and 10:30 P.M.). Tickets are $43.95 per person.

AUSTRALIA'S THUNDER FROM DOWN UNDER

Ages Up to 5	Ages 6–15	Ages 16–20	Ages 21 & Up	Senior Citizens
Not Suitable	Not Suitable	Not Suitable	☆☆☆	☆

Shopping

In keeping with the medieval flavor of Excalibur, many of its shops also follow the theme and are located in the Medieval Village area on the second level, which is where you'll find restaurants, the wedding chapels, a pub, the food court, and a cast of costumed characters interacting with visitors.

Shops and merchandise kiosks, mainly found in the Medieval Village area, include the following:

- **Airbrush/Caricature Booth**: Allow one of the talented artists to create a portrait or comical caricature of you and your family. This is a favorite among kids.
- **Amazing Pictures**: Create a one-of-a-kind photo souvenir.
- **Bico Jewelry**: Check out this exotic line of jewelry from Australia. Ideal for men and women of all ages, these trendy charms and necklaces make perfect (and unusual) gifts or souvenirs.
- **Casino Players**: Gifts relating to casino games are sold here.
- **Dragon's Lair**: This shop sells crystals, armor, and other medieval-theme gifts and souvenirs.
- **Excalibur Shoppe**: Here you'll find everything from T-shirts to coffee mugs all imprinted with the Excalibur logo. This is the place to shop for souvenirs.
- **Frontier Kingdom**: Southwestern gifts and Western wear is sold here.
- **Gold Castle Jewelers**: You guessed it—it's a jewelry store.
- **Jester's Court**: This shop offers a selection of toys and gifts ideal for kids.
- **Kids of the Kingdom**: Toys and kids' clothing are available here.
- **Kingdom Pearl Factory**: Pick your own oyster, open it up to find a pearl, and then make your own jewelry.
- **Marshall-Rousso**: This designer clothing shop offers men's and women's clothing.

- **The Medieval Hatter**: Fun and unique hats, as well as novelty items, are sold here.
- **Merlin's Mystic Shoppe**: Throughout the day and evening, see professional magicians demonstrate magic tricks and illusions that can then be purchased. The free magic shows are fun to watch, especially for kids and teens.
- **Spirit Shoppe**: Here you can purchase newspapers, magazines, convenience items, snacks, sodas, and liquors twenty-four hours per day.
- **Sweet Habits**: Satisfy your sweet tooth at this colorful candy shop.

Day Spa, Salon, and Fitness Facilities

When you're ready to pamper yourself, relax, or work out, Excalibur offers a midpriced day spa, fitness center, and full-service salon. While these facilities aren't as luxurious or exotic as the spas at the Bellagio or The Venetian, for example, the services offered are top-notch and more affordable.

Royal Treatment Spa & Fitness Center
☎702-597-7772

For a daily fee of $15 (for resort guests) and $20 (non-guests), visitors to the Royal Treatment Spa & Fitness Center are given access to a redwood sauna, eucalyptus steam room, heated whirlpool, relaxation lounge, exercise room, locker and shower facilities, and vanity amenities. Robes and sandals are also provided. This spa and fitness facility is open to guests age eighteen and up.

═FAST FACT

To build the giant Excalibur castle's exterior, more than 3.2 million concrete blocks and 2.5 million concrete slabs were used.

For an additional fee (ranging from $45 to $135), the day spa offers a wide range of treatments. Spa hours are 6:00 A.M. to 9:00 P.M., and reservations for these treatments can be made between one and five days in advance. Different types of massages, body wraps, facials, and body scrubs are among the treatments offered. A complete menu of available treatments and services, along with prices, can be found on Excalibur's Web site. All treatments include access to the spa facilities for the day.

Kristina's Hair Salon

✆702-597-7255

Kristina's Hair Salon is a full-service salon offering a range of services to both men and women. Services include cuts, shampoo, perms, manicures, and pedicures. An appointment is recommended but not required. You'll find this salon located on the third level of the main castle. The salon is open from 9:00 A.M. to 5:00 P.M.

Dining Options

Keeping with its family-friendly atmosphere, Excalibur offers a range of inexpensive dining options, suitable for the entire family. From fine dining to casual dining, this resort has it all.

Fine Dining

If you're looking for a fancy steak dinner, Excalibur is home to one of the finest restaurants in all of Las Vegas. The Steakhouse at Camelot is an award-winning steak and seafood restaurant that offers an incredible dining experience.

The Steakhouse at Camelot ($$$)

✆702-597-7449

Featuring top-quality steak and seafood entrées, this upscale restaurant is the perfect place to enjoy an elegant meal, celebrate a special occasion, or have a romantic dinner for two. The restaurant is open from 5:00 P.M. to 10:00 P.M. (11:00 P.M. on Fridays and Saturdays). Reservations are recommended.

Whatever the occasion, people of all ages will enjoy this American-style restaurant, where an extensive wine selection is available. As you step through the doors of the Steakhouse at Camelot, you'll be transported away from the hustle and bustle of the casinos and crowds. You'll be entertained by live piano music as you enjoy the delicious entrées expertly prepared by award-winning chef Frank Suosmaa and his culinary team. Entrées range in price from $19.95 to $70.

Come to the Steakhouse at Camelot to enjoy a delicious multi-course meal, but make sure you leave room for dessert. The crème brûlée, for example, is amazing and the perfect way to end the meal. While this is primarily a steak and seafood restaurant, you'll find a few chicken dishes, soups, and salads on the menu as well, insuring that just about everyone will find something to enjoy. This is a dining experience you won't want to rush through, so if you intend to catch a show, plan your schedule accordingly.

Sir Galahad's Prime Rib House ($$/$$$)

✆702-597-7448

Open for dinner only, this Tudor-style prime rib house offers delicious prime rib carved tableside, in addition to a nice selection of other entrées. Creamed spinach and Yorkshire pudding complete Sir Galahad's dining experience. If you're planning a party, private dining rooms are available for up to twenty people. Entrées are priced under $25 per person. On the menu, you'll find steak, chicken, and seafood dishes. While it's definitely a formal dining establishment, it's somewhat less formal and less expensive than the Steakhouse at Camelot. Reservations are recommended.

Regale Italian Eatery ($$)

✆702-597-7443

At this dinner-only establishment, you'll find a menu chock-full of Italian entrées, such as pizzas and pastas, served in an Italian village setting. This restaurant is headed by Chef Mark Pocaro. Live music is performed nightly from 5:00 P.M. to 10:00 P.M. (except on Wednesday and Thursday nights). All entrées are priced between $10 and $20. Reservations are recommended.

Casual Dining

Excalibur also offers a handful of less expensive, less formal dining options. Family-friendly is the word of the day at these restaurants.

Round Table Buffet ($/$$)

This Las Vegas–style buffet offers a wide selection of entrées, salads, and desserts at one price that's extremely reasonable ($9.99 per person for breakfast, $10.99 per person for lunch, and $14.49 per person for dinner).

Since this is an all-you-can-eat establishment, bring a hearty appetite! Seating is on a first-come basis, so be prepared to wait for seating during peak meal times. A Sunday brunch is also offered for $12.99 per person.

TRAVEL TIP

The closest monorail stop to the Excalibur is located about a five-minute walk away, at the MGM Grand. It's easiest to follow the walkway that goes from Excalibur to New York–New York, then cross Las Vegas Boulevard to enter the MGM Grand. The monorail allows you to travel up and down the Las Vegas Strip in order to reach other mega-resorts and attractions.

Sherwood Forest Café ($/$$)

Located on the casino level, near the resort's front desk area, Sherwood Forest Café is open twenty-four hours a day. This is the place to go for an inexpensive meal or snack. This café offers an extensive coffee-shop menu, with breakfast, lunch, and dinner items served all day and night. There's also a selection of Chinese specialties available in the evening, and a separate children's menu offered throughout the day and night. Full table service is provided. Meal prices range from $9.95 to $25 per person.

The Village Food Court ($)

In addition to the fine-dining and casual restaurant options at Excalibur, if you're looking for food that's fast and cheap, there's no need to go any farther than the Village Food Court.

Open for breakfast, lunch, dinner, and snacks throughout the day or night, here you'll find a central seating area and the following food options:

- **Café Espresso**: Gourmet coffees, cappuccino, espresso, and a full array of pastries are the specialty here.
- **Krispy Kreme Doughnuts**: Here you'll find the famous doughnuts in many varieties.
- **Cold Stone Creamery**: The Creamery offers soft-serve and traditional ice cream treats.
- **McDonald's**: Just look for those famous golden arches. Need anything more be said? If you're traveling with kids, chances are this will be a regular stop at mealtime. It's the perfect dining option for families on the go.
- **Quizno's**: Enjoy an Italian-style sub sandwich.
- **Pizza Hut Express**: Pizza is served for lunch, dinner, or a snack.
- **Manchu WOK**: Fresh and hot Chinese fast food is available here.

Lounges and Bars

Throughout the Excalibur resort, you'll find a handful of bars and lounges, some open twenty-four hours per day. Enjoy a drink as you gamble within the casino. Geared toward adults, these bars and lounges offer a relaxing and inviting atmosphere.

Excalibur's Casino

While Excalibur may have all of the amenities and charm of a family-oriented resort, it also offers an impressive, full-service casino designed for adult guests. One of the nice things about this casino is that there are plenty of low minimum-bet gaming tables and many penny, nickel, and quarter slot machines. Thus, the casino caters to casual gamblers as well as to high rollers.

Within Excalibur's 100,000-square-foot gaming area you'll find:

- 2,250 slot, video poker, and video keno machines
- 48 blackjack tables
- 7 roulette wheels
- 5 craps tables with double odds
- 2 Pai Gow poker tables
- 3 Caribbean Stud poker tables
- 4 Let It Ride tournament tables
- 1 mini-baccarat table
- 1 Big Six wheel
- 1 Casino War table
- 20 poker tables (featuring Seven Card Stud, Texas Hold 'em, and Omaha)
- A 104-seat keno lounge (plus the ability to play keno in the restaurants)
- A 150-seat race and sports book with big-screen TVs and interactive wagering

As with nearly all of the casinos in Las Vegas, free gaming lessons are available daily. If you've never gambled in Las Vegas before, it's an excellent idea to participate in free lessons to learn the basic rules of each game as well as the etiquette before putting your money on the line.

☝ TRAVEL ESSENTIAL

Earn rewards just for spending your money gambling! It's easy! Join the One Club by visiting the One Club desk located on the casino level at the resort or pointing your Web browser to ✑*www. myoneclub.com*. Accumulate points at Excalibur's casino, as well as at Mandalay Bay, Luxor, Monte Carlo, Circus, Circus, and several other casinos located throughout the country.

Useful Information for Guests

For resort guests, Excalibur offers free valet parking as well as self-parking. Acres of covered and surface parking provide close and easy access to the hotel and casino.

Several different walkways, many covered and offering a moving platform, connect Excalibur to New York–New York and Luxor. At both of these mega-resorts, you'll find a wide range of additional family-oriented activities and attractions.

CHAPTER 10

The Four Seasons

WHEN YOU FIRST STEP into the Four Seasons in Las Vegas, you'll immediately notice that something sets it apart from the other mega-resorts on the Strip: There's no casino. The Four Seasons is a traditional resort that's physically connected to Mandalay Bay, yet it's totally separate. The resort has its own main entrance, front desk, staff, restaurants, day spa, and amenities.

Mega-Resort Overview

✉3960 Las Vegas Boulevard South, Las Vegas, NV 89109
📞877-632-5000
📞702-632-5000
🖥*www.fourseasons.com*
Room and Suite Rates: $$$

The Four Seasons is one of the most luxurious resorts along the Strip. This is a top-notch resort, with 424 deluxe guest rooms and 86 suites, starting in price at $250 per weekday night and going up considerably from there. Each room is loaded with all of the finest amenities and furnishings you'll need for an extremely comfortable stay, and the service is impeccable.

The Four Seasons is family-friendly *and* small-dog-friendly. One way this resort makes family vacationing more pleasurable is with its Summer Family Specials. During the summer season, when a family books one deluxe guest room between Sunday and Thursday, a second, connecting guest room for children is available at the discounted weekday rate of $150 per night. This package also includes a $50 room credit, which can be applied to meals or incidentals, plus tickets to Mandalay Bay's popular Shark Reef attraction, as well as one complimentary in-room children's movie or one hour of in-room video games.

Because the Four Seasons is connected to Mandalay Bay, guests can also enjoy that resort's attractions and amenities, such as the eleven-acre water park that kids and teens will love. In terms of guest services, families with kids receive special treatment at the Four Seasons. Upon check-in, kids receive a special welcome gift, complimentary milk and cookies, have access to kid-size bathrobes in the guest rooms, and are able to order from a children's menu at the resort's award-wining restaurants.

TRAVEL ESSENTIAL

On a complimentary basis, microwave ovens, bottle warmers, refrigerators, strollers, playpens, and other infant- and kid-oriented essentials are available upon request from the resort's concierge.

For affluent adults traveling alone or with their kids, the Four Seasons truly sets the standard for luxury accommodations along the Las Vegas Strip.

FOUR SEASONS OVERALL FAMILY-FRIENDLINESS RATING

Ages Up to 5	Ages 6–15	Ages 16–20	Ages 21 & Up	Senior Citizens
☆☆☆	☆☆☆	☆☆☆	☆☆☆	☆☆☆

▲ The Four Seasons is family-friendly *and* luxurious.

Guest Room Accommodations

Accessible via three private elevators, the Four Seasons' guest rooms and suites are all located on five floors (thirty-five through thirty-nine) in one of the Mandalay Bay towers. The resort's lobby, spa, and restaurants are all located within a connected low-rise building.

Each guest room within the Four Seasons offers 500 square feet of living space that incorporates a large bathroom with marble fixtures and a separate shower and bathtub. All rooms offer a spectacular view of either the Las Vegas Strip or the surrounding desert. The list of amenities offered within the rooms is extensive and includes everything you'd expect from a world-class resort. Fine-quality bed linens and down comforters/duvets provide for extreme comfort and luxury at night. For families, multibedroom suites or adjoining deluxe rooms are available.

The Four Seasons offers two-bedroom guest suites ranging in price between $835 and $1,210 per night. These are ideal for families, although a much cheaper option is to reserve two connected deluxe guest rooms. The suites, however, offer a separate entry foyer, executive work area, living room, dining room, pantry, separate powder room, and a master bedroom and a second bedroom, each with its own bathroom. Suites range in size from 1,705 to 2,705 square feet.

≡FAST FACT

Guest rooms are equipped with a large television set, offering cable programming and pay-per-view movies. Connected to the television is a DVD player. The resort's concierge can provide a selection of family-friendly movies, or they can be rented (or purchased) from a nearby Blockbuster store.

Featured Attractions and Activities

While the Four Seasons has its own exclusive day spa, restaurants, and pool, it also shares a separate pool area with Mandalay Bay (this area includes a variety of water park activities, such as water slides and a wave pool, that are ideal for kids).

The resort itself offers no shows or activities, but the concierge can help guests book show tickets, tours, or activities such as golf, tennis, horseback riding, calm-water rafting, hiking, hot-air balloon rides, bicycling, or boating.

With two hours' notice, the concierge can also schedule private, in-room babysitting services, allowing parents to enjoy a night on the town knowing that their kids are being supervised by a bonded and licensed childcare provider within their own hotel room.

The Four Seasons has created a niche for itself, not just by offering extremely elegant accommodations, but also by creating a quiet resort environment that promotes relaxation, without having to deal with large crowds, casinos, or the hustle and bustle of the Las Vegas Strip (although you're literally minutes away from all of the Las Vegas excitement that can be found along the Strip).

The Spa: An Oasis of Serenity

The Spa, located within the Four Seasons' main building (near the private elevators that lead to the guest rooms), offers the ultimate in luxury. While not as large in size as other world-class day spas located along the Strip (such as the Canyon Ranch SpaClub), the Spa is an award-winning facility that offers a wide array of treatments, plus a fully equipped fitness center.

Within the Spa's sixteen private treatment rooms, seven types of facials, ten types of body treatments, and six types of massage treatments are among the offerings. The Four Seasons Signature Treatment (eighty minutes, $215), for example, includes body scrub, body wrap, massage, aromatherapy, and scalp treatment. Fifty- or eighty-minute massages are also available, and for an additional fee can be performed within your hotel room, rather than within one of the Spa's treatment rooms.

≡FAST FACT

In its August 2003 issue, *Travel + Leisure* magazine ranked the Four Seasons Las Vegas number six on its list of the Top 100 Continental U.S. and Canadian hotels. It was also ranked the first AAA Five Diamond Hotel in Las Vegas. *Zagat* ranked the resort number four in the country in 2004.

For the ultimate in relaxation, several spa packages are available for both men and women. The five-hour Five Diamond Package ($635), includes a Bali Sea Scrub, the choice of an eighty-minute facial, a fifty-minute body treatment, and the choice of any eighty-minute massage. Specifically for men, the Spa offers the "A Man for Four Seasons" package, which includes a fifty-minute gentleman's facial, the choice of any eighty-minute massage, and a fifty-minute seaweed body mask.

If you'd prefer to simply work out, the fitness center offers private personal trainers along with a selection of cardiovascular machines and a separate weight room (offering Cybex and free weights). The fitness center is available free of charge to resort guests over the age of eighteen.

Within the men's and women's locker rooms, you'll find a sauna, steam room, and whirlpool, plus chilled towels and bottled water. Hours of operation are 8:00 A.M. to 7:00 P.M. (spa) and 6:00 A.M. to 9:00 P.M. (fitness center).

Dining Options

Within walking distance of the Four Seasons are literally dozens of fine-dining restaurants at neighboring resorts, including Mandalay Bay. Within the Four Seasons itself, you'll find two restaurants: the Verandah and the newly renovated Charlie Palmer Steak House. Room service is also available twenty-four hours per day.

Fine Dining

The Four Season offers two fine-dining restaurants, both of which have special children's menus.

The Verandah

This restaurant offers indoor and outdoor seating and serves a large selection of traditional American favorites, including fresh seafood. The dining room seats 170 and serves until 10:00 P.M. Breakfast, lunch, and dinner are served, starting at 6:30 A.M., within a lovely and quiet Mediterranean setting.

For lunch, a special two-course "business lunch" is available for $22. The restaurant guarantees that you'll be in and out within one hour. Full vegetarian and Kosher menus are available.

Charles Palmer Steak

This fine-dining restaurant offers a nice selection of steak and seafood entrées. It's open for dinner only. The restaurant features an ever-changing menu. All beef served at Charles Palmer Steak is certified Angus and has been dry-aged for twenty-one days. Popular menu selections often include a sixteen-ounce New York strip steak, a twenty-eight-ounce Kansas City rib eye, a six-ounce filet mignon, and a forty-eight-ounce porterhouse steak for two. A full wine list is available to complement the meal. Contact the concierge for reservations.

Casual Dining

For casual dining, room service is available. The Verandah also offers a light menu for breakfast, lunch, and dinner, as well as traditional afternoon tea (served between 2:00 P.M. and 5:00 P.M. daily). Within a five-minute walk, an additional fifteen dining options are available at Mandalay Bay.

CHAPTER 11

Luxor

AS YOU CRUISE ALONG the Las Vegas Strip, you'll see castles, landmarks from other cities and countries, roller coasters on rooftops, and plenty of larger-than-life architecture. When you pass by Luxor, you'll feel as if you've been transported back to ancient Egypt.

The landmark structure of this resort is the incredibly large pyramid that houses the main lobby, the entertainment areas, and many of the guest rooms. Shining from the top of this thirty-story (350-foot-high) pyramid every night is the brightest light beam in the world. It can be seen from ten miles in space.

Mega-Resort Overview

✉3900 Las Vegas Boulevard South, Las Vegas, NV 89119-1000

☎888-777-0188

☎702-262-4000

✍*www.luxor.com*

Room and Suite Rates: $$/$$$

Luxor is owned and operated by the Mandalay Resort Group, which also owns and operates the Excalibur, Mandalay Bay, Circus, Circus, and the Monte Carlo in Las Vegas, plus several other casino and resort properties throughout America.

This family-oriented hotel has an ancient-Egyptian theme encompassing every aspect of the resort itself, starting with its pyramid shape. This theme is enhanced through the property's realistic décor and the shows presented here. Just inside the front door, you can't miss the life-size, 35-foot-tall replica of the Great Temple of Ramses II, one of the truly stunning architectural wonders of ancient Egypt.

In a nutshell, the Luxor offers activities, shows, and attractions for the whole family. It's the adults, however, who will better appreciate the extreme attention to detail that this resort offers in the ancient-Egyptian theme that is present everywhere.

Luxor has been a popular, family-friendly destination in Las Vegas since it opened in 1993.

LUXOR OVERALL FAMILY-FRIENDLINESS RATING

Ages Up to 5	Ages 6–15	Ages 16–20	Ages 21 & Up	Senior Citizens
☆☆	☆☆	☆☆☆	☆☆☆	☆☆☆

Guest Room Accommodations

The 4,408 rooms and suites in the Luxor offer comfort and convenient amenities. Many of the rooms have a stunning view of the Las Vegas Strip, the nearby mountains, or the hotel's pool. Suites with a Jacuzzi and/or concierge and valet service are available.

The main Luxor building is pyramid shaped, so all rooms in the main building have a slanted wall on the exterior (window) side. The rooms in the towers have square walls. All rooms are decorated in what the hotel calls an "updated Egyptian style." The tower rooms contain both a bathtub and a separate shower, while the basic rooms in the main pyramid structure contain only a shower.

Luxor offers both midpriced and luxury resort accommodations, with basic rooms priced between $79 and $289 per night. The basic Pyramid Rooms (within the resort's main pyramid structure) offer one king-size bed or two queen-size beds. More luxurious and spacious suites are available in a variety of configurations. The resort's two twenty-two-story towers also offer basic room accommodations, as well as a variety of more luxurious suites. Smoking and nonsmoking rooms are available.

▲ Luxor is a side trip to Ancient Egypt.   Photo ©The Las Vegas News Bureau.

 TRAVEL TIP

Basic room amenities include air conditioning, a color TV, cable and pay-per-view movies, computer hookup with high-speed Internet access, telephone, and AM/FM radio and alarm. An iron and ironing board and hairdryers are available for free upon request. For an additional daily fee, rollaway beds ($25), cribs ($15), and refrigerators ($15) are available.

Save Money when Booking Your Luxor Reservations

If you're looking for the lowest room rates, Luxor guarantees that if you book your reservations online at Luxor's own Web site (*www.luxor.com*), you will receive the lowest rate available for the dates of your stay.

While you'll still want to shop around on the other travel-related Web sites, be sure to check the rates at Luxor's Web site before booking your reservation. If you find a better rate elsewhere, call the hotel and they will match the rate.

By booking online, you'll automatically receive $10 off the published room rate per night and receive extra discounts, such as two complimentary (adult) admission passes to the Oasis Spa, $10 off an admission ticket to *Midnight Fantasy*, two free admission tickets to the King Tut Museum, plus $35 in retail savings.

Featured Attractions and Activities

In addition to the ancient Egyptian theme, which is a favorite among kids and teens, what makes Luxor an ideal family-oriented resort destination are the many attractions, rides, and shows that are family-friendly. The majority of these activities are located in the Pharaoh's Pavilion area, which is separated from the resort's adult-oriented casinos, bars, and lounges.

IMAX RideFilms

✆702-262-4555

Luxor offers three different IMAX RideFilms, which are technologically advanced, rather turbulent, motion-simulator thrill rides. The rides operate throughout the day and evening. Tickets are $6. They're not suitable for very young children, senior citizens, or anyone with physical limitations. Pregnant women, and people with back or neck problems, etc., should avoid these three attractions.

In Search of the Obelisk takes passengers on a trip to the dig site of an ancient subterranean civilization. *Reboot* (✐*www.reboot. com*) is based on the popular children's TV series and takes passengers on a whirlwind ride through Mainframe City. *Dracula's Haunted Castle: The Ride* is a thrill ride and horror film wrapped up into one experience. It's definitely a bit scary and more suitable for teens and adults.

IN SEARCH OF THE OBELISK

Ages Up to 5	Ages 6–15	Ages 16–20	Ages 21 & Up	Senior Citizens
Not Suitable	☆☆	☆☆	☆☆	☆☆

REBOOT

Ages Up to 5	Ages 6–15	Ages 16–20	Ages 21 & Up	Senior Citizens
☆	☆☆☆	☆☆	☆☆	☆☆

DRACULA'S HAUNTED CASTLE: THE RIDE

Ages Up to 5	Ages 6–15	Ages 16–20	Ages 21 & Up	Senior Citizens
Not Suitable	☆	☆☆☆	☆☆☆	☆☆

King Tut's Tomb Tour and Museum

☏702-262-4555

King Tut's Tomb and Museum at Luxor is the only full-scale reproduction located outside Egypt of Carter's discovery. During the fifteen-minute self-guided walking tour, you'll see exact reproductions of the tomb itself, as well as the artifacts that were found inside.

The museum is open daily from 9:00 A.M. to 11:00 P.M. An optional audiotape tour is available in multiple languages. Tickets are $5 per person.

≡FAST FACT

It was in 1922 that Howard Carter discovered the tomb of King Tutankhamen in Egypt—one of the greatest archaeological finds of all time. Since then, the priceless artifacts that were uncovered have toured the world.

While adults will find this museum fascinating and educational, young children will likely be bored. By visiting this museum, guests will develop a much greater appreciation for ancient Egypt and the artisans of the day.

KING TUT'S TOMB TOUR AND MUSEUM

Ages Up to 5	Ages 6–15	Ages 16–20	Ages 21 & Up	Senior Citizens
Not Suitable	☆	☆☆	☆☆	☆☆☆

Games of the Gods Arcade

People young and old who enjoy video games will enjoy Games of the Gods, which offers many of the latest arcade games, virtual reality games, and a karaoke video recording studio (where you can make your own MTV-style music video). This arcade is located on the attractions level of the Luxor.

OVERALL GAMES OF THE GODS ARCADE EXPERIENCE

Ages Up to 5	Ages 6–15	Ages 16–20	Ages 21 & Up	Senior Citizens
☆☆	☆☆☆	☆☆☆	☆☆	☆

One of the newest attractions within the Games of the Gods Arcade is the Maxflight VR2002 Programmable Roller Coaster. Using state-of-the-art flight-simulator technology, the Maxflight VR2002 lets you take a virtual ride on a roller coaster that you've designed yourself.

 TRAVEL ESSENTIAL

Get around the Strip by tram. In addition to the Las Vegas Monorail that travels up and down the Strip (the closest stop to Luxor is at the MGM Grand), there's a free tram that runs every three to four minutes, traveling between Luxor, Mandalay Bay, and Excalibur. It operates twenty-four hours per day.

The motion-based Indy 500 Racing Simulator, also located within the Games of the Gods area, puts you in the driver's seat against up to seven other opponents in a simulated high-speed race. You can also strap into Xtreme Powerboat to experience an action-filled powerboat racing simulation.

MAXFLIGHT VR2002 PROGRAMMABLE ROLLER COASTER

Ages Up to 5	Ages 6–15	Ages 16–20	Ages 21 & Up	Senior Citizens
Not Suitable	☆☆	☆☆☆	☆☆☆	☆

INDY 500 RACING SIMULATOR

Ages Up to 5	Ages 6–15	Ages 16–20	Ages 21 & Up	Senior Citizens
Not Suitable	☆☆	☆☆☆	☆☆☆	☆

XTREME POWERBOAT

Ages Up to 5	Ages 6–15	Ages 16–20	Ages 21 & Up	Senior Citizens
Not Suitable	☆☆	☆☆☆	☆☆☆	☆

The Swimming Pools

Open year-round (hours of operation vary based on the season), the Luxor's swimming pools are among the largest in Las Vegas. The pools are outdoors, on the west side of the main pyramid. All are heated to eighty degrees and have Jacuzzis. Private cabanas and rafts can be rented. The pool is available to all guests of the hotel. Towels are provided.

It's Showtime at Luxor

Luxor offers several different shows. *Blue Man Group Live*, based on the hit off-Broadway show, is suitable for the entire family and offers a one-of-a-kind musical entertainment experience. The IMAX movie theater also provides for a memorable experience.

Save Money on Luxor's Attractions

Many of the attractions at Luxor require separate admission fees. For a flat fee of $24.95 per person, however, you can purchase a money-saving "Passport to Adventure" attraction pass, which includes:

- One IMAX movie ticket
- Three IMAX RideFilms admissions
- One Pirates 4D admission ticket
- One pass to King Tut's Tomb and Museum
- One pass to the Virtual Reality Roller Coaster

This pass offers a full day's worth of fun and interactive indoor entertainment. All attractions take place within the Pharaoh's Pavilion area of the Luxor resort.

Blue Man Group Live

✆702-262-4400

✐*www.blueman.com*

Blue Man Group has a permanent home at the Luxor. These non-speaking performance artists wear blue makeup from head to toe and entertain audiences by performing music using very unusual instruments and by doing unusual mime movements. For example, according to the group, "The PVC instrument used during the performance is made from hundreds of feet of PVC tubing. Pitch is determined by the length of the tube. It is by far the coolest instrument ever made, partly because of its sound and partly because it changes color."

 TRAVEL TIP

Blue Man Group Live is suitable for the entire family, but young children (and some adults, for that matter) simply may not get it . . . the show is that unusual.

The two-hour show is extremely visual, highly unusual, and definitely worth seeing. Because the 1,219-seat theater at the Luxor has been custom-designed for this performance troupe, the Las Vegas version of the show is more extravagant than what's presented in other cities. Showtimes are 7:00 P.M. and 10:00 P.M., and tickets are $65 and $75.

BLUE MAN GROUP LIVE

Ages Up to 5	Ages 6–15	Ages 16–20	Ages 21 & Up	Senior Citizens
☆	☆☆☆	☆☆☆	☆☆☆	☆☆

Luxor IMAX Movie

✆702-262-IMAX

This family-oriented attraction offers a movie experience seen on a screen measuring nearly seven stories high. The IMAX movie frames are ten times the size of a conventional 35-millimeter film— resulting in awe-inspiring 2-D and lifelike 3-D images that envelop viewers and place them into other worlds, from the far reaches of outer space to the lowest depths of the sea.

In addition to the massive screen, the 312-seat theater offers a 15,000-watt, state-of-the-art sound system that is far more advanced than what you'd hear in an average movie theater. The sound in this theater actually surrounds you, creating a totally immersive experience.

Each day at least three different IMAX movie presentations are shown. The IMAX theater operates throughout the day and evening. Tickets are $9.95, and can be purchased up to five minutes before each scheduled show.

The feature films rotate periodically, but might include:

NASCAR 3D

Find out what it feels like to be in the driver's seat during a NASCAR race as you travel at 200 miles per hour around a track. You'll also learn what it takes to be a professional driver as you watch NASCAR racing from the inside. The movie uses state-of-the-art 3-D technology to add realism and excitement to the moviegoing experience. Kids and teens will love this IMAX film.

LUXOR IMAX MOVIE: *NASCAR 3D*

Ages Up to 5	Ages 6–15	Ages 16–20	Ages 21 & Up	Senior Citizens
Not Suitable	☆☆☆	☆☆☆	☆☆☆	☆☆

Everest

Go with professional climbers to the top of Mt. Everest and see the hardship and tragedy that climbers have endured. This is an action-packed documentary that's suitable more for teens and adults.

LUXOR IMAX MOVIE: *EVEREST*

Ages Up to 5	Ages 6–15	Ages 16–20	Ages 21 & Up	Senior Citizens
Not Suitable	☆	☆☆☆	☆☆☆	☆☆☆

Haunted Castle 3D

Take a visually stunning journey through a realistic, computer-generated haunted castle and discover what secrets are inside.

LUXOR IMAX MOVIE: *HAUNTED CASTLE 3D*

Ages Up to 5	Ages 6–15	Ages 16–20	Ages 21 & Up	Senior Citizens
Not Suitable	☆☆☆	☆☆☆	☆☆	☆☆

Pirates 4D

☎702-262-4400

Actor/comedian Leslie Nielsen stars in this high-seas adventure movie that features a wide range of special effects. You'll experience the film from within an interactive theater, so as you're watching the 3-D movie, you'll also *feel* some of the effects and become immersed in the comical adventure. Tickets are $6.95 and can be purchased up to fifteen minutes before a scheduled showtime. The show runs throughout the day from 9:00 A.M. to 6:00 P.M. You'll see, feel, and hear the action. This is a very different moviegoing experience that what an IMAX theater or a traditional movie theater offers.

PIRATES 4D

Ages Up to 5	Ages 6–15	Ages 16–20	Ages 21 & Up	Senior Citizens
☆	☆☆☆	☆☆☆	☆☆☆	☆☆☆

Shopping

Luxor offers a handful of gift and souvenir shops, most found within the Giza Galleria shopping area of the resort.

Giza Galleria

Giza Galleria is open Sunday through Thursday from 9:00 A.M. to 11:00 P.M., and on Fridays and Saturdays from 9:00 A.M. to midnight.

This mini-mall offers a variety of shopping experiences, including:

- **Cairo Bazaar**: Egyptian-theme gifts and souvenir items are available here.
- **Dandera's Bath & Body**: Body care products, soaps, and bubble-bath products are among this shop's offerings. Take what you buy back up to your room and transform the bathroom into your own personal day spa.
- **Exclusivo**: Men and women can shop for clothing here.
- **Ice Cream & Candy Store**: This is a great place to grab dessert while on the go or to satisfy your sweet tooth.
- **Luxor and Las Vegas Souvenir Store**: Here you'll find a wide range of merchandise featuring the Luxor logo and other Las Vegas–theme items.
- **Tie & Sock Shop**: This store features a selection of neckties, cigars, socks, and other accessories for men.

- **Tiny Tuts**: This children's store carries fun clothing and toys for children of all ages.
- **Treasure Chamber**: More Egyptian-theme gifts and souvenirs are available at this shop.

Other shops located throughout the Luxor complex include:

- **Blue Man Group Store**: Pick up some souvenirs from this unique show experience. Audio CDs, videos, and other products are available.
- **Innerspace**: You'll find some rarities at this art and jewelry shop.
- **The Luxor Logo Shop**: This shop carries a wide range of merchandise featuring the Luxor logo and other Las Vegas–theme merchandise.
- **Nile Newsstand**: Newspapers and magazines are among this shop's offerings.
- **Sobek's Sundries**: You can get personal items, magazines, drinks, and other items here.
- **Tut's Treasures**: The King Tut Museum shop offers a selection of Egyptian- and King Tut–theme gifts.

Day Spa, Salon, and Fitness Facilities

The Oasis Spa is Las Vegas's only world-class day spa that's open twenty-four hours per day. In addition to offering workout facilities, a wide range of fairly priced treatments is available.

The Oasis Spa
☎702-730-5720
☎800-258-9308
Based on research conducted by the world's foremost archaeologists, the pharaohs of ancient Egypt led a very pampered and lavish lifestyle. While you're staying at Luxor, you're invited to treat yourself to royal treatment at the Oasis Spa.

≡FAST FACT

The Oasis Spa is a 12,000-square-foot facility that features a full range of affordable amenities, including the fitness center, aromatic steam baths and showers, hot and warm whirlpools, a dry sauna, and an extensive menu of treatments ranging from body wraps and scrubs to massages, facials, hydrotherapy, aromatherapy, personal training, and tanning.

The Oasis Spa features a full-service hair and nail salon (by appointment only). The spa itself is open twenty-four hours a day; however, appointments for the various treatments and massages book up fast, so schedule appointments in advance. (Appointments can be scheduled up to five days in advance.)

Once an appointment is scheduled, plan on arriving thirty minutes early to allow for check-in and time to change. A Spa Facility Day Pass, which provides full access to the spa and fitness center, is included with any spa treatment priced at $45 or more.

Admission to just the spa and fitness facilities, which include lockers, showers, Jacuzzi, sauna, weight room, steam room, and cardiovascular machines (with no optional treatments), is $25 per day.

Dining Options

Like all of the mega-resorts, Luxor offers a selection of fine-dining and casual-dining experiences. The food court area or the buffet offer inexpensive meal options for families.

Fine Dining

Prepare yourself to be treated like Egyptian royalty when you dine at any of these restaurants located in Luxor's giant pyramid building.

Isis ($$$)

☎702-262-4773

The stars shine brightly indoors at this fine-dining establishment that overlooks Luxor's casino from the mezzanine level. Seasonal dishes, Continental cuisine, and calorie-conscious offerings are what you'll find on the menu. Dinner is served nightly from 5:30 P.M. until 11:00 P.M. The restaurant is closed on Tuesdays and Wednesdays. Plan on spending at least $45 per person for dinner. Reservations are recommended.

Sacred Sea Room ($$$)

☎702-262-4772

Fresh seafood (flown in daily) is the specialty at this fine-dining restaurant. It's decorated lavishly with murals and hieroglyphic reproductions depicting scenes of fishing on the Nile. Dinner is served nightly from 5:00 P.M. until 11:00 P.M. Plan on spending at least $40 per person. Reservations are recommended.

Luxor Steakhouse ($$$)

☎702-262-4778

If you want to dine like a true pharaoh and you're in the mood for nothing less than top-quality USDA prime cuts of beef, the Luxor Steakhouse offers elegant dining with specialties including New York strip steak, filet mignon, and roast prime rib. The menu also offers a selection of seafood, chicken, and pork entrées, soups, salads, and, of course, desserts. Dinner is served nightly from 5:00 P.M. to 11:00 P.M. Plan on spending at least $40 per person. Reservations are recommended.

Fusia ($$$)

☎702-262-4774

Featuring what the chef calls "New Chinese Cuisine," Fusia offers such specialties as twice-cooked duck and white miso–lacquered sea bass. Dine on blue crab rock shrimp rolls or spicy salt-and-pepper calamari as an appetizer or a mid-afternoon snack. Open daily from 5:00 P.M. to 11:00 P.M. Plan on spending at least $25 per person. Reservations are recommended.

Casual Dining

Following are several family-oriented, more casual dining options available at Luxor.

Pharaoh's Pheast Buffet ($$)

During your visit to Las Vegas, you'll probably want to experience a classic Las Vegas–style buffet. This particular buffet offers an endless supply of all-you-can-eat entrées, appetizers, salads, and desserts for one price. Breakfast is served from 6:30 A.M. to 11:00 A.M. Lunch is offered from 11:00 A.M. to 4:00 P.M. Enjoy dinner between 4:00 P.M. and 10:00 P.M. No reservations are accepted, so be prepared for a wait. Prices range from $10.75 to $16.95 per person.

Pyramid Café ($/$$)

Open twenty-four hours and located on the casino level of Luxor, the Pyramid Café serves a full-service, sit-down breakfast, lunch, and dinner in a coffee shop–style atmosphere. A full menu is available. If you're looking for a relatively fast and inexpensive meal, this is an excellent dining choice, and a good alternative to the buffet. Meals start at about $10 per person. A kids' menu is available.

Nile Deli ($/$$)

There were no delicatessens in ancient Egypt, but chances are the pharaohs would have enjoyed a classic turkey club sandwich, a potato knish, blintzes, chopped chicken liver, or potato pancakes. The Nile Deli offers "kosher-style" deli foods in a New York–theme setting. Open daily for breakfast, lunch, and dinner, this is an inexpensive dining option suitable for the entire family. The Nile Deli is located on the casino level of the hotel, near the Luxor Theater. Hours of operation are 6:00 A.M. to 10:00 P.M. Meals start at about $10 per person.

Luxor Food Court ($)

When you're looking for fast and cheap food or snacks, look no further than the Luxor Food Court. It's located on the attractions level of the hotel. Here you'll find a selection of fast-food classics they never had in ancient Egypt, such as McDonald's, Nathan's Hot Dogs, Little Caesar's Pizza, Swenson's Ice Cream, and Luxor Coffee Company.

The food court is open daily from 6:00 A.M. until midnight. It's cheap, it's convenient, and there's enough variety to keep everyone you're traveling with happy.

Nightclubs, Lounges, and Bars

When it comes to adults-only nighttime entertainment, RA is one of the most popular nightclubs in Las Vegas. Throughout the mega-resort, you'll also find a handful of bars and lounges.

RA: The Nightclub (For Adults Only)

✆702-262-4400

✎*www.ralv.com*

When the sun goes down, the fun begins at this modern-day nightclub with an ancient Egyptian twist. Dance into the night as lasers, lights, and a pulsating sound system go into full gear while nonstop dance music is played. The 19,000-square-foot nightclub offers a spacious dance floor, stage, two large full-service bars, and plenty of booths and tables. There are also two cigar lounges, a sushi bar, special VIP booths, and a variety of other amenities designed to make every night a memorable party experience.

Wednesday nights, RA hosts "Pleasuredome," what the Luxor calls "the hippest, sexiest house party on the Las Vegas Strip." It features the best club music from Los Angeles and New York and RA's provocative cage-dancing contest. Thursday night is the weekly Deca Dance party, where music from the 1980s is played.

Live performances by top recording artists also take place throughout the year at RA. The club is open Wednesdays through Saturdays from 10:00 P.M. to 6:00 A.M. An upscale dress code is strictly enforced and no minors are admitted. There is a $20 cover for men and $10 for women. Tickets can be purchased in advance.

Nefertiti's Lounge

Open seven days a week, Nefertiti's Lounge offers a full-service bar and ongoing entertainment throughout the evening. Whether you need to take a break from the sightseeing, you're gearing up for a night of gambling, or you're meeting friends or coworkers for a nightcap, the lounge offers a place to relax and have a drink.

Luxor's Casino

No matter how you enjoy risking your money, when it comes to casino-style games of skill and chance, Luxor's Casino offers all of the popular table games, such as blackjack, craps, roulette, baccarat, Pai Gow, Caribbean Stud poker, Let It Ride, poker, and keno. There are also 2,600 slot machines, video poker machines, and video keno machines allowing you to risk between a nickel and $100 per play. Slot players can try to win millions of dollars or cars on progressive games.

≡FAST FACT

While playing your favorite casino games, you can earn points that can be redeemed for free accommodations, show tickets, and a variety of other "prizes." Be sure to join the One Club by visiting the membership desk located on the casino level at the resort or by pointing your Web browser to *www.myoneclub.com.*

If gambling in the hustle and bustle of a busy casino isn't for you, the Luxor offers more comfortable poker rooms, where games of Seven Card Stud and Texas Hold 'em are almost always in progress.

Sports fans can bet on their favorite events or sporting competition while watching the seventeen giant-screen TVs or 128 individual viewing monitors in the race and sports book area of the casino.

CHAPTER 12

Mandalay Bay and THEhotel at Mandalay Bay

ALONG WITH THE BELLAGIO, The Venetian, and Wynn Las Vegas, Mandalay Bay can easily be considered one of the more luxurious mega-resorts on the Strip. Having cost more than $950 million to build, this resort offers guests a wide range of amenities, even in the standard guest rooms.

Mega-Resort Overview

✉3950 Las Vegas Boulevard South, Las Vegas, NV 89119
☎877-632-7000
☎702-632-7777
🖰*www.mandalaybay.com*
Room and Suite Rates: $$$/$$$$

Mandalay Bay is designed to appeal to an affluent clientele, including businesspeople, honeymooners, seniors, and couples traveling alone. For families, what Mandalay Bay offers is the ultimate in luxury, comfort, and superior service but at a price. Many of the attractions offered at this resort, such as the indoor Shark Reef, the beach and pool area, and the Broadway-style entertainment, are suitable for the entire family.

▲ Mandalay Bay is a top-notch resort.

Along with the other amenities and activities you'd expect to find in a world-class resort, Mandalay Bay houses a stadium-size entertainment venue, where major events and concerts are regularly held.

The majority of the restaurants offer a fine-dining experience, while the resort's lovely day spa offers guests a full range of services to pamper their minds and bodies simultaneously.

TRAVEL TIP

Mandalay Bay is located in the South End of the Las Vegas Strip, about two miles from the McCarran International Airport.

Instead of offering a traditional Las Vegas musical revue or magic show, Mandalay Bay brings the excitement of Broadway theater to the Strip, with an award-winning, all-star cast presenting the smash-hit, family-oriented musical *Mamma Mia!*

Mandalay Bay is a luxurious resort unto itself; however, within this resort is a second, separate but fully integrated resort, called THEhotel at Mandalay Bay. Featuring 1,120 suites with separate living and sleeping areas as well as its own restaurants, services, and amenities, THEhotel offers the ultimate in luxury. To make THEhotel reservations, call ✆877-532-7800. (This resort within a resort was formally a Four Seasons property. For details about the new Four Seasons, see Chapter 10.)

▲ THEhotel at Mandalay Bay.   Photo provided by PR Newswire Photo Service.

MANDALAY BAY OVERALL FAMILY-FRIENDLINESS RATING

Ages Up to 5	Ages 6–15	Ages 16–20	Ages 21 & Up	Senior Citizens
☆	☆☆	☆☆☆	☆☆☆	☆☆☆

Guest Room Accommodations

What Mandalay Bay calls a standard room (starting at a published rate of $149 per night and going up considerably), most of the other resorts along the Strip would call a deluxe room or even a suite. The average standard room is 515 square feet, and includes a master bath and a long list of amenities, including a separate bathtub and shower, robes, makeup mirror, hairdryer, his and hers closets, two phone lines with data ports, a 27-inch television, two queen-size or one king-size bed, floor-to-ceiling windows, and an iron with ironing board.

Mandalay Bay also offers more spacious Deluxe Rooms, as well as suites in multiple configurations. The 500 suites at Mandalay Bay are large (between 690 and 6,670 square feet) and offer a wet bar with refrigerator, spa tub, and a handful of other luxuries.

The guest accommodations within THEhotel at Mandalay Bay are all suites, offered in a variety of sizes and configurations, but all providing maximum luxury and comfort. During nonpeak travel times, basic suites start at just $159 per night and go up considerably.

TRAVEL ESSENTIAL

The Bathhouse Spa at THEhotel at Mandalay Bay (☎877-632-9636) is a two-story, $25 million, 14,000-square-foot facility. It's open daily from 5:00 A.M. to 10:00 P.M.

At 750 square feet, the basic suites within THEhotel are considered spacious by Las Vegas standards. Each room offers a wet bar and 42-inch plasma television. The bathrooms feature marble and granite décor, plus a separate tub and shower. There's also high-speed Internet access and a fax/printer in every room, among other amenities. THEhotel also has its own day spa, fitness facilities, restaurant, café, and lounge.

Save Money when Making Your Reservations

You can save money by booking your reservation online at the Mandalay Bay Web site. In addition to finding special "online only" rates, when you book online you'll automatically receive $250 in Mandalay Place Savings Certificates, a coupon for a two-for-the-price-of-one breakfast at the House of Blues, an upgrade to a Honeymoon suite for an additional $35 (when you check in Sunday through Thursday), or an upgrade to an Executive Suite for an additional $50 (when you check in Sunday through Thursday).

Depending on the dates you'll be traveling, when you book online, a basic room can start as low as $119 per night, which is a bargain for this luxurious resort complex.

Featured Attractions and Activities

In addition to attracting conventiongoers, business travelers, and sports fans attending high-profile events, thanks to the assortment of activities and attractions this mega-resort offers, it's a common destination for families.

Take your pick of the many major attractions that Mandalay Bay has to offer.

≡FAST FACT

Research shows that there are only twelve golden crocodiles remaining in the entire world. The Shark Reef is home to five of them.

The Shark Reef

☎702-632-4555

Shark Reef is North America's only predator-based aquarium. Within the 1.6 million gallon tank, you'll see sixteen different types of sharks, along with 100 other animal species, including sawfish, giant rays, green sea turtles, piranha, and golden crocodiles. In all, Shark Reef offers fourteen different exhibits, showcasing more than 2,000 sea creatures.

Many people are fascinated by the world under the sea, yet few get a chance to see the exotic creatures that live beneath the oceans. As a state-of-the-art and extremely well-designed indoor aquarium complex, Shark Reef offers an up-close and exciting look at sharks and other sea creatures.

≡FAST FACT

Most aquariums house their animals in habitats using seawater pumped directly from the ocean. Due to its remote desert location, Shark Reef's curators create their own seawater, using a state-of-the-art process.

Open daily from 10:00 A.M. to 11:00 P.M., Shark Reef is suitable for people of all ages. This is a self-paced, walk-through attraction, where you can spend anywhere from one to three hours. It's a unique and extremely fascinating attraction that's well worth the price of admission ($15.95 for adults and $9.95 for children).

SHARK REEF

Ages Up to 5	Ages 6–15	Ages 16–20	Ages 21 & Up	Senior Citizens
☆	☆☆☆	☆☆☆	☆☆☆	☆☆☆

House of Blues

☏702-632-7600

In addition to offering New Orleans–style dining, House of Blues is a live music venue that hosts nightly concerts by well-known (and not-so-well-known) performers. Bob Dylan, Sheryl Crow, the Blues Brothers, B. B. King, Indigo Girls, Yes, Cheap Trick, Al Green, Stevie Nicks, and Chris Isaak have been some of the performers at this Las Vegas House of Blues location.

The venue accommodates 1,800 guests. For an up-to-date concert schedule, contact the box office, Ticketmaster (☏702-474-4000/✐www. ticketmaster.com), or the House of Blues Web site at ✐www.hob.com.

HOUSE OF BLUES

Ages Up to 5	Ages 6–15	Ages 16–20	Ages 21 & Up	Senior Citizens
Not Suitable	Not Suitable	☆☆	☆☆	☆☆

The Swimming Pool

Most Las Vegas hotels and resorts offer a few swimming pools, maybe a waterfall or two, and if you're lucky, a whirlpool or waterslide. Mandalay Bay, however, offers an 11-acre tropical sand-and-surf beach. There are also three swimming pools, nine private bungalows, sixteen cabanas (which can be rented), and a variety of beachside lounges, restaurants, and shops.

Relax on a sandy beach, take a swim in the wave pool, or enjoy a swim in the resort's traditional swimming pool. With 1,700 tons of sand, 1,640,270 gallons of water, and a wave pool that measures 41,178 square feet (with adjustable waves up to 6 feet for boogie boarding and surfing), the surf and beach area of Mandalay Bay is nothing short of impressive.

 TRAVEL TIP

Throughout the year, outdoor concerts are held on the beach. Hall and Oates, Billy Idol, REO Speedwagon, Rick Springfield, and the Go Go's are just a few of the performers who have appeared at this popular outdoor concert venue. Ticket prices for these concert events vary.

This area offers a wonderful way to relax and unwind. Surrounding the entire beach area is exquisite landscaping featuring a tropical motif, complete with palm trees and exotic plants. The adjoining "Lazy River" flows at 2 miles per hour and allows guests to take a relaxing ride on a raft.

TROPICAL SAND-AND-SURF BEACH

Ages Up to 5	Ages 6–15	Ages 16–20	Ages 21 & Up	Senior Citizens
☆☆	☆☆☆	☆☆☆	☆☆☆	☆☆

☝ TRAVEL ESSENTIAL

It's tee time! While staying at Mandalay Bay, you have the option to play golf at one of six courses located in the Las Vegas area, including Bali Hai Golf Club, Desert Pines Golf Club, Royal Links Golf Club, and Stallion Mountain Country Club. Book tee times by calling ☎702-632-6185.

It's Showtime at Mandalay Bay

When it comes to entertainment at Mandalay Bay, there's no shortage of options. In addition to an ever-changing lineup of musical acts at House of Blues, major sporting and concert events taking place regularly at the Mandalay Bay Events Center, and the resort's resident show, *Mamma Mia!*, you and your family can enjoy some or all of what this mega-resort offers.

Mamma Mia!

☎877-632-7400
✐*www.mamma-mia.com*

The smash-hit Broadway musical *Mamma Mia!* has found a home in Las Vegas. The all-star, extremely talented cast and the hit music of Abba will delight you. The group's most popular songs have been ingeniously woven together into a comic musical with an intricate and utterly ridiculous plot. People of all ages leave the theater laughing and dancing down the aisles.

The plot involves a mother, a daughter, three possible dads, and a pending wedding. This show continues to be presented throughout the world and has already been seen by over 10 million theatergoers. Many of Abba's mega-hit songs are featured, including "Dancing Queen," "Money, Money, Money," "S.O.S.," "Take a Chance on Me," and, of course, "Mamma Mia."

Even if you've already seen *Mamma Mia!* on Broadway, it's definitely worth seeing again . . . and again. If you're looking for an upbeat and highly entertaining show for the entire family, this is the one show in Las Vegas that's a must-see. Showtimes are 7:00 P.M. Monday through Thursday, and 5:00 P.M. and 9:00 P.M. on Saturday and Sunday. There are no shows on Fridays. Tickets are $45, $75, and $100.

MAMMA MIA!

Ages Up to 5	Ages 6–15	Ages 16–20	Ages 21 & Up	Senior Citizens
Not Suitable	☆☆☆	☆☆☆	☆☆☆	☆☆☆

Mandalay Bay Events Center

This 12,000-seat sports and entertainment complex is the setting for many concerts, major sporting events, and television specials that take place throughout the year.

Some of the biggest events in Las Vegas happen within this entertainment complex. For ticket information and a listing of special events, call Ticketmaster at ✆702-474-4000 or visit ✍*www.ticketmaster. com* on the Web.

Shopping

Although Mandalay Bay doesn't offer a shopping promenade or mall like some other resorts along the Strip, you will find a selection of fine stores offering gifts, souvenirs, clothing, and other merchandise.

- **Bali Trading Company**: An assortment of South Seas treasures and gifts are available here, including one-of-a-kind hand-carved works of art.
- **House of Blues Store**: Buy souvenirs and memorabilia from this theme restaurant and concert venue.
- **Jack Gallery**: Contemporary art is featured in this gallery and store.
- **Jungle Juice Spirits**: Las Vegas souvenirs and merchandise are available here along with various liquor items for the over-twenty-one crowd.

- **Le Paradis**: Watches and fine jewelry are sold at this upscale jeweler.
- *Mamma Mia!* **Store**: Souvenir merchandise from *Mamma Mia!* is available here, including the show's soundtrack.
- **Mandalay Bay Floral**: This is a full-service florist. Have fresh flowers or arrangements delivered to your room or anywhere in the world.
- **Mandalay Bay: The Store**: Mandalay Bay merchandise is offered along with tropical casual wear. It's located across from the registration desk in the lobby.
- **Pearl Moon Boutique**: Designer swimwear, spa merchandise, workout gear, hats, sunglasses, and beach footwear are the types of items you'll find at this boutique.
- **Portfolio**: This store's specialty is women's shoes and clothing.
- **Rangoon News Bureau**: Newspapers, magazines, sundries, and snacks are available at this shop, located at the elevator lobby on the casino level.
- **Reflections**: Fine glass pieces and other art are offered here.
- **Stars Memorabilia**: If you're looking for celebrity memorabilia, you'll find a large selection of photographs, autographs, and other items at this store.
- **Surf Shack**: This shop offers everything you'll need when spending a day at the pool or beach, including sun care products and bathing suits.
- **The Wave**: Located at the elevator lobby on the casino level, this shop offers golf shirts embroidered with the Mandalay Bay wave logo.
- **Tropical Gifts and Stuff**: Logoed merchandise plus a selection of children's playthings are available from this shop, which is located next to the elevator at beach level.

Day Spa, Salon, and Fitness Facilities

When you're ready to relax and pamper yourself, Mandalay Bay offers one of the most upscale and luxurious day spas on the Strip.

There's also a full-service salon and complete fitness facilities. In addition to the main spa located within Mandalay Bay, there's also the Bathhouse Spa, which is part of THEhotel at Mandalay Bay. This is a totally separate facility that's open to hotel guests and non-guests for a daily fee.

Spa Mandalay

☎877-632-7300

Staffed with talented, certified professionals, the spa at Mandalay Bay houses twenty-six fully equipped treatment rooms. Treatments and services offered range from classic and traditional therapies, such as Swedish massage or reflexology, to more exotic treatments you'd typically find only at the world's most exclusive day spas. The spa is also equipped with waterfalls, Jacuzzis, and whirlpools, separate men's and women's locker room facilities, and several saunas and steam rooms.

There's also a 4,500-square-foot fitness and personal training center, including a full line of Life Fitness machines for both cardio-vascular and circuit training. Personal trainers and group classes in water aerobics and yoga are available.

The $27 per-day entrance fee (for hotel guests) for the spa includes use of the redwood sauna, eucalyptus steam room, heated whirlpools, cold plunge, relaxation lounge, shower facility, exercise room, and vanity amenities. Robes, slippers, towels, and a full line of health and beauty products are also provided. The spa's treatments all cost extra and vary in price. Visit the Mandalay Bay Web site for a complete menu of available spa treatments, classes, and prices.

TRAVEL TIP

To ensure that you get the most out of your spa experience, be sure to arrive at the spa at least forty-five minutes before your scheduled treatment or service. This allows you time to check in, change, and utilize some of the spa's facilities before your appointment.

Reservations for specific treatments are taken up to three weeks in advance for people planning to stay at the resort. The spa's management reports that weekend appointments typically fill up quickly, so guests should make their appointments as early as possible, although walk-in appointments are accepted provided slots are open in the schedule. The daily entrance fee to the spa is waved when you schedule any treatment or service costing over $50.

Thanks to the lavish design and décor of the spa facility, the selection of top-notch treatments, and the superior service, Spa Mandalay is definitely one of the most luxurious day spas in Las Vegas. The spa also offers its own café, featuring a selection of healthy menu options. Spa Mandalay is open daily from 5:00 A.M. to 10:00 P.M. to hotel guests and non-guests who are at least eighteen years of age.

A Robert Cromeans Salon
✆702-632-6130

A team of John Paul Mitchell Systems hairdressers staff this exclusive, full-service salon, which offers what it calls "five-star treatment" to all of its visitors. Make your appointment(s) as early as possible to ensure that the services you want will be available when you want them. Hours of operation are 10:00 A.M. to 7:00 P.M. (Monday through Friday), 8:00 A.M. to 6:00 P.M. (Saturday), and 10:00 A.M. to 5:00 P.M. (Sunday).

Dining Options

Dining at Mandalay Bay is just one of many ways you can relax and enjoy your time in Las Vegas. Following is a rundown of the dining options available at this mega-resort.

Fine Dining
Mandalay Bay offers an assortment of truly exquisite fine-dining options. Some of these establishments enforce dress codes, and reservations are certainly recommended, especially during peak mealtimes.

To make reservations at any of these fine-dining establishments, call ✆877-632-5300.

3950 ($$$)

Open for dinner only, 3950 serves contemporary "classic cuisine," which means that the freshest seafood and the highest quality cuts of prime beef are used as the primary ingredients. Menu items include: Beluga Caviar ($100 per ounce), Maine Lobster Cocktail Appetizer ($17), Sweet Maine Lobster Entrée ($55), Rack of Lamb ($42), Filet Mignon ($35), and a wide selection of seafood, meat, poultry, soups, and salads. Plan on spending at least $50 per person.

Aureole ($$$)

Restaurateur Charlie Palmer offers visitors a chance to experience the seasonal American dishes, created by Chefs Joe and Megan Romano (a husband-and-wife team), that made his award-winning New York City restaurant famous. To accompany your meal, choose from an extensive selection of rare French and American wines. This is the largest of Mandalay Bay's fine-dining establishments.

Wolfgang Puck's Trattoria del Lupo ($$$)

The chef to the stars, responsible for creating such restaurants as Spago and the California Pizza Kitchen, has helped to develop a classic Italian restaurant for Mandalay Bay.

According to the resort, "The restaurant experience is much like a stroll into a small, secluded piazza in Milan with views of the pasta, charcuterie and bakery production areas as well as wonderful food displays and several communal tables." The menu offers a nice selection of traditional as well as contemporary dishes, all adapted from many regions of Northern and Southern Italy. To prepare some of these dishes, a wood-burning rotisserie and pizza oven is used. Open daily for lunch and dinner.

Shanghai Lilly ($$$)

Shanghai Lilly offers a classical selection of Cantonese cuisine with Szechuan specialties and influences. The restaurant features four private dining rooms and chefs who have been brought in directly from the top restaurants in Hong Kong. Open for dinner only.

Casual Dining

In addition to offering several of the finest of fine-dining establishments in Las Vegas, Mandalay Bay features a handful of specialty and theme restaurants. Many of these eating establishments are less formal, a bit less expensive, and offer guests a broad range of dining choices.

Red, White and Blue ($$)

This restaurant offers three distinct American dining experiences—"red" represents regional seafood specialities, "blue" is a classic American deli, and "white" is a counter of delicious desserts. Open for breakfast, lunch, dinner.

Border Grill ($$)

Adapted from the award-winning restaurant with the same name in Los Angeles, Border Grill is owned and operated by Mary Sue Milliken and Susan Feniger, the popular hosts of the Food Network's *Too Hot Tamales* television series. In 1985 these two chefs took a road trip into Mexico. During their travels they discovered a wide range of authentic recipes and cooking techniques, which they used as influences for the various menu selections offered at the Border Grill.

Open daily for lunch and dinner, the restaurant has a reputation for taking traditional Mexican food and successfully "translating" it for the American market.

China Grill's Café and Zen Sum ($$)

From the creators of China Grill, this eating establishment is open daily for lunch and dinner. While the focus of this restaurant continues to be preparing every dish on grills or in woks using an array of flavorful sauces, the café offers a conveyor dim sum bar that's perfect for a quick and casual meal.

Rumjungle ($$)

Also from the creators of China Grill, Rumjungle combines entertainment with dining as guests are treated to a dancing firewall that transforms into a wall of water as people enter this restaurant. As for the food itself, all main dishes are prepared over a large open fire pit that can be seen from the main dining room. It serves as a lovely backdrop for the restaurant's dance floor.

The menu is mostly tropically inspired, with many items served on flaming skewers, "Rodizio" style. The bar offers a wide assortment of exotic drinks. Whether you're going to eat or drink, you'll be entertained by Latin, Caribbean, and African music until early in the morning. Open daily for dinner.

Red Square ($$)

If you're looking for something exciting to do at night, Red Square features a frozen ice bar, a wonderful selection of more than 100 frozen vodkas, martinis, and Russian-inspired cocktails. Dining selections include an extensive caviar list and a menu of Russian, French, Italian, and American specialties. Open daily for dinner.

House of Blues ($$)

Combine a full menu with live blues music and you have the Las Vegas location of House of Blues. Menu items include Creole/Cajun staples such as jambalaya, gumbo, and étoufée as well as Southern favorites such as fried catfish, barbecued ribs, wood-fired pizza, and burgers. Open daily for breakfast, lunch, and dinner. Like many theme restaurants, this one offers a gift and merchandise shop.

The International House of Blues Foundation Room is a private club open to members and VIP guests. It's also used for special events. Located on the forty-third floor of the resort, this room combines fine dining with a spectacular view of the Las Vegas Strip and surrounding valley.

Raffels Café ($/$$)

Open twenty-four hours, this is an upscale café that overlooks the resort's tropical gardens, lagoon, and pools.

The Noodle Shop ($/$$)

Enjoy a casual meal from a traditional Cantonese noodle kitchen. In addition to a wide range of noodle items, congee, rice, and barbecue dishes are offered at the restaurant's counter or at tables. Open for lunch and dinner, the Noodle Shop also features late-night dining. You'll find this restaurant next to the casino's high-stakes gaming area.

Bay Side Buffet ($$)

Open for breakfast, lunch, and dinner, the Bay Side Buffet offers an all-you-can-eat menu at a flat rate. The buffet itself overlooks the resort's 11-acre lagoon.

 TRAVEL ESSENTIAL

Get around the Strip by tram. In addition to the Las Vegas Monorail that travels up and down the Strip (the closest stop to Mandalay Bay is at the MGM Grand), there's a free tram that runs every three to four minutes, traveling between Luxor, Mandalay Bay, and Excalibur. It operates twenty-four hours per day.

Lounges and Bars

While many of the restaurants and cafés in Mandalay Bay offer full bar service, the resort also features a handful of stand-alone bars and lounges for the over-twenty-one crowd.

Coral Reef Lounge

Located in the heart of the casino, this full-service lounge/bar also offers a sushi bar.

Island Lounge

You'll find this lounge on the casino floor. Throughout the afternoon and night, live entertainment is presented.

Orchid Lounge

Live entertainment and exotic drinks are served throughout the afternoon and evening. This is one place to stop for a fresh cup of coffee in the morning, too.

Mandalay Bay's Casino

As you explore the casino area of Mandalay Bay, you'll be surrounded by an extraordinary atmosphere created using flowing water, lush foliage, and exotic architecture—not to mention over 2,400 slot machines/video poker machines, 122 table games, a poker room, baccarat, and a race and sports book (with seventeen large screens and 300 seats). There's also a high-stakes gaming area.

CHAPTER 13

The MGM Grand

YOU WON'T FEEL LIKE YOU'RE IN KANSAS anymore when you step through the entrance of the MGM Grand, which was inspired by the Emerald City from *The Wizard of Oz*. You can't miss the larger-than-life lion statue guarding the entrance to this popular mega-resort.

Mega-Resort Overview

✉3799 Las Vegas Boulevard South, Las Vegas, NV 89109

✆800-929-1111

✆702-891-1111

✎*www.mgmgrand.com*

Room and Suite Rates: $$/$$$/$$$$

The MGM Grand is conveniently located at the corner of Tropicana Avenue (across the street from the New York–New York Hotel & Casino). This resort is a city unto itself. It comprises a cluster of tremendous emerald green structures, including four thirty-story towers.

This mega-resort offers its guests just about everything a vacationer could want from a Las Vegas resort, including a wide range of guest room accommodations, a glitzy casino, shows and concerts, restaurants, special events, a swimming pool, plus a luxurious day spa.

▲The MGM-Grand.   Photo ©Ferras AlQuaisi.

When the MGM Grand opened back in 1993, one of its major attractions was a theme park designed primarily for young people. In recent years, however, this theme park has been closed and other kid-oriented amenities the resort offered have been discontinued. The MGM Grand's main focus appears to be on its casino gaming and convention business, although it still offers some amenities and activities suitable for families.

The theme of this resort is the Golden Age of Hollywood, showcasing several classic films, including *Wizard of Oz* and *Casablanca*. Looking at this resort from the outside, it's impossible to miss the 100,000-pound, 45-foot-tall bronze lion statue that stands proudly at the property's main entrance. Inside, guests and visitors alike are treated to an up-close look at real-life lions in the Lion Habitat.

≡FAST FACT

Initially built at a cost of over $1 billion, the 114-acre resort was recently renovated at an additional cost of over $575 million.

The Hollywood Theatre within the resort regularly hosts a stable of world-renowned musical performers and comedians. *La Femme*, a French music and dance show, has its American home at the MGM Grand. This glamorous show features amazing choreography, plus thirteen performers wearing intricate costumes.

One of the most convenient things about staying at the MGM Grand is that it houses one of the Las Vegas Monorail stations, so guests can easily travel up and down the Strip to visit other resorts and attractions.

The MGM Grand is as luxurious as ever; however, the reduction in family-oriented activities and amenities over the past few years is a bit disappointing.

MGM GRAND OVERALL FAMILY-FRIENDLINESS RATING

Ages Up to 5	Ages 6–15	Ages 16–20	Ages 21 & Up	Senior Citizens
☆	☆☆	☆☆	☆☆☆	☆☆☆

Guest Room Accommodations

The MGM Grand features 5,034 guest rooms in varying price categories. Travelers on a budget will find that the resort's 600 Emerald Tower rooms offer elegant and well-equipped accommodations at affordable rates.

The majority of the rooms at MGM Grand are called "deluxe" rooms. These are approximately 446 square feet, which is larger than comparably priced rooms at most other resorts and casino hotels. Basic amenities include black-and-white marble bathrooms, spacious closets, and in-room movies (offered on a pay-per-view basis). Although these rooms are comfortable, like most hotel rooms located in a casino they're designed to provide a place for guests to sleep, but little more. After all, if you're spending too much time relaxing in your hotel room, you're not in the casino gambling, at a restaurant eating, or taking in a show.

The 751 suites within the MGM Grand offer many different combinations of amenities, from full kitchens to wet bars, dining and living rooms, and in-room spas. Ranging in size from 675 square feet to more than 6,000 square feet, these accommodations offer a variety of options.

The Player Suites are the smallest rooms in this price category. Each offers an oversized bedroom connected to a separate living area. These rooms are available with your choice of two queen-size beds or one king-size bed. Spa Suites are slightly larger than the MGM Grand's Player Suites. Each Spa Suite has a whirlpool and separate shower, a spacious bedroom with a king-size bed, a separate living area, a wet bar, and a dining table with seating for four. (They're best suited for couples traveling without kids.)

The 775-square-foot Vista Suites offer more space in the bedroom and living area with two entrances to a central bathroom. Two televisions, a wet bar, a king-size bed, and a dining area with seating for four are standard. Lobby Suites are corner-style, *L*-shaped, 950-square-foot rooms with one bedroom, a dining area, a bar/snack area, whirlpool, and two televisions.

═FAST FACT

If you enjoy visiting the MGM Grand, imagine what it would be like to live here full-time! The Residences at MGM Grand offer luxurious, fully furnished condominiums, ranging in price from $350,000 to well over $1.5 million. Ground breaking for the first of six forty-story condominium-hotel towers was in late 2004.

As the suite prices increase, the amenities and level of luxury increase. The MGM Grand's Glamour Suites, for example, offer 1,270 square feet of living space. Included in these suites are a wet bar, a dining area with seating for four, two bathrooms, and a large bedroom with a sleigh-bed, a marble vanity, and a spacious walk-in closet.

If you're looking for a room with a spectacular view of the Las Vegas Strip, consider reserving one of MGM Grand's Patio Suites. The hotel offers fourteen Patio Suites; each has 1,300 square feet of living space, two-story vaulted ceilings, and a 786-square-foot outdoor patio area with a private whirlpool. Amenities for these rooms include a big-screen television, office area with two desks, separate dining area, two baths, his and her sinks, an oversized tub in the master bath, and plenty of closet space.

In 1999, the hotel opened the Mansion, an invitation-only group of twenty-nine private villas. These Tuscan-Mediterranean-theme accommodations are modeled after 200-year-old Italian villas and range from 2,400 to 12,000 square feet.

Depending on the time of year, deluxe room rates vary from $99 to $350 per night. Suites and villas are priced between $199 and $15,000 per night.

Featured Attractions and Activities

Like most mega-resorts in Las Vegas, the MGM Grand has several attractions and activities that the whole family will love. The following sections detail some of the family favorites.

The MGM Grand Lion Habitat

Lions, tigers, and bears, oh my! Farther along the Strip, The Mirage may offer a stunning display of white tigers, but if you want to see lions up close the MGM Grand is definitely the place to visit. This $9 million attraction showcases up to five adult lions daily. These lions are direct descendants of MGM Studios' famous marquee lion, Metro. Guests can view all of the lions up close, from the safety of a clear, glassed-in tunnel that runs directly through the lions' indoor habitat.

If you have a half-hour or so with nothing to do, this is a great activity for people of all ages, and you can't beat the price! Kids especially will enjoy watching the lion cubs at play. Admission is free, and the Lion Habitat is open daily from 11:00 A.M. to 10:00 P.M.

THE MGM GRAND LION HABITAT

Ages Up to 5	Ages 6–15	Ages 16–20	Ages 21 & Up	Senior Citizens
★★	★★★	★★	★★	★★

CBS Television City

How many times have you watched television and wondered, "What were those writers and producers thinking?" Well, this free attraction offers you a chance to get a sneak peek at upcoming television shows, and then offer your feedback to the producers and advertisers.

After watching tapes of various TV shows (which you choose), you'll be asked to complete a detailed survey. The pilots of shows you'll be watching are presented by the CBS Television Network, MTV, VH1, and Nickelodeon. This activity is suitable for TV viewers over the age of ten. It's a free activity that offers a behind-the-scenes glimpse of TV shows still in development. Hours of operation are 10:00 A.M. to 10:00 P.M.

CBS TELEVISION CITY

Ages Up to 5	Ages 6–15	Ages 16–20	Ages 21 & Up	Senior Citizens
Not Suitable	★★	★★	★★	★★

The Swimming Pool

The 27,000-square-foot Grand Pool area is divided into five pool sections, including a 1,000-foot gently flowing river "pool." The Grand Pool area features private cabanas, cocktail service, and a poolside restaurant. Use of the pool is free to hotel guests, so don't forget to pack a bathing suit.

Hours of operation vary based on the time of year; however, there's always at least one pool and one whirlpool open year-round. Pool hours will also vary based on weather conditions, but most areas are open daily from 9:00 A.M. to 5:00 P.M.

☛ TRAVEL ESSENTIAL

Enjoy playing golf at the top-rated Shadow Creek golf course, an option available only to guests of the MGM Grand, New York–New York, Mirage, Bellagio, Treasure Island, and Primm Valley Resorts in Las Vegas. Priced at $500 per round, this includes limousine transportation to and from the golf course, a caddy, and a golf cart.

It's Showtime at the MGM Grand

In addition to the ever-changing lineup of special shows, concerts, and sporting events held at the MGM Grand, the resident show, *La Femme*, was imported directly from Paris. In addition, there's an all-new Cirque du Soleil show appearing here that opened in late 2004.

Cirque Du Soleil's "KA"

☎800-929-1111

☎702-891-7777

✎*www.cirquedusoleil.com*

In November 2004, the MGM Grand became home to yet another totally original Cirque du Soleil show, called *KA*. This show combines acrobatic performances with martial arts, elaborate costumes, and original puppetry, plus special effects created using multimedia technology and pyrotechnics. Through dance, specialty acts, and effects including the dramatic use of fire and smoke, this show tells the epic story of a pair of twins who embark on a journey to fulfill their destinies.

KA has a strong Asian influence and features a cast of seventy-two artists. The custom-built theater holds 1,951 guests. With its original story line, acts, and musical score, this Cirque du Soleil production is unlike any other show in Las Vegas.

Tickets are $99, $125, and $150. Shows run Fridays through Tuesdays (with no shows on Wednesdays and Thursdays). The show begins at 7:00 P.M. or 8:00 P.M. depending on the day, with a second performance (on certain days) held at 10:30 P.M.

CIRQUE DU SOLEIL'S "KA"

Ages Up to 5	Ages 6–15	Ages 16–20	Ages 21 & Up	Senior Citizens
Not Suitable	Not Suitable	☆☆☆	☆☆☆	☆☆☆

La Femme

☎702-891-7777
☎800-929-1111

The French performing troupe known as Le Femme performs nightly at MGM Grand. The latest edition of the show offers seven new performances featuring twelve talented and beautiful dancers, each wearing a one-of-a-kind costume.

This is a replica of the world-famous show *Crazy Horse* in Paris and showcases spectacular choreography. This is an unusual and extremely sophisticated show that incorporates nudity, making it suitable only for adults (twenty-one and older). The concept for this show was developed in Paris, back in 1951. Its goal was to make the traditional striptease acceptable to a wide audience. Using costumes, music, dramatic lighting effects, and glamorous sets, *Le Femme* is a classy and highly erotic show that's suitable for men, women, and couples. After seeing this visually appealing and entertaining show, you'll begin looking at the female form as true art. Tickets are $59, and showtimes are 8:00 P.M. and 10:30 P.M. (no shows on Tuesdays).

LA FEMME

Ages Up to 5	Ages 6–15	Ages 16–20	Ages 21 & Up	Senior Citizens
Not Suitable	Not Suitable	Not Suitable	☆☆☆	☆☆☆

The Grand Garden Arena and Hollywood Theater

☎800-929-1111

While the Grand Garden is a 17,157-seat arena that often hosts concerts by some of the biggest names in the music industry and high-profile sports events, the Hollywood Theater offers a much more intimate setting. This 740-seat theater often hosts entertainers such as Tom Jones, comedians Carrot Top and George Carlin, and master illusionist David Copperfield. Ticket prices for each event vary; tickets can typically be purchased up to three months in advance.

Shopping

The MGM Grand offers a relatively small selection of gift shops within the Star Lane Shops area and the Studio Walk area of the resort. For the ultimate in shopping experiences, visit the Forum Shops at Caesars Palace or the Fashion Show Mall, also located along the Strip.

Day Spa, Salon, and Fitness Facilities

The Grand Spa (℡702-891-3077) is a 30,000-square-foot facility that features more than thirty treatment rooms, saunas, steam rooms, whirlpools, and relaxation lounges. In short, it provides everything you could possibly need to pamper your mind, body, and soul.

 TRAVEL TIP

The Fitness Center features state-of-the-art exercise equipment, including virtual reality climbers and bikes, treadmills, cross-trainers, free weights, and computerized circuit-training equipment.

Whether you're in search of a traditional massage or something a bit more extravagant and unusual (such as a facial or sea-salt scrub), chances are you'll find it at this full-service spa. There's a daily $25 admission fee to use the spa and fitness center facilities. All treatments and services are extra. The spa is open from 6:00 A.M. to 8:00 P.M.

Dining Options

While the MGM Grand no longer offers a family-oriented theme park, the mega-resort does still have a strong emphasis on offering an array of dining experiences. You'll find an unusually large selection of fine-dining establishments as well as more casual restaurants throughout the property.

Fine Dining

No matter what your taste buds are craving, from fast food to fine cuisine prepared under the supervision of one of the world's foremost chefs, you'll find it at MGM Grand. Hours of operation vary for each restaurant, and in most cases, reservations are either required or highly recommended, so plan accordingly. Room service is also available twenty-four hours a day to hotel guests.

SeaBlue ($$$)

☎702-891-3486

This is an upscale seafood restaurant operated under the supervision of Chef Michael Mina. It's open daily for dinner only, between 5:30 P.M. and 10:30 P.M. This intimate restaurant seats only 154. Entrées include Angry Lobster and North Sea Cod as house specialties. Reservations are recommended.

Fiamma Trattoria ($$$)

☎702-891-7600

Enjoy what the chef calls a combination of classic and contemporary Italian cuisine. Open daily for lunch (11:30 A.M. to 2:30 P.M.) and dinner (5:30 P.M. to 10:30 P.M.). Florentine Steak and Yellow Fin Tuna Carpaccio are among the specials of the house. Plan on spending between $45 and $60 per person. Reservations are recommended.

Emeril Lagasse's New Orleans Fish House ($$$)

☎702-891-7374

World-renowned chef and TV personality Emeril Lagasse offers his New Orleans–style selection of modern Creole and Cajun cooking at this seafood restaurant. Barbecued shrimp, lobster, fresh fish (flown in daily from around the world), and Emeril's famous double-cut pork chops are all featured menu items. Open daily for lunch

(11:30 A.M. to 2:30 P.M.) and dinner (5:30 P.M. to 10:30 P.M.); the average per-person meal price is $38 to $45, not including alcoholic beverages. Reservations are recommended.

Nobhill ($$$)

✆702-891-7337

Open daily for dinner only, this restaurant offers a selection of San Francisco–inspired cuisine. Meals are prepared using organic poultry and produce flown in from San Francisco. Menu selections include Avocado Alexis, "Palace" Green Goddess Salad, North Beach Cioppino, Chicken Tetrazzini, Steak "Rossini," and Seasonal Fresh Fruit Tart Tatin. Plan on spending between $50 and $65 per person. Dinner is served from 5:30 P.M. until 11:00 P.M. nightly. Reservations are recommended.

Craftsteak ($$$)

✆702-891-7318

This is primarily a steakhouse; however, a nice selection of soups, salads, seafood, chicken, veal, duck, and quail dishes are also available. Open for dinner only (5:30 P.M. until 10:00 P.M.). Plan on spending at least $75 per person. Reservations are recommended.

Shibuya ($$/$$$)

✆702-891-3100

In an effort to offer virtually any type of cuisine you have an appetite for, the MGM Grand has added Shibuya to its selection of award-winning fine-dining restaurants. Shibuya provides guests with an authentic Japanese dining experience.

 TRAVEL ESSENTIAL

The chefs at Shibuya combine traditional ingredients with modern cooking techniques to create a delicious and memorable meal. Three different dining experiences are offered here: sushi, Teppan, and à la carte specialties.

This restaurant is open for dinner only, from 5:30 P.M. to 10:30 P.M. on Sundays through Thursdays, and until 11:00 P.M. on Fridays and Saturdays. Average per-person prices range from $4 to $19 for the sushi bar, up to $22 for the à la carte menu, and between $38 and $65 for Teppan-style dining. Reservations are required.

Diego ($$/$$$)
✆702-891-3200

Traditional Mexican cuisine is offered here for lunch and dinner. The hours are 11:30 A.M. to 2:30 P.M. for lunch and 5:30 P.M. to 11:00 P.M. (or midnight, depending on the night) for dinner. Average per-person prices range from $25 to $40. Reservations are recommended.

Pearl ($$)
✆702-891-3110

Open for dinner only (6:00 P.M. to 11:00 P.M.), Pearl offers a large selection of contemporary Chinese, Cantonese, and Shanghainese specialty dishes. Plan on spending around $65 per person. This restaurant offers an extensive wine list. Reservations are recommended.

Wolfgang Puck Bar & Grill ($$/$$$)
Wolfgang Puck, the chef to the stars and owner of Spago in Hollywood, has opened a chain of restaurants throughout the country specializing in Italian cuisine and pizza. Like all of the restaurants in the chain, this one offers a family dining environment, especially for pizza lovers. Other menu options include grilled fish and meat.

It is open daily for lunch and dinner (11:00 A.M. to 11:00 P.M.). The average per-person meal costs $18 to $25 for lunch and $28 to $40 for dinner. Seating is on a first-come basis. This café was totally remodeled and opened again in July 2004.

Casual Dining
For more casual, family-oriented dining options, check out any of these restaurants:

Grand Wok and Sushi Bar ($/$$)

Lunch and dinner are available at this midpriced restaurant that offers Asian cuisine, including sushi. The restaurant serves from 11:00 A.M. to 11:00 P.M.; however, the extensive sushi bar is only open Mondays through Thursdays between 5:00 P.M. and 10:00 P.M., Fridays and Saturdays between 11:00 A.M. and 1:00 A.M., and Sundays between 11:00 A.M. and 11:00 P.M. Plan on spending under $15 per person.

'Wichcraft ($/$$)

Offering breakfast, lunch and dinner, 'Wichcraft is a spinoff of a New York City–style sandwich shop, serving primarily hot and cold sandwiches. Open from 8:00 A.M. until 8:00 P.M. daily. The average sandwich costs under $10. Limited seating is available.

Grand Buffet ($$)

Las Vegas is known for its all-you-can-eat buffets, so if you have a big appetite and you're in the mood for a casual-dining experience, drop by the buffet for a wide selection of foods at a reasonable price. Open daily for breakfast (7:00 A.M. to 11:00 A.M.), lunch (11:00 A.M. to 2:30 P.M.), and dinner (4:30 P.M. to 10:00 P.M.); seating is on a first-come basis, so be prepared for a wait. A champagne brunch is served on weekends from 10:00 A.M. to 2:30 P.M.

▣ TRAVEL TIP

The Grand Buffet offers an inexpensive dining experience for the whole family. The per-person price for this all-you-can-eat extravaganza is $11.99 (breakfast), $14.99 (lunch), $21.99 (dinner), and $24.99 (brunch).

The food selections change daily, but there are always at least eight main entrées, often including freshly cooked ham, turkey, and prime rib. There's also an extensive salad and dessert bar. The quality of the food at the buffet certainly surpasses fast food but doesn't touch what's served at MGM Grand's fine-dining establishments. Of course, since you're in a casino environment, you can play keno from your table as you eat.

Studio Café ($/$$)

In Las Vegas, the casinos never close and the nightlife keeps going until the wee hours of the morning. No matter what time of day (or night) it happens to be, if you're hungry, the Studio Café is open and ready to serve.

The menu offers a wide range of inexpensive American items, plus a separate menu featuring Chinese cuisine. The average per-person meal cost is from $9 to $15. Seating is on a first-come basis, but reservations are accepted for large groups. The Studio Café offers an excellent option for sit-down, full-service casual dining that's better than traditional fast food.

The Rainforest Café ($$)

✆702-891-8580

✐*www.rainforestcafé.com*

When you walk through the main entrance of any Rainforest Café, you'll find yourself stepping into a lifelike rain forest, complete with trees, waterfalls, rain, audio-animatronic animals, live parrots, and a 10,000-gallon saltwater aquarium.

As you dine, don't be surprised if a tropical rainstorm erupts around you. Thanks to flashy special effects, you won't get wet, but the experience truly enhances the dining experience, and kids love it!

 TRAVEL ESSENTIAL

The Rainforest Cafés, which are now located throughout the country, offer the ultimate in theme-restaurant dining for the entire family. Because this is a theme restaurant, the prices are a bit higher than a traditional family-style restaurant, but you're paying for the ambiance. There's also an extensive Rainforest Café gift shop that's chock-full of kid-oriented and animal-theme merchandise and souvenirs.

Menu selections include pastas, salads, sandwiches, and a wide assortment of incredible desserts. If you've never experienced a Rainforest Café, it's worth checking out either for lunch or dinner. Since these restaurants are basically the same in every city, if you've already dined at a Rainforest Café in your home city, you might consider experiencing one of the many other theme restaurants in Las Vegas.

The Rainforest Café is open Monday through Thursday from 8:00 A.M. to 11:00 P.M., and Friday and Saturday from 8:00 A.M. to midnight. Plan on spending between $12 and $20 per person. Reservations are recommended.

Stage Deli ($)

Outside New York City, finding an authentic New York-style deli sandwich is virtually impossible, but that's exactly what's offered at the Stage Deli at MGM Grand. If you're looking for a delicious, fast, and inexpensive sandwich, this is the place to stop. Pastrami on rye is the specialty, but you'll find turkey, roast beef, and a wide range of other deli meats here. The sandwiches themselves are overstuffed (extra large).

This is a walk-up style restaurant offering sandwiches to go, but seating for adults is available at the race and sports book next to the Grand Theater. You can also take your food back to your room. Open daily 7:30 A.M. to 9:00 P.M.

Cabana Grille ($/$$)

Enjoy breakfast or lunch while relaxing at or near the resort's lovely pool. The menu offers a wide range of options, including some great snacks for when you get the munchies by the pool.

Farmer's Market Food Court ($)

Ideal for kids and open for lunch and dinner, this food court features McDonald's, Hamada Express, Nathan's Famous Hot Dogs, Mamma Ilardo's Pizza, and Häagen-Dazs ice cream.

Starbucks Coffee ($)

The MGM Grand offers two Starbucks locations on resort property. Here you'll find a wide range of the gourmet coffees that have made Starbucks famous. Within Las Vegas there are now over thirty Starbucks retail locations. Visit the company's Web site (✑*www.starbucks.com*) for a complete listing.

Nightclubs, Lounges, and Bars

For the over-twenty-one crowd, nighttime is an exciting time at the MGM Grand. Several nightclubs, lounges, and bars are available. Studio 54 offers the ultimate dance club experience, while some of the other lounges feature live entertainment and full bar service.

Studio 54

✆702-891-7254

It's a blast from the past at Studio 54 at MGM Grand. The 20,000-square-foot nightclub features three separate dance floors and four bars that come to life as chart-topping dance music is played on a state-of-the-art sound system. While the original Studio 54 in New York was open only to VIPs, celebrities, and the "in crowd," the velvet rope of this club will open to anyone over the age of twenty-one.

Club hours are 10:00 P.M. to 3:00 A.M. nightly. (The club is closed Sundays and Mondays.) Some nights feature special themes. For example, Thursday nights' theme is "Dollhouse." A "front of the line pass" for admission is priced at $30 or $40, depending on the night. Normal admission is $20 for guys and free for women. The club has a dress code restricting T-shirts, tank tops, baggy jeans, flannel shirts, hats, tennis shoes, and work boots, so dress accordingly.

If you're looking to relive the 1970s, love to dance, and want a fun-filled evening, drop by Studio 54 for an after-dinner celebration.

More Nightlife at MGM Grand

Other bars and lounges within the MGM Grand include:

- **Tabu**: This is a modern lounge with its own private VIP area. It's a classy cross between a lounge and a nightclub. Every

Wednesday, this lounge offers a fashion show, featuring designs offered at local boutiques.

- **Zuri**: This is a 100-seat, full-service bar located in the main lobby.
- **Showbar Lounge**: This lounge features bands that perform nightly.
- **Teatro**: This relatively new nightspot features a full-service bar and an upscale atmosphere. It's open from 4:00 P.M. until 4:00 A.M. and is located along the newly renovated Studio Walk area of the resort.

The MGM Grand's Casino

The MGM Grand offers more than just a simple casino to keep you occupied and entertained. The casino here is huge—equivalent to the size of four football fields. And the space is jam-packed with gaming machines, ranging from nickel to $500 per-play slot machines. The 165 gaming tables include baccarat, Pai Gow poker, minibaccarat, Caribbean Stud poker, craps, roulette, blackjack, Let It Ride, casino war, Big Six, and Spanish 21. There's also a poker room, keno lounges, and a race and sports book.

Gamblers can join the Players Club to earn valuable bonus points by using their membership cards in slot machines and at gaming tables. Benefits include cash back; exclusive merchandise; discounted or complimentary rooms, food, and beverages; room upgrades; show tickets (and preferred seating); express check-in; and invitations to special events.

To join the Players Club, fill out a registration form at the Players Club Promotions Booth in the casino or visit the resort's Web site.

CHAPTER 14

The Mirage

THE MIRAGE, WHICH OPENED in November 1989 and cost $630 million to build, truly offers something for everyone, including top amenities at competitive, midpriced rates. Owned and operated by MGM Mirage, which also owns and operates several other mega-resorts and casinos along the Strip and elsewhere in the United States, The Mirage is located between Caesars Palace and Treasure Island. It's perfectly located in the heart of the Las Vegas Strip. The resort itself encompasses three thirty-story buildings, as well as a cluster of villa-style apartments and bungalows.

Mega-Resort Overview

✉3400 Las Vegas Boulevard South, Las Vegas, NV 89109
✆800-627-6667
✆702-791-7111
✑*www.mirage.com*
Room and Suite Rates: $$/$$$/$$$$

The Mirage isn't just a resort with a focus on comfortable accommodations. It also offers guests plenty of entertainment options. In front of the property is a lagoon with waterfalls and grottos, as well as a volcano that erupts every fifteen minutes.

Inside, guests and visitors alike are treated to a variety of free and inexpensive attractions, including a 20,000-gallon aquarium in the registration area, a white tiger exhibit, and an interactive live dolphin exhibit.

 ## TRAVEL ESSENTIAL

If you have a cell phone, wireless PDA, or handheld device that's capable of surfing the Internet, you can access a wide range of information about The Mirage from its mobile-optimized Web site. Point your handheld device's Web browser to ✎*http:// mobile.mirage.com.*

If you're looking for accommodations that truly represent Las Vegas in the twenty-first century, with much of the luxury, amenities, glitz, and glamour that the city has to offer, The Mirage is where you'll want to stay. While it's not a family-oriented resort in the traditional sense, it does offer a handful of family-oriented attractions, activities, and dining options, as well as several types of guest accommodations suitable for families traveling with kids and/or teens.

THE MIRAGE OVERALL FAMILY-FRIENDLINESS RATING

Ages Up to 5	Ages 6–15	Ages 16–20	Ages 21 & Up	Senior Citizens
☆☆	☆☆☆	☆☆☆	☆☆☆	☆☆☆

Guest Room Accommodations

As mentioned earlier, no resort in Las Vegas designs its rooms for guests to spend too much time in them—after all, you're supposed to be out gambling, shopping, or seeing the sights. Nevertheless, The Mirage offers extremely comfortable accommodations.

The resort offers 3,044 rooms, which include 281 suites. Typical guest rooms (referred to as "deluxe" rooms) offer one king-size bed or two queen-size beds, plus a wide range of amenities and furnishings. These rooms are priced anywhere from $109 per night up to

$450 (or more). Hospitality Suites feature a bedroom with king-size bed, one-and-a-half baths, and a parlor area. There's also a dining area that can seat six and an adjacent wet bar. The bedroom can be closed off from the hospitality area.

Two-bedroom Hospitality Suites are also available. These rooms typically have a king-size bed in one bedroom and two queen-size beds in the second bedroom (making them perfect for families).

The Tower Suites feature a bedroom with a king-size bed and a separate parlor area with a wet bar. Some of the suites also offer two bedrooms, plus a spectacular view of the city. Meanwhile, for the ultimate in luxury, the Penthouse Suites (located on the top two floors of The Mirage tower) offer one or two bedrooms, a separate living/dining area with a wet bar, and a wide range of other amenities.

TRAVEL TIP

Guest room amenities include in-room mini-bar, iron, ironing board, private safe, hairdryer, telephone, and high-speed Internet access.

The Petite Suites offer all of the amenities of the resort's full-size suites but on a smaller scale. The bedroom and living area are separated by a large armoire housing a swivel entertainment center. These suites offer two bathrooms, a wet bar, and a marble entry. Eight villa apartments and six lanai bungalows, each with a private pool, are also available.

Suites at The Mirage range in price from $275 per night up to well over $2,500 per night. All of the rooms throughout this resort were redesigned and renovated back in 2002.

Featured Attractions and Activities

Suitable for families, The Mirage offers a range of free and inexpensive activities and attractions. The resort itself is also located in the heart of the Strip, which makes it extremely easy to get to other resorts and attractions via taxi, by walking, taking the Las Vegas Monorail, or riding a free shuttle bus.

Here's some of what there is to see and do within The Mirage:

The Mirage Volcano

In front of The Mirage is a 54-foot volcano that erupts every fifteen minutes between dusk (around 7:00 P.M.) and midnight. Flames shoot into the sky, spewing smoke and fire 100 feet above the waters below. It offers a great photo opportunity.

The volcano is a free attraction that can be seen from along the Strip by passersby and resort guests alike. It's just one of the attractions that make The Mirage an exciting place to visit.

≡ FAST FACT

To simulate the lava flowing as the volcano erupts, over 3,000 lights are used in conjunction with audio special effects.

THE MIRAGE VOLCANO

Ages Up to 5	Ages 6–15	Ages 16–20	Ages 21 & Up	Senior Citizens
☆	☆☆	☆☆	☆☆	☆☆

The Royal White Tiger Habitat

Open twenty-four hours a day, this free attraction allows guests and visitors to view some of the royal white tigers raised and trained by Siegfried and Roy. These illusionists have dedicated their lives to preserving this endangered species of tiger. The open-air environment allows guests to view the tigers up close, while allowing the tigers freedom to roam in a large, open area that's designed to resemble the Himalayan Mountains where these exotic and beautiful creatures are from.

THE ROYAL WHITE TIGER HABITAT

Ages Up to 5	Ages 6–15	Ages 16–20	Ages 21 & Up	Senior Citizens
★★	★★	★★	★★	★★

Siegfried & Roy's Secret Garden and Dolphin Habitat

☏702-791-7111

The Secret Garden is the home to many of Siegfried and Roy's rare animals, including exotic panthers, white lions of Timbavati, and the royal white tigers of Nevada. The largest animal is a ceremonial Thai elephant. By developing this attraction, Siegfried and Roy hope to increase public awareness of the plight of all endangered and rare animals. This attraction demonstrates what is possible when humans and animals work and play together. It also provides guests of all ages an extraordinary opportunity to get up close to some of the most exotic and beautiful creatures on the planet. The attraction offers an entertaining, thought-provoking, and educational experience.

≡FAST FACT

Missing from The Mirage are two Las Vegas legends—Siegfried and Roy. These master magicians and illusionists were the headline act at The Mirage between February 1990 and October 2003. While you can still see Siegfried and Roy's Royal White Tigers at The Mirage, their memorable show is now part of Las Vegas history. For more information, go to ✐www.siegfriedandroy.com.

There is a $12 (per adult) admission fee, which includes access to the Secret Garden and the Dolphin Habitat. Children under ten years of age are admitted free of charge. An audio tour, featuring the voices of Siegfried and Roy, is available to guests as they see the various exhibits. The Secret Garden is open 11:00 A.M. to 3:30 P.M. weekdays and 10:00 A.M. to 7:00 P.M. weekends. Winter hours are 10:00 A.M. to 3:30 P.M.

SIEGFRIED & ROY'S SECRET GARDEN

Ages Up to 5	Ages 6–15	Ages 16–20	Ages 21 & Up	Senior Citizens
☆☆	☆☆☆	☆☆☆	☆☆☆	☆☆☆

The Dolphin Habitat is a 2.5 million-gallon dolphin pool area and home to a family of Atlantic bottle-nose dolphins. (There are seven dolphins in all.) Four connected pools, an artificial coral reef system, and a sandy bottom replicate the dolphin's natural environment. The facility houses only dolphins that were born at this site or relocated from other facilities. No animals were taken from the wild for this project.

The Dolphin Habitat is an educational facility. Guests are offered a chance to see dolphins in their natural habitat and learn about their role in nature. Guided tours are provided throughout the day. Guests are able to get up close to the dolphins; however, there is no physical interaction with them. Throughout the day, dolphin experts have spontaneous "interactions" with the animals. This is not a preplanned or rehearsed animal show like one you would see at SeaWorld. The Dolphin Habitat will be of particular interest to children and teens. Hours of operation are 11:00 A.M. to 7:00 P.M. weekdays and 10:00 A.M. to 7:00 P.M. weekends. Winter hours are 11:00 A.M. to 5:30 P.M.

TRAVEL ESSENTIAL

Be sure to visit the underground area of the Dolphin Habitat for an underwater view of the dolphins and an excellent photo opportunity.

SIEGFRIED & ROY'S DOLPHIN HABITAT

Ages Up to 5	Ages 6–15	Ages 16–20	Ages 21 & Up	Senior Citizens
☆☆	☆☆☆	☆☆☆	☆☆☆	☆☆☆

The Aquarium

When guests enter the resort, one of the first sights they'll notice is a 20,000-gallon saltwater aquarium. Stocked with ninety species of angelfish, puffer fish, tangs, and other exotic sea creatures, including three different kinds of sharks, the aquarium also houses more than 1,000 coral-reef species from around the world. It is one of the most elaborate and technically advanced coral-reef aquariums in the world. The tank itself is 53 feet long, with water that is 6 feet deep. This is a free exhibit, open twenty-four hours a day.

 **TRAVEL TIP**

Located just beyond the main entrance of The Mirage, you'll find the Atrium area. This free attraction features a wide variety of exotic and beautiful flowers and plants, plus over 500 palm trees and orchids. This area is designed to resemble a lush tropical rain forest. As you're exploring the resort, take a few minutes to stroll through the Atrium.

Video Game Arcade

Offering about thirty video games, this arcade combines the latest in video gaming with classic games. Most cost $.50 or $1 per play. You'll find the arcade near the entrance to the pool area. The arcade is open from 9:00 A.M. to 10:00 P.M. Sunday through Thursday, and from 9:00 A.M. to midnight on Friday and Saturday.

Swimming Pool

The outdoor pool area at The Mirage features a series of lagoons, inlets, and waterfalls and is open to all resort guests. In May 2003, a $7 million renovation of this area was completed. Two swimming pools, three spas, private cabanas (available for rental), an outdoor café, and beautiful landscaping are what you'll now find there. The pools' hours vary by season. Call ✆702-791-7111, ext. 7487, for hours of operation during your visit.

It's Showtime at The Mirage

In addition to entertainers performing nightly within the resort's various lounges, the main headliner at The Mirage is Danny Gans. He's been performing his one-man show at The Mirage since 2000, but became the resort's star performer when *Siegfried & Roy* closed.

Danny Gans

✆800-963-9634

As a master impressionist, comedian, singer, and actor, Danny Gans has been named "Entertainer of the Year" multiple times in Las Vegas. He appears every Tuesday, Wednesday, Thursday, Saturday, and Sunday night at 8:00 P.M., within a 1,265-seat theater. Now the resident headline act at The Mirage, Danny Gans offers a fun-filled show that's more suitable for teens and adults than for kids.

While there's no doubt that Danny Gans is a master entertainer, this show isn't in the same league as any of the Cirque du Soleil productions, Celine Dion, *Mamma Mia!* or any of the other Las Vegas shows that command a $100 per-seat ticket price.

Danny Gans has been a performer at The Mirage for years. At the time this book was being written, he was performing in the theater that was formally home to *Siegfried & Roy*.

In 2006, this theater will become the home of a new Cirque du Soleil performance being created in collaboration with the living members of the Beatles, as well as the deceased group members' widows. This will be a $100 million production that's sure to become one of the hottest and most talked-about shows on the Strip. While the original Beatles won't actually be appearing in this show, many of their famous songs and recordings will be incorporated into the performance in an innovative and entertaining way.

DANNY GANS

Ages Up to 5	Ages 6–15	Ages 16–20	Ages 21 & Up	Senior Citizens
Not Suitable	Not Suitable	☆	☆☆	☆☆☆

Shopping

The Mirage is just a short walk from the world-famous Forum Shops at Caesars Palace, but in The Mirage itself you'll find an assortment of fine stores, open from 9:00 A.M. to midnight, including:

- **Actique**: Sportswear and designer fashions for women are available in this store.
- **D. Fine**: A large selection of men's designer fashions can be found here.
- **DKNY**: Designer Donna Karan New York showcases her latest clothing and shoe line here.
- **Impulse**: This shop offers a selection of gifts, souvenirs, costume jewelry, sundries, and other items, and is open twenty-four hours.
- **La Perla**: This is a clothing and accessory boutique for him and her.
- **The Mirage Collection**: Mirage-logoed merchandise, plus souvenirs from *Siegfried & Roy* and Danny Gans are sold here. Open twenty-four hours.
- **The Mirage Shop**: Mirage souvenirs can be purchased here, twenty-four hours per day.
- **Moschino**: The popular fashion designer has a boutique located within The Mirage.
- **Shadow Creek**: A pro shop for golf enthusiasts, open daily from 7:00 A.M. to 10:00 P.M.
- **Watch Boutique**: Looking for a new watch or jewelry? Check out the selection offered here.

Spa and Salon

✆800-456-4564 (Spa)
✆702-791-7472 (Spa)
✆702-791-7474 (Salon)

To cater to an ever-growing health-conscious clientele, The Mirage features an extensive spa and salon that offer the latest fitness, health, and beauty programs. Within the spa, you'll find an aerobic studio, separate men's and women's facilities, sauna, steam bath, whirlpool, private massage rooms, and a juice bar. Personal training sessions are also available.

Spa equipment and services also include stationary bicycles, treadmills, and stair climbers, a full line of Cybex weight training machines, free weights, aromatherapy, body exfoliation, and sea-weed facial masks. Besides the daily fee required to use the fitness and spa facilities, additional fees apply for special services, such as massages, facials, and personal training sessions. The spa is open from 6:00 A.M. to 7:00 P.M.

The beauty salon provides a complement of services including hairstyling, from cuts to coloring. Nail treatments, facials, and makeup services are also available by appointment. The salon is open from 9:00 A.M. to 7:00 P.M.

Dining Options

At The Mirage, you'll find an excellent selection of dining options, no matter what your budget or what type of meal you're looking for.

Fine Dining

In addition to a handful of fine-dining restaurants and other eating establishments that offer more casual, less expensive dining options, twenty-four-hour room service is available to resort guests. Reservations are strongly recommended for all of The Mirage's fancier restaurants. The dress code for these fine-dining establishments is "casual elegance."

To make a reservation (which is highly recommended) at any of the fine-dining restaurants, call ✆866-339-4566. You can also make your reservations online by visiting The Mirage's Web site and clicking on the "Dining" option.

Kokomo's ($$$)

Kokomo's specializes in steaks and seafood. Although it is located indoors, in the heart of The Mirage's main building, the dining room re-creates a tropical rain forest, making guests feels as if they're out-doors, surrounded by waterfalls and exotic plant life.

The restaurant is open daily for dinner only (5:00 P.M. to 10:30 P.M.). Reservations are recommended.

Mikado ($$$)

Open nightly for dinner from 6:00 P.M. to 11:00 P.M., Mikado offers a large menu of traditional Japanese foods, including sushi. Other menu items include lobster, steak, chicken, and shrimp, all cooked and served Teppanyaki-style. A complete selection of entrées is also available from an à la carte menu. A sushi bar is located in the garden area of the restaurant. A large selection of wines, including sake, is available with dinner. The average meal price per person is about $50. Reservations are recommended.

Moongate ($$$)

Offering classic Szechuan and Cantonese entrées from China, this restaurant features a dining room that is decorated using classical Chinese architecture. One of the house specialties is a combination platter of deep-fried prawns, egg rolls, barbecued spareribs, and crab rangoons.

Moongate is open nightly for dinner from 5:30 P.M. to 11:00 P.M. The average meal price per person is between $40 and $50. A large selection of fine wines is also available. Reservations are recommended.

Onda ($$$)

Created by Boston-based chef Todd English, Onda offers classic regional dishes from Italy, as well as delicious American cuisine. Menu items include homemade pasta, breads, fresh seafood, and meats. Onda is open nightly for dinner from 5:30 P.M. to 11:00 P.M. A large selection of fine California and Italian wines is available with dinner, which is served in a dining room decorated with imported tiles and marble. The average price per person is about $50. Reservations are recommended.

Renoir ($$$)

Serving an extensive menu of contemporary French cuisine, Renoir is open for dinner from 5:30 P.M. to 9:30 P.M. (Tuesdays through Saturdays). A special five-course tasting is available for a flat rate of $90 per person. The décor of this restaurant includes silk-covered walls and brocade upholstery, plus artwork from French Impressionist Pierre-Auguste Renoir. Reservations are recommended.

Men are asked to wear jackets when dining at Renoir, which is located next to the Moongate restaurant.

Samba Brazilian Steakhouse ($$$)

This unique Brazilian grill offers the "Rodizio" style of cooking, which focuses mainly on entrées consisting of chicken, beef, vegetables, and fish. An all-inclusive dinner menu is priced under $30 per person; however, an à la carte menu is also available. For this, plan on spending upward of $50 per person. Dinner is served nightly from 5:30 P.M. to 11:00 P.M. Reservations are recommended.

A live Samba trio performs every night, helping to add an upbeat ambiance to everyone's dining experience. The Samba Grill offers a beverage list that includes a large assortment of tropical specialty drinks in addition to South American wines. Separating itself from the clutter of run-of-the-mill and theme restaurants in Las Vegas, Samba Grill offers an unusual and highly enjoyable dining experience for people of all ages.

TRAVEL TIP

Throughout the year, The Mirage hosts a wide range of big-name musicians, comedians, and entertainers who perform special shows. For example, comedians such as Jay Leno, Ray Romano, Wayne Brady, and David Spade all appeared recently. Contact the resort's concierge or call ☎702-791-7111 for details about special events.

Casual Dining

For guests and visitors looking for a more relaxed, less expensive dining experience that's more suitable for the entire family, the following options are available at The Mirage.

Caribe Café ($$)

Open twenty-four hours a day, this coffee shop offers an extremely diverse menu, including salads, sandwiches, exotic desserts, and all-American breakfasts. Breakfast, lunch, dinner, and snacks are served.

Carvings: The Mirage Buffet ($$)

Offering more than 150 menu items each day, this is a classic, Las Vegas–style, all-you-can-eat buffet. It's open daily for breakfast, lunch, and dinner. Because of the popularity of the buffet, be prepared for a wait to be seated, particularly during peak periods. This buffet recently underwent a massive redesign and reopened in June 2004.

Carvings now offers twelve different food stations, including Chinese, Italian, sushi, and American cuisine. There's also a full-service bar and an open kitchen, so you can see much of the food being prepared. Among the popular offerings are all-you-can-eat shrimp and crab legs, plus a mouthwatering array of desserts. Diners are provided with large, square-shaped plates to pile on the food.

One unusual thing about this buffet is that while it's huge (the dining room seats 584 people), it offers a relatively quiet dining atmosphere, with no loud casino noise in the background. The tables are nicely spaced and the décor is bright and festive. Carvings offers top-quality food at a very fair price. It is one of the best dining values on the Strip and is ideal for families.

The California Pizza Kitchen ($$)

Located next to the casino's race and sports book, this chain restaurant offers wood-fired gourmet pizzas and a nice selection of other Southern California-inspired foods. Open Sunday through Thursday for lunch and dinner, hours are from 11:00 A.M. to midnight daily (and on Fridays and Saturdays until 2:00 A.M.).

Coconuts Ice Cream Shop ($)

A wide selection of desserts is served day and night, including freshly made ice creams, sorbets, and frozen yogurts. There's also a coffee bar (Coffee Express) that serves muffins, cookies, and a variety of gourmet coffees, making it a great place to stop for a quick and inexpensive breakfast or snack. Open daily from 11:00 A.M. to 11:00 P.M.

Paradise Café ($$)

Located near the pool area, this café offers a light menu. It's an ideal place to stop for a quick and inexpensive snack. It's open seasonally.

The Roasted Bean ($)

This is an inexpensive coffee shop, serving gourmet coffees, pastries, and sandwiches. It's open for breakfast, lunch, and dinner between 7:00 A.M. and midnight.

Lounges and Bars

The following lounges and bars are open to the over-twenty-one crowd only:

- **Ava**: If you're in the mood for a drink and live entertainment, check out this Polynesian-theme lounge and full-service bar.
- **Baccarat Bar**: You'll find this lounge, featuring live piano music, at the center of The Mirage's casino. Full bar service is available.
- **Onda Lounge**: Located near the Onda restaurant, this lounge offers live piano music and full bar service.

The Mirage's Casino

The large, 100,000-square-foot and lavishly decorated casino at The Mirage is designed to resemble a Polynesian village. It offers keno and more than 2,400 slot and video poker machines, plus table games such as craps, blackjack, and baccarat. There's also a separate poker room and a race and sports book.

CHAPTER 15

New York-New York Hotel & Casino

WHERE ELSE BUT IN Las Vegas can you see the Eiffel Tower, a 45-foot-tall bronze lion, a giant pyramid, a medieval king's castle, and the Empire State Building all within a several-block radius? Each mega-resort along the Strip has its own unique theme. At the New York-New York Hotel & Casino (operated by MGM Mirage), the theme is a celebration of and dedication to the Big Apple. Originally built at a cost of $485 million, this property features twelve New York City-style buildings and replicas of the city's most famous landmarks (all created at one-third actual size).

▲New York-New York and it's familiar sites.   Photo ©The Las Vegas News Bureau.

Mega-Resort Overview

✉3790 Las Vegas Boulevard South, Las Vegas, NV 89109

✆800-693-6763

✆702-740-6969

✐*www.nynyhotelcasino.com*

Room and Suite Rates: $$/$$$/$$$

With published room rates starting at just $69, this is one of the least expensive mega-resorts on the Strip; however, deluxe rooms and suites are priced upward of $600 to $2,500 per night. Be sure to check the various travel-related Web sites for lower room rates. The New York-New York Web site also offers online-only rates and special package deals that'll save you money.

Since it opened in January 1997, New York-New York has attracted city dwellers and country folk alike, all visiting this property for a taste of the big city, while at the same time experiencing the excitement of Las Vegas.

≡FAST FACT

Located near the base of the 150-foot-tall Statue of Liberty replica, at the front of the resort, there's a September 11th tribute and memorial. Guests from around the world continue to place personal items and mementos at this memorial in order to pay tribute to the heroes and victims of this tragedy.

For families, New York-New York is an attractive property for several reasons. First, it's affordable. Second, it's located in an ideal location, toward the center of the Strip, making it easy to get to other resorts and attractions relatively quickly and affordably. New York-New York also offers a few shows, activities, and attractions that are family-friendly, such as the Manhattan Express roller coaster and the Coney Island Emporium.

NEW YORK–NEW YORK OVERALL FAMILY-FRIENDLINESS RATING

Ages Up to 5	Ages 6–15	Ages 16–20	Ages 21 & Up	Senior Citizens
☆	☆☆	☆☆	☆☆☆	☆☆☆

Guest Room Accommodations

The New York-New York Hotel & Casino is an ideal place for families to stay. An assortment of room accommodations and suites are available. The rooms themselves are spacious, offering a single king-size bed or two queen-size beds, a television, seating area, closet, and full bathroom. Some suites contain wet bars, while others offer whirlpool baths and other amenities.

In August 2004, all of the 1,370 standard guest rooms at New York-New York were remodeled at a cost of over $30 million. Now called Park Avenue Deluxe Rooms, each offers the following amenities: a 27-inch flat-screen television, a desk equipped with high-speed Internet access, a private safe, a lighted makeup mirror, a glass shower enclosure, a full-length mirror, iron and ironing board, hairdryer, lighted armoires, and a seating area.

Featured Attractions and Activities

Nearly all of the attractions and activities offered at New York-New York are family-friendly—exceptions are Cirque du Soleil's *Zumanity*, the resort's casino, the bars, and the lounges. If you're looking for a much more family-oriented Cirque du Soleil performance, check out *Mystère* (at Treasure Island) or "*O*" (at the Bellagio).

While visiting New York-New York, the Manhattan Express roller coaster and the Coney Island Emporium are definitely worth experiencing. Comedian Rita Rudner's show is funny, uplifting, entertaining, and suitable for teens and adults alike.

Manhattan Express:
The Coney Island–Style Roller Coaster

Imagine a high-speed roller coaster that starts indoors, but through a series of twists, loops, and turns quickly takes riders outdoors (along the perimeter of the New York-New York resort) as they see the Las Vegas Strip whiz by.

The Manhattan Express roller coaster is one of the fastest and most exciting thrill rides on the Strip. With a maximum height of 203 feet and drops of 144 feet, riders travel at speeds up to sixty-seven miles per hour. Experience this high-speed and turbulent ride on one of five four-car, sixteen-passenger trains as you blast your way along the 4,777 feet of track.

Because of its popularity, be prepared for a wait if you're planning to ride during peak times (holidays and weekend evenings and nights). For the best view of the Strip, experience this ride at night. Ticket prices are $12.50 for the first ride and $6 for re-rides. Hours of operation are 10:00 A.M. to 10:30 P.M. (11:30 P.M. during peak periods).

MANHATTAN EXPRESS: THE CONEY ISLAND–STYLE ROLLER COASTER

Ages Up to 5	Ages 6–15	Ages 16–20	Ages 21 & Up	Senior Citizens
Not Suitable	☆	☆☆☆	☆☆☆	☆

Coney Island Emporium

Guests and visitors of New York-New York will enjoy this light-hearted re-creation of Coney Island, complete with multiple kiddie rides, carnival games (that offer prizes), snacks, and over 200 state-of-the-art arcade games. Participate in laser tag, ride the bumper cars, or experience a virtual reality game. Arcade games cost anywhere from $.50 to $2 per play. Many award tickets that can be collected and redeemed for prizes. The Coney Island Midway games are priced between $1 and $2 per play and prizes are awarded.

TRAVEL TIP

> If you're looking for more theme park-style thrill rides, be sure to visit Circus, Circus's Adventuredome indoor theme park, as well as the rides atop the Stratosphere Tower.

The Coney Island Emporium is located away from the casino, on the resort's second level, next to the Manhattan Express. This area offers ongoing, hands-on entertainment for children, teens, and adults alike. Kids and teens can easily spend several hours here. Hours of operation are 8:00 A.M. to midnight (2:00 A.M. on Fridays and Saturdays).

CONEY ISLAND EMPORIUM

Ages Up to 5	Ages 6–15	Ages 16–20	Ages 21 & Up	Senior Citizens
☆☆	☆☆☆	☆☆	☆☆	☆☆

It's Showtime at New York-New York

The real New York City may have dozens of Broadway shows, but the New York-New York Hotel & Casino features comedy by Rita Rudner, plus a groundbreaking show created by Cirque du Soleil.

Cirque du Soleil's *Zumanity*

📞866-606-7111

📞702-740-6815

✉*www.zumanity.com*

Since 1984, Cirque du Soleil has memorized and entertained over 50 million circusgoers with its unique blend of original music, intricate and imaginative costumes, amazing sets, thought-provoking story lines, innovative choreography, and unusual circus acts. The French circus troupe continues to tour throughout the world, while also offering several exciting family-oriented shows right here in Las Vegas.

Zumanity, however, is something new and different. It's an adults-only cabaret-style circus. This show is highly entertaining and thought-provoking, and the circus acts are amazing to watch, but *Zumanity* is also edgy and pushes the envelope in terms of its themes. If you see this show, enter the theater with an open mind.

 TRAVEL ESSENTIAL

Instead of waiting at the box office to purchase your show tickets, you can visit the New York–New York Web site (*www.nynyhotel casino.com*) and purchase your theater tickets online for *Zumanity* and Rita Rudner before you even leave home.

This show is ideal if you're visiting Las Vegas for a romantic get-away weekend, for example, but it's definitely not suitable for kids or teens. *Zumanity* is presented in a 1,259-seat custom-built theater and features a fifty-person cast. Nobody under age eighteen will be admitted. Showtimes are 7:30 and 10:30 P.M. Tuesday through Saturday. Tickets range from $65 to $105.

CIRQUE DU SOLEIL'S *ZUMANITY*

Ages Up to 5	Ages 6–15	Ages 16–20	Ages 21 & Up	Senior Citizens
Not Suitable	Not Suitable	☆☆☆	☆☆☆	☆☆

Rita Rudner

✆800-693-6763

✆702-740-6815

www.ritarudner.com

You've seen her on HBO, as well as on virtually every television talk show from David Letterman, Oprah, and Jay Leno to *Live with Regis and Kelly*. She's also toured America, performing at comedy clubs everywhere.

Now based in Las Vegas, well-known comedienne Rita Rudner performs a ninety-minute, family-friendly comedy act nightly within the 451-seat Cabaret Theater at New York-New York. This show is lighthearted, funny, and thoroughly entertaining. It's definitely worth seeing! Showtimes are 8:00 P.M. (9:00 P.M. on Friday and Saturdays). Tickets are $53.70.

RITA RUDNER

Ages Up to 5	Ages 6–15	Ages 16–20	Ages 21 & Up	Senior Citizens
Not Suitable	☆	☆☆☆	☆☆☆	☆☆☆

Rita Speaks Out!

In addition to being a headline performer each night at New York-New York, Rita Rudner is happily married and the mother of a young daughter. Some of what you'll hear in her standup comedy routine focuses on her family. Her entire ninety-minute show offers clean, family-friendly entertainment. While most comedians rely on adult language to get laughs, Rita's show is clean, but very funny. This is a great show for the whole family.

≡FAST FACT

One of the New York City landmarks replicated at New York–New York is the 300-foot-long, 50-foot-high Brooklyn Bridge, which more than 15 million people cross by foot each year while visiting Las Vegas. The real Brooklyn Bridge's foot traffic is only approximately 940,000 pedestrians per year.

Shopping

Although New York-New York doesn't offer a mall-like shopping experience, throughout the resort you'll find unusual shops, including:

- **Cashman's Photo Magic**: Using the latest computer technology, your image will be superimposed onto any one of more than 200 scenarios, such as fictional magazine covers. This is also the place to go for thirty-minute photo processing or camera supplies.
- **Grand Central Watch Co.**: Browse the large selection of gold and platinum jewelry, including wedding bands and watches.
- **Harley-Davidson Shop**: T-shirts and other Harley-Davidson-logoed merchandise is sold here.
- **Houdini's Magic Shop**: Ongoing demonstrations by skilled magicians make this shop a fun place to browse through, even if you're not looking to purchase.
- **I Love New York**: Here you'll find more than 2,000 novelty and apparel items, many with a New York theme. This is the place to buy New York-New York merchandise.
- **Manhattan Express Show**: After you experience the roller coaster, drop into this shop to purchase a souvenir photo of your ride, along with a handful of other roller coaster–related items.
- **Soho Village**: New York-theme fashions and gifts, plus evening wear, gift baskets, fine cigars, and cigar accessories are among the items offered in this shopping area.
- **The News Stand**: Newspapers, magazines, paperback books, health and beauty aids, snack foods, tobacco products, sundries, and beverages are sold here.
- **Vegas Express**: This railroad-theme specialty store features children's apparel, toys, collectibles, and gifts for all ages. A large selection of Las Vegas-theme gifts are also available.

Pool, Spa, and Fitness Facilities

New York-New York offers an outdoor swimming pool area open to people of all ages. The fitness area offers cardiovascular equipment, free weights, and Tuff Stuff circuit-training equipment. Hours are 6:30 A.M. to 7:00 P.M. daily. Call ☎702-740-6955 for information.

🧳 TRAVEL TIP

While the Spa at New York-New York offers many of the services and amenities you'd want, it doesn't compare to the world-class service and treatments you'll receive at the Canyon Ranch SpaClub, located within The Venetian (☎877-220-2688/✍*www.canyonranch.com*).

When you're ready to kick back, relax, and be pampered, the spa facility offers men and women a wide range of treatments and services, including massages, facials, aromatherapy soaks, body scrubs, and mist-on tanning. Treatments range from twenty-five to seventy-five minutes in length. Prices vary, but are very competitive with other spas located on the Strip. The spa is open daily from 8:00 A.M. to 6:00 P.M.

Access to just the spa facilities is $20 per day; however, discounted multiday passes are available. (Use of the spa facilities is included when you book an optional spa treatment, such as a massage, facial, or body scrub.)

The spa facilities, open to resort guests and non-guests, include separate men's and women's locker room facilities, relaxation lounges, showers, steam rooms, dry saunas, whirlpools, vanity amenities (robes and slippers are provided), and access to the fitness center.

The Regis Signature Salon, which is part of the spa, offers complete hair, nail, and skin care, along with body wraps and waxing services. Advance reservations should be made for spa or salon treatments.

≡ FAST FACT

In 2004, the entire outdoor pool area was remodeled. Cabanas can now be rented and there's a lovely café and bar that can be enjoyed while relaxing by the pool.

Dining Options

New York-New York offers a few fine-dining options, but has a much greater focus on affordable, casual dining that's family-friendly.

Fine Dining

Gallagher's Steakhouse and Il Fornaio provide the perfect atmosphere for a formal business dinner, intimate celebration, or simply a fine-dining experience with the family. Each restaurant in New York-New York offers a theme menu and atmosphere.

Gallagher's Steakhouse ($$$)

✆702-740-6450

The original Gallagher's Steakhouse was founded in 1927 in New York City. Today, its award-winning steak and fresh seafood entrées are served right here in Las Vegas. Open daily for dinner (4:00 P.M. to 11:00 P.M., and until midnight on Fridays and Saturdays). Prime rib, porterhouse steak, and filet mignon are among the house specialties.

Il Fornaio ($$$)

✆702-740-6403

Award-winning Italian cuisine that's made from authentic regional recipes is offered here. Homemade pastas, rotisserie meats, mesquite-grilled fish, wood-fired pizzas, fresh salads, and hearth-baked bread are among the specialty items found on the menu. The restaurant is open daily, 8:30 A.M. to 11:30 P.M. (until 12:30 A.M. on Fridays and Saturdays), for breakfast, lunch, and dinner.

Casual Dining

The food choices at New York-New York are as diverse as what you'd find walking along the streets of New York City. This is especially welcome if you're on a budget or looking for kid-friendly food that's served quickly. The multitude of choices includes:

Il Fornaio Panetteria ($$)

An ideal first stop in the morning (or for lunch), this bakery offers a wide selection of pastries, coffees, sandwiches, and salads, along with fresh Italian bread, cookies, and cakes.

Chin Chin Café ($$)

Straight from Los Angeles, this popular Chinese restaurant offers a contemporary atmosphere and some of the best fried rice you'll find anywhere. The exhibition-style kitchen allows you to watch the skilled chefs prepare the meals. The food isn't cheap, nor is it fast food, but Chin Chin Café offers a casual-dining experience the whole family can enjoy for lunch, dinner, or a between-meal snack. An extensive dim sum selection is also offered.

America ($$)

Open twenty-four hours, this restaurant features American-style cuisine selections from across the country. If you're staying at New York-New York, it's the ideal family-dining restaurant, because it's always open and affordable. A selection of American wines and beers is also offered.

Gonzalez y Gonzalez ($$)

If you're in the mood for authentic Mexican cuisine, you'll find it here. In addition to offering traditional New York-style Mexican food items, the restaurant itself is decorated with lanterns and piñatas, plus offers a tequila bar.

Nathan's Famous Hot Dogs ($)

Those world-famous hot dogs and French fries are available from this Nathan's fast-food establishment, located in the Coney Island Emporium area. Quality fast food that's suitable for the whole family is served here. It's ideal if you're in a hurry, on a budget, or simply wanting to enjoy the atmosphere of the Emporium area while having a snack.

Häagen-Dazs Ice Cream ($$)

This ice cream counter offers Häagen-Dazs ice cream and an assortment of other treats.

Schrafft's Ice Cream ($)

This ice cream counter offers an assortment of ice cream-based treats, including sundaes.

The Village Eateries ($)

This is New York-New York's version of a food court. It's an ideal place to go for a quick and cheap bite to eat. You'll find a variety of inexpensive menu options from Broadway Burger, Greenwich Village Coffee Company, Ice Cream Shop, Greenberg's Deli, Sirrico's Pizza, and Fulton Fish Frye.

The ESPN Zone ($$)

This theme restaurant is a cross between a sports bar and a family-friendly restaurant. Video monitors throughout the restaurant show sporting events, while the décor consists of a wide range of sports-related memorabilia. This is a fun place to eat and drink. Young people will love the sports video games and other activities this restaurant offers. Open for lunch and dinner (11:30 A.M. to 12:30 A.M. daily and until 1:30 A.M. on Fridays and Saturdays).

Grand Central Coffee Company ($)

Gourmet coffees and pastries are served here, starting at 7:00 A.M. daily. On weekends it's open until 2:00 A.M.

New York Pretzel ($)

Grab a pretzel as a quick snack, just as you can in New York City from those famous street vendors. The big difference here is that the pretzels aren't stale. Open 10:00 A.M. until 11:00 P.M. (and until 1:00 A.M. on Fridays and Saturdays).

Stadium Snack Bar ($)

Hot dogs, pretzels, nachos, and other quick and inexpensive "fast food" items are served here, starting at 8:00 A.M.

Krispy Kreme Doughnuts ($)

Those famous doughnuts that people can't seem to get enough of are available here, starting at 7:00 A.M. daily. They're also available at the Stadium Snack Bar.

Lounges and Bars

If you're not looking for a full meal, but want to relax and have a drink, enjoy live entertainment, or sing along with the entertainment, New York-New York offers several lounges and bars for the twenty-one-and-over crowd.

The Bar at Times Square

This lively bar features dueling pianos and fun-filled sing-alongs for older audiences (you must be of legal drinking age). N.Y.P.D. (New York Piano Duos) performs nightly. The bar itself is modeled after a New York City pub. It's open twenty-four hours, with live musical performance daily until 2:00 A.M.

Nine Fine Irishmen

As you've probably guessed from the name, this is an authentic Irish pub serving traditional Irish food and drinks, along with live entertainment.

Coyote Ugly

Based on the popular movie, this is a fun-filled bar featuring beautiful waitresses with an attitude. It's a Southern-style bar with plenty of hospitality.

ESPN Zone

In addition to being a theme restaurant with a full menu, ESPN Zone is a full-service sports bar.

Big Apple Bar

Open twenty-four hours, this New York-style bar features ongoing live entertainment and an extensive drink menu.

The Lobby Bar

One of the first things you'll see when you set foot through the main entrance of New York-New York is this bar. It's located adjacent to the registration desk.

New York–New York's Casino

New York-New York's 84,000-square-foot casino is designed to make you feel as if you're outside, exploring New York City. This, however, is an entirely indoor casino offering classic Las Vegas-style gaming.

 TRAVEL ESSENTIAL

If you have a cell phone, wireless PDA, or handheld device that's capable of surfing the Internet, you can access a wide range of information about New York-New York from its mobile-optimized Web site. Point your handheld device's Web browser to *http://mobile.nynyhotelcasino.com.*

Here, you'll find seventy-two gaming tables and 2,200 slot machines. Visitors can try their hand at blackjack, craps, roulette, mini-baccarat, progressive Pai Gow poker, Caribbean Stud poker, Let It Ride, Big Six, casino war, and keno, all available in the main casino area. For those who prefer to follow professional sports, the casino also offers a race and sports book.

CHAPTER 16

Treasure Island

LOCATED NEXT TO THE famous Mirage resort and operated by MGM Mirage, Treasure Island shares over 100 acres of property with The Mirage and is located in a perfect location along the Strip. Treasure Island, however, is somewhat less expensive and slightly less elegant than its sister properties, yet offers similar accommodations and services. Treasure Island, which opened in October 1993, is an excellent choice for families traveling with children and teens, in part because of its pirate motif.

Mega-Resort Overview

✉3300 Las Vegas Boulevard South, Las Vegas, NV 89109
📞800-944-7444
📞702-894-7111
✐*www.treasureisland.com*
Room and Suite Rates: $$/$$$/$$$$
All public areas of Treasure Island maintain the theme of a Caribbean hideaway, based loosely on a village created by Robert Louis Stevenson in his novel *Treasure Island*. Surrounding the front of the resort is Buccaneer Bay Village, a replica of a thriving Old World village. The large cove area in front of the resort is where a free twenty-minute show, called *Sirens of TI*, can be seen several times each evening. *Sirens of TI* offers music, dancing, special effects, and

a somewhat ridiculous story line. It features very lighthearted, family-friendly entertainment.

TREASURE ISLAND OVERALL FAMILY-FRIENDLINESS RATING

Ages Up to 5	Ages 6–15	Ages 16–20	Ages 21 & Up	Senior Citizens
☆☆	☆☆☆	☆☆☆	☆☆☆	☆☆☆

Guest Room Accommodations

European fabrics and custom-woven carpeting provide an elegant background upon which traditional wood furnishings are used to create a comfortable living space within the guest rooms and suites. Each room features floor-to-ceiling windows with an excellent view of the mountains, the Strip, or the resort's lovely pool area. The color scheme features soft earth tones.

Basic guest rooms contain a single king-size bed or two queen-size beds, desk, television, bureau, high-speed Internet access, and small table with two chairs. Other amenities include a marble bath and shower, hairdryer, makeup mirror, and in-room safe.

▲ See *Sirens of TI* at Treasure Island.   Photo ©The Las Vegas News Bureau.

 **TRAVEL TIP**

For an additional $25 per night, you can reserve a basic guest room on an upper-level floor that offers an amazing view of the Las Vegas Strip.

Types of Rooms Offered

In addition to 2,885 guest rooms, Treasure Island features 220 suites (ranging in price from $159 to $2,500 or more per night). The suites are divided into five categories based on price, size, and amenities offered. If you're looking for family accommodations that are more comfortable than reserving two connecting basic guest rooms, a suite offers a slightly more expensive solution.

Suite options include:

Petite Suites

These suites are larger than basic guest rooms. Like the regular guest rooms, the suites are elegantly styled with traditional furnishings and custom fabrics. Each of these suites features a king-size bed and a separate sitting area, as well as his and her bathrooms. They're ideal for couples.

Executive Suites

These suites, a bit larger than the Petite Suites, offer a king-size bed, a comfortable sitting area, and luxurious his and her bathrooms. They're most suitable for couples.

Tower Suites

The Tower Suites offer the ideal combination of elegance and comfort in spacious surroundings. Each suite has a king-size bed, a large sitting and dining area, and elaborate his and her bathrooms and walk-in closets.

Luxury Suites

These suites have a large bedroom with a king-size bed and a separate living room and dining area. Each Luxury Suite features his and her bathrooms, a whirlpool bathtub, and a variety of in-room amenities, including a wet bar.

Premier Suites

The Premier Suites are Treasure Island's most spacious suites. They offer top-of-the-line amenities and facilities. Located on the top floors of the towers, they offer panoramic views of the city and the resort's theatrical ship battle. Amenities include a full entertainment center, wet bar, Jacuzzi, and walk-in closet.

Featured Attractions and Activities

Because of its location, getting to and from any of the major attractions along the Strip is easy, whether you choose to walk, drive, take a taxi, utilize the Las Vegas Monorail, or try the free shuttles that are available.

Treasure Island is located directly across the street (less than a three-minute walk) from the Fashion Show Mall, which, in addition to the Forum Shops, offers some of the best shopping in Las Vegas. Family-oriented activities and dining options are also available at this indoor mall.

Swimming Pool

The pool at Treasure Island is accented with shady awnings, brightly colored flowers, and dozens of palm trees. Complimentary towels and lounge chairs are provided to all guests. Cabana rentals are available for full and half days and include bottled water, juices, sodas, television with cable, telephone, rafts, and changing room. Sundries, including suntan lotion, dive masks, and sunglasses, are available for sale. A cocktail and snack bar is conveniently located poolside. This is an outdoor pool, so it's open seasonally.

It's Showtime at Treasure Island

The shows presented here are among Treasure Island's most popular activities. Out of all the Cirque du Soleil shows offered (*Mystère*, "O,"

Zumanity, and the newest show at the MGM Grand, *KA*), *Mystère* at TI is the most family-oriented.

Cirque du Soleil's *Mystère*

☏800-392-1999

✐*www.cirquedusoleil.com*

Cirque du Soleil is a Montreal-based circus troupe that has been in existence since 1984. This isn't your typical circus, however. Designed for adults but suitable for teens, Cirque du Soleil has several traveling tour groups and a permanent U.S. home in Las Vegas at Treasure Island, New York–New York, the MGM Grand, and the Bellagio, as well as at Pleasure Island at the Walt Disney World Resort in Orlando, Florida.

Cirque du Soleil's show *Mystère* is presented exclusively at Treasure Island and features seventy-two acrobats, comedians, actors, singers, dancers, and musicians from eighteen countries. In addition to the exhilarating performances, the live music, sets, and costumes are absolutely incredible.

TRAVEL ESSENTIAL

Nobody under the age of five will be admitted into the Cirque du Soleil theater. Make sure you make arrangements for your youngest travel companions if you want to see this show.

Mystère is performed twice nightly (except Monday and Tuesday) in a 1,600-seat theater designed exclusively for the show. Tickets are $95, and should be purchased in advance from the box office, since performances typically sell out.

Celebrating more than ten years in Las Vegas, *Mystère* is revamped every few months as new specialty acts are added and others are changed. It'll definitely appeal to a more mainstream, family-oriented audience than Cirque du Soleil's *"O"* and is one of the very best shows offered in Las Vegas. It's definitely worth the price of admission and shouldn't be missed! Showtimes are 7:30 P.M. and 10:30 P.M. (no shows on Wednesdays or Thursdays).

If you've never seen a Cirque du Soleil show, this one offers a night's worth of top-notch entertainment that's well worth the price of admission. Located down the Strip at the Bellagio, Cirque du Soleil presents another show, called "O." It's an even more unusual show that mostly takes place in water.

CIRQUE DU SOLEIL'S *MYSTÈRE*

Ages Up to 5	Ages 6–15	Ages 16–20	Ages 21 & Up	Senior Citizens
Not Suitable	☆☆	☆☆☆	☆☆☆	☆☆☆

Sirens of TI

From along Las Vegas Boulevard, in front of Treasure Island, catch this free show that happens every night. Complete with special effects, music, dance, acrobats, larger-than-life sets, and plenty of excitement, *Sirens of TI* is a twenty-minute show that takes place on a "stage" that's actually an expansive lagoon. It features scantily clad women, so it might not be optimum for the youngest family members. The story line of this show is utterly ridiculous, but it's somewhat entertaining and you can't beat the admission price.

When choosing your viewing location, make sure you can clearly see the two pirate ships in the lagoon, or you'll only be seeing "half" of the show. Showtimes are 7:00 P.M., 8:30 P.M., 10:00 P.M., and 11:30 P.M. daily.

SIRENS OF TI

Ages Up to 5	Ages 6–15	Ages 16–20	Ages 21 & Up	Senior Citizens
Not Suitable	Not Suitable	☆☆	☆☆	☆☆

Shopping

In addition to the shops and boutiques located inside Treasure Island, the resort is a short walk from the Fashion Show Mall, a rather large indoor mall located along the Strip. It's also a short walk (or cab ride) from the Forum Shops, which feature dozens of upscale shops and theme restaurants.

Within Treasure Island, you'll find these shops:

- **Captain Kids**: A selection of Treasure Island merchandise, toys, and plush animals are sold here.
- **Island Provisions**: Poolside supplies and sundries, such as suntan lotion, are available here.
- *Mystère* **Store**: This boutique offers official Cirque du Soleil merchandise and gifts not available elsewhere (except from the Cirque du Soleil main order catalog). The soundtrack from *Mystère* and other Cirque du Soleil shows can be purchased here, along with clothing items and other distinctive gifts.
- **Sirens Apparel and Lingerie**: A selection of women's fashions and intimate apparel is offered at this shop.
- **The $10 Boutique**: Take the familiar dollar-store concept and multiply it by ten. All of this store's merchandise is priced under $10.
- **The Candy Reef**: Chocolates, candies, and a selection of other sweets are sold here. If you have a sweet tooth, you're sure to find something to satisfy your cravings.
- **The Lobby Store**: Jewelry, gifts, souvenirs, and merchandise with the resort's logo are sold here.
- **The Siren's Cove Shop**: Here you'll find gifts, souvenirs, and merchandise imprinted with the resort's logo.
- **The Watch Shop**: Looking for a new watch? The Watch Stop offers a wide selection of watches and fine jewelry.
- **Treasure Island Store**: Find Calvin Klein fashion apparel, along with souvenirs and sundries, here.

Day Spa, Salon, and Fitness Facilities

Between October 2004 and spring 2005, the TI Spa and Salon (☎702-894-7472) was closed for renovation. Upon reopening, it began offering top-notch services, treatments, and facilities designed to truly pamper guests. Amenities at the spa include men's and women's locker room facilities (complete with saunas, whirlpools, and steam baths).

Workout attire, robes, and sandals are provided. There is a daily admission fee to use the spa facilities that can be billed directly to your room. Services and treatments offered within the spa are billed separately.

≡FAST FACT

Treasure Island (TI) comprises three thirty-six-story buildings and houses over 2,885 guest rooms, including 220 suites. The theme of this mega-resort re-creates an elegant Caribbean hideaway.

The exercise room within the spa offers stationary bicycles, treadmills, stair climbers, Cybex weight-training machines, and free weights. There's also a full-service juice bar and complete vanity amenities available.

The TI Salon offers a full complement of services, including hair-styling, haircutting, pedicures, manicures, and facials. Hours of operation are 7:00 A.M. to 7:00 P.M. daily.

Dining Options

Pretending you're a pirate as you explore TI and The Mirage (which offers the white tigers attraction) will help you develop a hearty appetite. As you'd expect from a large Las Vegas mega-resort, you have many dining options at TI, including an amazingly delicious family-oriented Mexican restaurant, called Isla Mexican Kitchen & Tequila Bar, which is open for lunch and dinner.

Fine Dining

Many of Treasure Island's fine-dining establishments have a "dressy casual" dress code and do not allow children under the age of five. Thus, these restaurants aren't designed for families with young children. Be sure to check with the restaurant's host or the resort's concierge for details.

The Buccaneer Bay Club ($$$)

✆866-286-3809

Located on the second level of the resort and overlooking Buccaneer Bay, this restaurant gives diners an excellent view of the Strip and the nightly *Sirens of TI* show. Indulge in such entrées as Cornish game hen, sautéed Chilean sea bass, or shrimp scampi sauté. Dinner is served nightly from 5:00 P.M. to 10:30 P.M. Like all of the fine-dining establishments at Treasure Island, this one is perfect for an intimate dinner, a business dinner, or a celebration of a special occasion (such as an anniversary). Reservations are recommended.

Francesco's ($$$)

✆866-286-3809

This restaurant offers a wide selection of Italian specialties, including fresh pasta, antipasti, and Mediterranean-style seafood. Francesco's itself is decorated with original artwork created by celebrities such as Tony Bennett and Phyllis Diller. It also has an open kitchen, so you can see the chefs at work as they prepare your meal. Dinner is served nightly from 5:30 P.M. to 11:00 P.M. Reservations are recommended.

Isla Mexicana Kitchen & Tequila Bar ($$/$$$)

✆866-286-3809

Open between 11:00 A.M. and 2:00 A.M. for lunch, dinner, and late-night snacks, this restaurant offers traditional Mexican cuisine with what Chef Richard Sandoval calls a "modern twist." Isla Mexicana features an open-style kitchen, modern décor, and an extensive menu. Even the dishes the food is served on were custom-designed to create a more visually appealing and theme-oriented dining experience.

The food's presentation is truly artwork on a plate. Even if you're not a big fan of Mexican food, this restaurant offers entrées that'll cater to everyone's palate.

Popular entrées include tacos, enchiladas, tamales, burritos, soups, salads, beef, and fish. For a dinner entrée, the Isla Grilled Filet Mignon ($32) is amazing, while the Grilled Mexican Sliced Chicken Breast is equally scrumptious. For an appetizer, there's a rolling gua-camole cart. A server prepares the guacamole specifically to your taste, right before your eyes.

 **TRAVEL TIP**

A free monorail service connects Treasure Island with The Mirage. It's just one of the great services offered at this mega-resort.

In addition to the menu items, Isla Mexicana offers a full-service bar, specializing in a handful of specialty drinks such the Mexican Cucumber. When you're ready for dessert, there's a family-style sampler dish ($18) that features a selection of items that'll satisfy everyone's sweet tooth.

Isla Mexicana offers excellent prices, great food, and superior service that's worth experiencing for either lunch or dinner. Reservations are recommended.

The Steak House ($$$)
&866-286-3809

Open daily for dinner only (5:30 P.M. to 11:00 P.M.), the Steak House offers a fine selection of steak and seafood dishes, along with appetizers, soups, salads, side dishes, and desserts. Veal chops, filet mignon, lobster tail, and lamb chops are among the specialties of the house. "Dressy casual attire" is recommended. A full-service bar is also offered, as is an extensive wine selection. Reservations are recommended.

Casual Dining

Since it's probably not within your budget to have every meal at one of Treasure Island's fine-dining restaurants, TI also offers several casual-dining alternatives suitable for the entire family. Reservations are not required for any of these cafés or restaurants.

Dishes: The Treasure Island Buffet ($)

Open daily for breakfast, lunch, and dinner, this all-you-can-eat buffet offers a wide selection of foods. The menu changes throughout the day, and daily specials are always offered. In addition to traditional buffet items, Dishes offers a country bakery, an American BBQ, Asian cuisine, a sushi bar, pastas, and wood-fired pizzas, plus an assortment of other culinary delights from around the world.

Like all buffets at the Las Vegas resorts, this one offers an excellent value. Guests are seated and served on a first-come basis, so be prepared to wait to get in, especially during peak times. This is one of the best buffet deals along the Strip. Recently, Dishes underwent a major redesign and renovation. It reopened in late 2004.

Starbucks Coffee ($)

The coffee you love from the Starbucks in your hometown is available at Treasure Island. Whether you want that morning dose of caffeine to get you moving, or you need to take time to relax during the day or evening, drop by Starbucks Coffee for gourmet coffee, cappuccino, espresso, Frappuccino, and fresh pastries. Open from 6:00 A.M. until 1:00 A.M.

Kahunaville ($$)

Open daily from 8:00 A.M. to 11:00 P.M., this tropical island–theme restaurant serves breakfast, lunch, and dinner, plus serves up live entertainment nightly. During the summer months, poolside dining is available. The menu offers a selection of regional cuisine with Asian, Mediterranean, and tropical influences.

Entrées include chicken, pork, salads, and pasta dishes, plus sandwiches. While this is a restaurant, the bar area is a popular nightspot for the over-twenty-one crowd. Here the bartenders actually perform tricks as they prepare and serve the drinks. For more information, check out the restaurant's Web site at ✐*www.kahunaville.com.*

Terrace Café ($$)

Enjoy the view of TI's pool area as you dine at this casual restaurant that's open twenty-four hours. The menu offers a large selection, allowing you to enjoy breakfast, lunch, dinner, or a snack anytime. The prices are very reasonable.

Canter's Deli ($$)

Open daily, starting at 7:00 A.M. (and remaining open at least until midnight), Canter's Deli is modeled after the world-famous Los Angeles–based deli that offers an incredible array of overstuffed sandwiches, many served on the deli's trademark sourdough rye bread. This deli has been a popular dining spot in Los Angeles since 1931. Now the famous sandwiches are available in Las Vegas.

Ben & Jerry's Ice Cream ($)

In the mood for a cool treat? The many famous flavors of Ben & Jerry's Ice Cream are served here. Some of the company's most popular ice cream flavors include Cherry Garcia, Chunky Monkey, New York Super Fudge Chunk, Phish Food, and just plain vanilla.

Krispy Kreme Doughnuts ($)

A large selection of those famous doughnuts are available here. It's a great place to stop for a quick and cheap breakfast or snack.

Nightclubs, Lounges, and Bars

For the over-twenty-one crowd, TI features a handful of bars, lounges, and nightclubs, each offering an array of specialty drinks and a distinctive and fun "after dark" atmosphere. Tangerine, for example, is one of the hottest nightspots along the Strip. Other bars and lounges include:

Isla Mexican Kitchen and Tequila Bar

Connected to the restaurant is a stand-alone bar, featuring a terrific selection of specialty drinks, including the Mexican Cucumber and, of course, tequila. Open daily from 11:00 A.M. until 2:00 A.M.

Kahunaville

Connected to the restaurant, this tropical hot spot serves a wide selection of alcoholic beverages influenced by the islands. The bartenders here really put on a show as they prepare and serve the drinks. Open daily from 8:00 A.M. until 3:00 A.M.

Mist

Open until 4:00 A.M. nightly, Mist offers a classy bar atmosphere that's ideal for socializing or watching televised sporting events.

Breeze Bar

Premium liquors and mixed drinks are the specialty of this full-service bar.

TRAVEL TIP

Check out the trendy Tangerine nightclub. It's an upscale Las Vegas nightclub that offers an indoor lounge and outdoor deck area, a disc jockey spinning a combination of rock and dance music, plus periodic live musical performances by a brass trio.

Treasure Island's Casino

Continuing the old Caribbean hideaway theme, Treasure Island's casino is decorated in gold and whitewashed tones and features artifacts from around the world. As for gaming, the casino offers over 2,000 slot and video poker machines, along with an assortment of gaming tables (including blackjack, roulette, Caribbean Stud, Pai Gow, Let It Ride, Big Six, craps, mini-baccarat, Spanish 21, and baccarat). There's also a large race and sports book, plus keno.

CHAPTER 17

The Venetian

LOCATED ON THE SITE of the old Sands Hotel (which was imploded on November 26, 1996), the $1.5 billion Venetian Resort complex is one of the most luxurious, prestigious, and state-of-the-art resorts in Las Vegas. Catering to an upscale (and older) clientele, this resort alone contains more hotel rooms (luxury suites) than the entire island of Bermuda. Upon stepping into The Venetian's main lobby for the first time, the experience can only be described as breathtaking, and the experience gets better from there! The architecture and artwork throughout this mega-resort have set new standards in luxury and beauty within Las Vegas.

Mega-Resort Overview

✉3355 Las Vegas Boulevard South, Las Vegas, NV 89109

✆888-283-6423

✆702-414-1000

⌨*www.venetian.com*

Room and Suite Rates: $$$$

According to The Venetian's management, "The resort appeals to world travelers, business professionals, conventioneers, and families—people who enjoy going far beyond the simple 'must see' attractions to experience a 'must see, stay, dine, shop, and enjoy' resort destination."

▲ Take a gondola ride through the Venetian.　　Photo ©The Las Vegas News Bureau.

The Venetian expertly mixes leisure and comfort in grand style—all dedicated to honor the beauty, romance, and spirit of Venice, Italy. Best of all, if you're traveling to Las Vegas from within the United States, no passport is required and everyone speaks English.

To ensure that the entire resort retains its truly Italian flair, two historians are on retainer, constantly making sure the famous landmarks that have been re-created throughout the resort maintain their authenticity. St. Mark's Square, Campanile Tower, Ca'd'Oro, Doge's Palace, the Grand Canal, and the Rialto Bridge are among the re-creations.

Since opening in 1999, The Venetian has undergone some major expansion. In addition to adding one of the most prestigious fine-art galleries in America as one of its main attractions, this mega-resort now houses a new $25 million, custom-designed theater, where the Broadway hit musical *Phantom of the Opera* will be presented nightly, starting in 2006.

Also added to The Venetian is Venezia at The Venetian, a $275 million expansion to the resort facility that houses an additional 1,013 guest rooms and suites in a "hotel within the hotel" environment. The rooms in this new, twelve-story addition feature 700 square feel of living space, 9-foot-high ceilings, a private bedchamber (with draped canopies), and a 130-square-foot bathroom decorated in fine Italian marble.

If you're looking for the ultimate in luxurious accommodations while in Las Vegas, you have three main options—The Venetian, the Bellagio, or the Four Seasons. The Venetian's Italian theme makes this mega-resort truly one-of-a-kind. To realize just how extraordinary it is, while in the main lobby or in many of the public areas, look up and view the stunning hand-painted murals on the ceilings.

THE VENETIAN OVERALL FAMILY-FRIENDLINESS RATING

Ages Up to 5	Ages 6–15	Ages 16–20	Ages 21 & Up	Senior Citizens
☆	☆☆☆	☆☆☆	☆☆☆	☆☆☆

Guest Room Accommodations

The Venetian is the first Las Vegas resort to offer suites exclusively. Guests enjoy a spacious 700 square feet of living space with finely appointed amenities that include a plush private bedchamber (featuring draped canopies), an oversized 130-square-foot bathroom (finished in Italian marble), and a sunken living room area that includes a convertible sofa, two upholstered chairs, a desk, and a game table. Additionally, the standard suites offer an in-room safe, a fully stocked mini-bar, a dedicated fax machine that doubles as a copier and computer printer, three telephones (with dual lines and data-port access), high-speed Internet access, and two 27- or 36-inch televisions with pay-per-view movies and cable programming.

These suites are almost double the size of the most luxurious deluxe rooms and basic guest rooms at other resorts and hotels along the Strip. Yes, you're going to pay more to stay at The Venetian. It's definitely one of the more pricey resorts in Las Vegas, but in this case, the high room rates are worth it.

≡FAST FACT

Among the additional amenities and services offered when you reserve one of the Concierge Suites within Venezia at The Venetian are personalized unpacking services, private elevator access, a duvet instead of a blanket, 100 percent cotton blend triple sheets on the beds, a 15-inch LCD television in the bathroom, fresh flowers, complimentary newspaper, a DVD library, and continental breakfast.

Featured Attractions and Activities

The Venetian offers a handful of activities. While kids and teens will love Madame Tussauds and the gondola rides offered both indoors and outdoors, the resort's resident show, *Phantom of the Opera*, is definitely more suitable for teens and adults, as opposed to kids.

Madame Tussauds

✐www.mtvegas.com

One of London's top visitor attractions has crossed the Atlantic. Madame Tussauds is an interactive wax museum that spans more than 28,000 square feet and features well over 125 masterfully crafted, life-size, and amazingly lifelike wax figures.

Film, television, and sports celebrities, plus Las Vegas icons, are all part of this exhibit, which is suitable for people of all ages. All of the clothing worn by the wax figures belonged to the actual celebrity counterparts, which adds to the incredible lifelike appearance of the figures.

Some of the figures you'll see include: "The Rock," Babe Ruth, Arnold Palmer, Bette Midler, Billy Idol, Cher, Dean Martin, Elvis Presley, Elton John, Frank Sinatra, Madonna, Britney Spears, Prince, Michael Jackson, Sammy Davis, Jr., Tina Turner, Wayne Newton, Brad Pitt, Eddie Murphy, Patrick Stewart, Mel Gibson, Jodie Foster, Whoopie Goldberg, Lucille Ball, Sarah Michelle Gellar, Oprah Winfrey, Larry King, Liberace, Jerry Springer, Princess Diana, Benjamin Franklin, Don King, Sylvester Stallone, Liza Minelli, plus dozens of others.

TRAVEL ESSENTIAL

One of the most recent additions is a salute to the hit television show *American Idol*. Talking wax figures of host Ryan Seacrest and judge Simon Cowell can be seen on a recreation of the popular *American Idol* set.

What makes this museum unique and fun is that visitors are encouraged to touch, photograph, and examine each of the life-size figures closely as they make their way through this attraction at their own pace. Plan on spending between one and three hours here, and don't forget to bring your camera. Kids and teens especially will enjoy posing with their favorite wax-figure celebrities. Madame Tussauds is open from 10:00 A.M. to 10:00 P.M. (closing times vary by season). Tickets are $20.95 for adults, $14.95 for senior citizens and students, and $9.95 for children (ages six to twelve). Special family admission packages are available.

MADAME TUSSAUDS

Ages Up to 5	Ages 6–15	Ages 16–20	Ages 21 & Up	Senior Citizens
☆	☆☆☆	☆☆☆	☆☆☆	☆☆☆

Gondola Rides

Why just walk or dine along the re-created Grand Canal when you can experience an authentic (and extremely romantic) gondola ride? This is a great way for honeymooners or those celebrating an anniversary or engagement to end a lovely evening after enjoying one of the resort's restaurants. It's also a fun midday activity with your kids. As you cruise along the canal, you'll be serenaded in Italian.

Hours of operation are 10:00 A.M. to 11:00 P.M. Same-day reservations are definitely required. Be sure to stop by Emporio D' Gondola to make your reservation, starting at 9:00 A.M. Outdoor gondola rides are not available when the weather is bad.

GONDOLA RIDES

Ages Up to 5	Ages 6–15	Ages 16–20	Ages 21 & Up	Senior Citizens
☆	☆☆☆	☆☆☆	☆☆☆	☆☆☆

Time Traveler: The Ride

☎702-733-0545

Here you'll find four different fast-paced, state-of-the-art motion-simulator rides that are fun and exciting for kids, teens, and adults alike. Each ride, including Time Traveler, Doom Castle, and Red Hot Planet, offers its own story line and totally different visual effects. Tickets are $9 per ride, $12 for two rides, and $18 for four rides.

TIME TRAVELER: THE RIDE

Ages Up to 5	Ages 6–15	Ages 16–20	Ages 21 & Up	Senior Citizens
Not Suitable	☆☆	☆☆	☆☆	☆

Guggenheim Hermitage Museum

☎702-414-2440

✍*www.guggenheimlasvegas.org*

Located near the main entrance of The Venetian is one of the most exclusive art galleries along the Strip. If you appreciate fine art, the likes of which you'd typically only see within one of the world's most prestigious museums or galleries, you'll definitely want to visit the Guggenheim Hermitage Museum. Hours are 9:30 A.M. to 8:30 P.M.

This museum is managed and operated by the Solomon R. Guggenheim Foundation. It was established to be a premier venue for the presentation of exhibitions based on the collections of the Guggenheim and Hermitage museums. All programming is generated by the directors and curatorial staffs of the Guggenheim and Hermitage museums. Exhibits change twice per year. For an additional $4 fee, you can rent an audio guide program that describes each of the paintings in detail as you walk through this stunning, self-paced exhibit hall.

Tickets are $15 for adults, $12 for senior citizens and Nevada residents, $11 for students with ID, $7 for children ages six to twelve. An annual pass is $45. You'll find $2-off-admission coupons distributed throughout the resort.

GUGGENHEIM HERMITAGE MUSEUM

Ages Up to 5	Ages 6–15	Ages 16–20	Ages 21 & Up	Senior Citizens
Not Suitable	Not Suitable	☆☆	☆☆☆	☆☆☆

The Swimming Pools

Within The Venetian Tower is a five-acre pool deck that's been modeled after a Venetian garden. Here, you'll find three swimming pools (with lifeguards on duty), two hot tubs, twenty cabanas (available for rent), a pool concierge desk, a retail shop, a café, poolside cocktail service, and outdoor showers. Lounge chairs and towels are provided. Hours of operation vary by season but tend to be between 8:00 A.M. and 7:00 P.M.

It's Showtime at The Venetian

One of the most popular Broadway shows in history now has a home in Las Vegas.

Phantom of the Opera

✆702-414-1000

✐www.thephantomoftheopera.com

After spending over sixteen years on Broadway, Andrew Lloyd Webber's *The Phantom of the Opera* has found a permanent home in Las Vegas, starting in 2006. This newly created, ninety-minute production is directed by twenty-time Tony Award winner Harold Prince and will be presented nightly within a theater that's been custom-designed at a cost of $25 million.

"This new production of *The Phantom of the Opera* offers audiences a theater of majesty and grandeur unlike any experienced in the world, to showcase the most successful musical ever," stated Rob Goldstein, president of The Venetian.

≡FAST FACT

Not only is the theater amazing, but *The Phantom of the Opera* features stunning sets, costumes, and makeup. For example, the Phantom's makeup takes two hours to put on before every performance. First, the actor's face is moisturized and closely shaved. Next, the prosthetics are fitted, before two wigs, two radio microphones, and two contact lenses are placed.

Phantom of the Opera premiered in London back in 1986 and has played more than 65,000 performances in twenty countries and 110 cities. More than 100 million people have seen this record-breaking and award-winning musical. When it makes its Las Vegas debut in 2006, this production will feature state-of-the-art special effects and an amazingly talented, Broadway-caliber cast. This is a spectacular production that will appeal to more mature theatergoers. For a more family-oriented theater experience, *Mamma Mia!* is presented nightly at Mandalay Bay.

At the time this book was written, showtimes and ticket prices were not available. Contact the resort's concierge or box office for details.

PHANTOM OF THE OPERA

Ages Up to 5	Ages 6–15	Ages 16–20	Ages 21 & Up	Senior Citizens
Not Suitable	Not Suitable	☆☆	☆☆☆	☆☆☆

Shopping

People who love to shop should, after exploring the Forum Shops, definitely make their way to the Grand Canal Shoppes for an experience they won't soon forget. This indoor mall is breathtakingly beautiful, offers a selection of more than eighty elegant shops, and features live performers throughout the day and evening. Call

☎702-414-4500 for further information or visit their Web site at ✍*www. grandcanalshoppes.com.*

 TRAVEL TIP

Within the Grand Canal Shoppes area, you'll find a handful of fine-dining restaurants, a food court (ideal for family dining), and several popular bars and lounges. The Food Court offers the Coffee Bean & Tea Leaf, Häagen-Dazs Ice Cream, Krispy Kreme Doughnuts, Original California Juice Bar, Panda Express, Munari Produce, Shake 'N Burger, Towers Deli, Tintoretto Bakery, and Vico's Burrito.

Serenading gondoliers, Venetian glassblowers, and live performers are on hand to lend added authenticity to your shopping experience. This classy indoor mall combines Venetian cobblestone walkways, arched bridges, and winding canals with a mix of unusual and beautiful shops. Hours of operation are 10:00 A.M. to 11:00 P.M. (midnight on Fridays and Saturdays).

Along with popular mall stores such as Brookstone, Banana Republic, Godiva, and Kenneth Cole, you'll find a large selection of designer label shops and distinctive boutiques.

Highlights include:

- **BCBG Max Azria**: Find contemporary women's fashions at this boutique.
- **Bernard Passman Gallery:** For more information about the artistry of Bernard K. Passman, check out the Passman Web site at ✍*www.passman.com.*
- **Burberry**: Men's and women's designer fashions and accessories are offered here.
- **Ca'd'Oro**: When The Venetian Hotel was first conceived, Ca'd'Oro signed on to become the pre-eminent jewelry store, helping set the tone for other stores at the Grand Canal Shoppes.

- **Canyon Ranch Living Essentials**: A wide variety of beauty products, spa accessories, and sportswear from the famous Canyon Ranch SpaClub are sold here, allowing you to recreate a spa experience in your hotel room or at home.
- **Davidoff**: Davidoff of Geneva has modernized the old-style men's smoking club.
- **Erwin Pearl**: Here you'll find jewelry, including gold, silver, pearls, Austrian crystal, hand enameling, and glass beading.
- **Houdini's Magic Shop**: At this shop, popular items include Houdini memorabilia, magic tricks, gags, pranks, and novelties.
- **Il Prato**: This shop is a wonderful source of collectible masks and fine paper goods.
- **Jimmy Choo**: Malaysian-born Jimmy Choo was Princess Diana's preferred shoemaker, thanks to his handmade satin, strappy sandals. Now his show fashions are available to the general public.
- **Lladro**: Fine porcelain art from the second half of the twentieth century is displayed and sold here.
- **Mikimoto**: The originator of cultured pearls since 1893, Mikimoto specializes in the finest Akoya cultured pearl and South Sea pearl jewelry collections.
- **Regis Galerie**: Art and antique lovers will discover an ambiance of centuries gone by as they explore this gallery, which specializes in nineteenth-century French antiques, period art glass, nineteenth- and twentieth-century bronzes, oil paintings, chandeliers, and other fine objects of art.
- **Tolstoys**: A unique store offering fine-contemporary and vintage writing instruments, quality time pieces, collectibles, and accessories for home and office.

 TRAVEL ESSENTIAL

Throughout the day, the Grand Canal Shoppes feature live performers, jugglers, singers, and living statues who entertain shoppers. There are plenty of photo opportunities, so be sure to bring your camera.

Day Spa, Salon, and Fitness Facilities

Throughout this book, you've read about the many world-class day spas located within the various mega-resorts. Without a doubt, one of the most luxurious full-service day spas is the Canyon Ranch SpaClub (☎877-220-2688; *www.canyonranch.com*), located in the heart of the Grand Canal Shoppes within The Venetian. If you're looking to truly pamper yourself, relax, and rejuvenate your mind and body, this is the place you should visit, whether it's for a standard massage or one of the spa's more exotic treatments.

TRAVEL TIP

In addition to a fully equipped fitness center, the Canyon Ranch SpaClub features a rock-climbing wall, priced at $50 per twenty-five-minute session. Private personal trainers, Pilates instruction, nutrition consultation, and other services are also available for a fee.

This 65,000 square-foot-facility is a full-service spa and fitness club located near the resort's five-acre pool deck. The facility offers more than 120 services, including massage and therapeutic body-work; hydro massage; aloe glaze; herbal wraps; mud, salt, and seaweed treatments; and Watsu.

The Canyon Ranch SpaClub also offers a complete fitness facility with classes, a wellness center staffed by physicians, nutritionists, and educators, a full-service salon, a retail store, and the Canyon Ranch Café (open for breakfast, lunch, and dinner).

The SpaClub is open to anyone over eighteen; however, resort guests receive priority in appointments for spa treatments and services. A $30 daily pass is available to use the facilities. You'll have access to fitness classes, a body composition analysis, plus use of the fitness center, cold dip, steam room, whirlpool, sauna, and locker rooms for the day. Robes, slippers, and complimentary beverages in the spa reception area are provided. Special multiday or multiservice package deals are also available. Personal fitness training, which covers cardiovascular exercise, strengthening, and stretching, is also offered.

The Canyon Ranch SpaClub is one of the more exclusive, luxurious, and pricey day spas in Las Vegas, although the fees are well worth it. Plan on spending $140 for a standard fifty-minute massage. The spa's signature Canyon Stone Massage (eighty minutes) is priced at $245, while the Euphoria treatment (100 minutes) is priced at $300. Another of the spa's signature treatments is the Canyon Ranch Mango Sugar Glo (fifty or 100 minutes), which includes a body scrub, massage, and hydrotherapy treatment in one.

≡FAST FACT

The Canyon Ranch SpaClub is modeled after the world-famous Canyon Ranch Spa located in Lenox, Massachusetts. There are also Canyon Ranch Spas located aboard the *Queen Mary 2* cruise ship and in Tucson, Arizona. Call ☎800-742-9000 for details.

Aside from the spa and fitness center, full salon services are offered. All appointments should be made as far in advance as possible. For salon information, call ☎702-414-3700. Salon hours are 9:00 A.M. to 7:00 P.M. daily. The Canyon Ranch Café (☎702-414-3633/7:00 A.M. to 6:00 P.M. daily) is the ideal place to end your spa experience with a healthy meal or snack. The café offers a full juice bar.

TRAVEL ESSENTIAL

Be sure to arrive for your massage or treatment appointment at least forty-five minutes early to allow ample time to check in, change, and enjoy the spa's facilities. Give yourself time to use the steam room, sauna, or whirlpool before and after your treatment.

Dining Options

As you'd expect from one of the most luxurious resorts in Las Vegas, The Venetian offers a handful of fine-dining as well as more casual, family-oriented options. The food court within the Grand Canal Shoppes, for example, offers quality food at very affordable prices.

Fine Dining

Whether strolling through a re-created sixteenth-century streetscape or dining along the replicated Grand Canal, visitors to The Venetian have a passport to a world of culinary delights. Reservations are recommended for these restaurants.

Postrio ($$/$$$)

✆702-796-1110

This San Francisco bistro was created by world-renowned chef Wolfgang Puck. It offers California cuisine with Asian and Mediterranean influences. Postrio is open daily for lunch and dinner. Open 11:30 A.M. to 11:00 P.M. (midnight on weekends). Steaks, seafood, and pasta dishes are the house specialties. Reservations are recommended.

Taqueria Canonita ($$$)

✆702-414-3773

This Stephan Pyles restaurant specializes in Mexican cuisine. It is open from 11:00 A.M. to 11:00 P.M., Sunday through Thursday, and 11:00 A.M. to midnight on Fridays and Saturdays. Chile rellenos, tacos al carbon, and shrimp quesadillas are among the specialties of the house. Reservations are recommended.

Delmonico Steakhouse ($$$)

✆702-414-3737

Guests of this restaurant will enjoy a classic American steakhouse with Creole influences, inspired by celebrity chef Emeril Lagasse. Open daily for lunch and dinner. Reservations are recommended.

Canaletto ($$/$$$)

✆702-733-0070

From the creators of Il Fornaio comes this fine-dining restaurant that serves authentic Northern Italian cuisine from the Veneto region. Freshly baked breads are an excellent addition to every meal. Open Sunday through Thursday from 11:00 A.M. to midnight, and Fridays and Saturdays from 11:00 A.M. to 1:00 A.M. Reservations are recommended.

Lutèce ($$/$$$)

✆702-414-2220

This upscale restaurant specializes in traditional French cuisine. Open daily for dinner (5:30 P.M. to 10:30 P.M.) and located on the casino level of the resort, Lutèce offers both indoor and outdoor seating. Reservations are recommended.

Pinot Brasserie ($$/$$$)

✆702-414-8888

Modeled after the famed Los Angeles eatery that was conceived by Joachim Splichal, this bistro offers an assortment of delicious Italian and French dishes, plus a large wine selection. Open for lunch and dinner. Reservations are recommended.

Royal Star ($$/$$$)

✆702-414-1888

Master Hong Kong chefs combine ancient traditions with modern creativity to offer California Chinese cuisine at its best. Open daily from 11:00 A.M. to midnight, Royal Star has become famous for its extensive dim sum menu.

Over fifty types of baked, steamed, and dessert dim sum are available, ranging in price from $3 to $8.75 each. This restaurant offers a quiet atmosphere, plenty of tables to accommodate families, plus a large selection of tasty dinner entrées (served 5:00 P.M. to 11:00 P.M.), such as Shan Yu Filet Mignon ($28), Kung Pau Chicken ($18), Hot Braised Shrimp ($23), Royal Peking Duck ($58), and Classic Ginger and Green Onion Lobster (market price). All of the food is expertly prepared to order. Royal Star can be described as "a new generation of traditional Chinese cuisine." Reservations are recommended.

Valentino ($$/$$$)

✆702-414-3000

This contemporary Italian restaurant is modeled after Piero Selvaggio's popular Italian restaurant that's known for its regional dishes. Valentino in Los Angeles has been named one of the best Italian restaurants in America. This second location can be found along "restaurant row" on The Venetian's casino level. Open for dinner only, from 5:30 P.M. to 11:00 P.M. The restaurant's wine cellar features more than 24,000 bottles of fine wines. Reservations are recommended.

Zeffirino ($$/$$$)

✆702-414-3500

Fine Italian cuisine, presented by chef-to-the-stars Paolo "Zeffirino" Belloni, is served for lunch and dinner (11:00 A.M. to 11:00 P.M.). House specialties include seafood with an Italian flair, such as filet of sole Piccola, lobster tail, and grilled fish. Reservations are recommended.

Casual Dining

Whether you are in a hurry, want a quick or affordable meal, or are looking for family-friendly dining options, here's what The Venetian offers.

Grand Lux Café ($)

The Grand Lux Café (from the creators of the Cheesecake Factory) offers relaxed dining, good service, and large portions. With over 150 menu items, the café is open twenty-four hours and is located on the Grand Canal Shoppes' casino level.

La Strada Food Court ($)

Included in this food court area are San Gennaro Grill, Pizzeria Enzo, Santa Lucia Café, Häagen-Dazs, Vico's Burritos, Panda, and Rialto Deli.

Bouchon ($$)
☎702-414-6200

Open for breakfast, lunch, and dinner, this is a classic French bistro and oyster bar. Reservations are optional.

AquaKnox ($$)
☎702-414-3772

Open for dinner only, here you'll find a menu that's chock-full of California-inspired seafood entrées. Reservations are optional.

The Grill at Valentino ($$)
☎702-414-3000

Serving lunch and dinner daily, this is a light Italian restaurant, specializing in gourmet pizzas, pastas, veal, and other traditional dishes. Reservations are optional.

Tsunami Asian Grill ($$)

Midpriced Asian dishes and sushi are among the menu offerings for lunch and dinner. If you're looking for a top-notch Chinese restaurant, however, check out Royal Star.

Noodle Asia ($$)

Dim sum and noodle dishes are served here for lunch and dinner. This restaurant is open until 3:00 A.M., so it's ideal for a late-night snack.

Canyon Ranch Café ($/$$)

For those who like to eat healthfully, this café is located within the Canyon Ranch SpaClub. According to the chef, it's where "good taste and good nutrition are a perfect combination." Open for breakfast, lunch, and dinner, the menu offers a variety of choices from around the world. Many of the dishes utilize fresh fruits and vegetables, plus fresh fish, lean meats, and protein-rich soy and beans. The food served here is free of preservatives and additives. Organic ingredients are used whenever possible. This café is open to everyone, not just guests of the spa.

Tintoretto Bakery ($)

Open from 7:00 A.M. until 1:00 A.M., a wide selection of freshly baked pastries, breads, and other items are available for breakfast or for a quick snack throughout the day. Gourmet coffees, Italian espresso, and cappuccino are also served.

Lounges and Bars

Throughout The Venetian, you'll find a selection of adults-only bars and lounges. All of the fine-dining restaurants also offer full-service bars. For nightclub-style entertainment, be sure to visit the Showroom (C2K) and Venus Lounge, both located within the Grand Canal Shoppes.

V Bar is a hip, upscale lounge that's open from 6:00 P.M. until 4:00 A.M. It offers DJs spinning virtually all night. La Scene Lounge offers live nightly entertainment, featuring high-energy bands.

The Venetian's Casino

Inside the replicated facade of the Doge's Palace is a 120,000-square-foot casino. The 110 table games include craps, blackjack, roulette, Let It Ride, Caribbean Stud poker, Pai Gow poker, mini-baccarat, Pai Gow tile, and a Big Six wheel. A race and sports book, keno lounge, and single-zero roulette are also offered. The casino also offers 2,100 slot machines, including the multiproperty, linked progressive games.

Like all of the popular casinos in Las Vegas, The Venetian offers a slot club that allows guests to earn points by using their membership card when playing the casino's slot machines. Members can earn complimentary meals, show tickets, discounted room rates, and other prizes.

CHAPTER 18

Exploring the Rest Of the Strip

LAS VEGAS IS DOING its best to live up to the advertising slogan "What happens here, stays here." Thus, many of the resorts on or near the Strip offer excellent accommodations and top-notch resort amenities and services, yet cater mainly to business travelers, adult vacationers, honeymooners, senior citizens, and gamblers. While some of these resorts also offer attractions, restaurants, shows, or other amenities that are family-friendly, they're included in this section because they don't have the overall family-friendliness that the mega-resort properties described earlier do.

Aladdin at a Glance

✉3667 Las Vegas Boulevard South, Las Vegas, NV 89109
☎877-333-9474
☎702-785-5555
✐*www.aladdincasino.com*
Room Rate: $$$/$$$$

With 2,567 rooms and suites, the theme of this hotel is 1,001 Arabian Nights. The 100,000-square-foot casino features over 2,093 slot and video poker machines, seventy-two gaming tables, plus a race and sports book. There is a separate gaming area for high-stakes players called the London Club. Twenty-one fine-dining and casual restaurants are located in the main resort area and Desert Passage shopping areas, including Elements Fresh Seafood and Prime Steaks (steaks and seafood), Tremezzo (Italian), Spice Market Buffet (a Las Vegas-style buffet), Zanzibar Café (a twenty-four-hour, casual restaurant), and the Bonsai Sushi and Sashimi Bar. There's also a Starbucks Coffee that's open twenty-four hours.

Shows and Attractions

The primary shows at the Aladdin are *"V" The Ultimate Variety Show*, *Steve Wyrick Mind Blowing Magic*, and *Fashionistas*. When it comes to shopping, Aladdin offers the Desert Passage, an indoor mall featuring 140 retail stores, including many unique shops and boutiques that you don't see in typical malls. A full-service day spa (the Elemis Spa) and health club are also available, as well as an outdoor pool located six stories above the Strip.

 TRAVEL TIP

At the time this book was written, plans were under way to transform the Aladdin into the Planet Hollywood Resort & Casino, which, like the restaurant chain, would have themes based on Hollywood's biggest motion pictures. Whether and when this transformation will actually happen is yet to be determined.

ALADDIN: OVERALL RESORT RATING BASED ON AMENITIES AND RATES

Ages Up to 5	Ages 6–15	Ages 16–20	Ages 21 & Up	Senior Citizens
☆	☆	☆☆	☆☆	☆☆

Bally's at a Glance

✉3645 Las Vegas Boulevard South, Las Vegas, NV 89109

✆800-634-3434

✍*www.ballyslasvegas.com*

Room Rate: $$/$$$/$$$$

Bally's has 2,814 rooms. This is a classic Las Vegas casino/resort. The 67,000-square-foot casino offers all of the slot machines and table games you'd expect from a world-class casino resort that's located in the heart of Las Vegas. Four fine-dining restaurants along with a handful of casual-dining establishments offer vacationers a choice between many types of cuisines at different price points.

Shows and Attractions

The primary show at Bally's is *Jubilee!* For about thirty years, Bally's has been a popular destination for Las Vegas vacationers. While this is a fully equipped resort, it offers amenities that are mostly suited to adults. Bally's is the longtime home to *Donn Arden's Jubilee!*, a classic Las Vegas–style variety show featuring showgirls, million-dollar sets, and a cast of over 100. The show is presented Saturday through Thursday, at 7:30 P.M. and 10:30 P.M. *Jubilee!* is open to people age eighteen and up.

Bally's is also one of the resorts with a Las Vegas Monorail stop.

BALLY'S: OVERALL RESORT RATING BASED ON AMENITIES AND RATES

Ages Up to 5	Ages 6–15	Ages 16–20	Ages 21 & Up	Senior Citizens
☆	☆	☆☆	☆☆	☆☆☆

Barbary Coast at a Glance

✉3595 Las Vegas Boulevard South, Las Vegas, NV 89109

✆888-227-2279

✐*www.barbarycoastcasino.com*

Room Rate: $/$$

A classic Las Vegas resort/casino, Barbary Coast has 200 rooms. The 30,000-square-foot casino offers all of the popular table games, a race and sports book, slot and video poker machines, and keno. Two fine-dining restaurants and one casual restaurant are offered.

Shows and Attractions

There are three bars and a lounge, some offering live musical entertainment. This is a relatively small, classic Las Vegas–style casino offering above-average room accommodations at low prices. This property will primarily appeal to gamblers, conventiongoers, and business travelers.

**BARBARY COAST: OVERALL RESORT RATING
BASED ON AMENITIES AND RATES**

Ages Up to 5	Ages 6–15	Ages 16–20	Ages 21 & Up	Senior Citizens
Not Suitable	Not Suitable	☆☆	☆☆	☆☆

Boardwalk Hotel & Casino at a Glance

✉3750 Las Vegas Boulevard South, Las Vegas, NV 89109

✆800-635-4581

✆702-735-2400

✐*www.boardwalklv.com*

Room Rate: $/$$

This hotel has 653 rooms. The theme is Coney Island midway/carnival. The 33,000-square-foot casino features 650 slots, twenty table games, and a race and sports book. There are two casual restaurants and a deli buffet.

Shows and Attractions

The primary shows are *Spectrum: A Tribute to Motown and R&B* and *Purple Reign* (a tribute to Prince). Now operated by MGM Mirage, the Boardwalk Hotel & Casino is a smaller, no-frills, inexpensive hotel located right on the Strip. Located next door to a Walgreen's pharmacy and the Monte Carlo, it is little more than a typical hotel (as opposed to a resort or mega-resort). The hotel itself offers few amenities other than clean, ordinary rooms, a swimming pool, and a small casino, but it does have the Strip's only 24-hour buffet.

 **TRAVEL TIP**

There are no fine-dining restaurants at the Boardwalk Hotel & Casino. The biggest benefit to this hotel is that it's clean and well-priced, making it perfect for vacationers on a budget.

BOARDWALK: OVERALL RESORT RATING BASED ON AMENITIES AND RATES

Ages Up to 5	Ages 6–15	Ages 16–20	Ages 21 & Up	Senior Citizens
☆	☆	☆	☆	☆

Casino Royale at a Glance

✉3419 Las Vegas Boulevard South, Las Vegas, NV 89109

✆800-854-7666

⟁*www.casinoroyalehotel.com*

Room Rate: $/$$

There are 152 rooms at this hotel. The theme is classic Las Vegas–style hotel and casino. The 30,000-square-foot casino features table games, slot and video poker machines, and a sports book. Dining options include the Outback Steakhouse, Denny's, Subway, and a pizza place.

Shows and Attractions

Offering low room rates, Casino Royale is a small, older hotel that is located in the heart of the Strip. Aside from two fast-food restaurants and a bar, a swimming pool, and the rather small casino, this property offers little in the way of entertainment. If you have your heart set on staying at a hotel or resort on the Strip, and the mega-resorts are booked solid, Casino Royale is a good alternative for gamblers and budget travelers.

CASINO ROYALE: OVERALL RESORT RATING
BASED ON AMENITIES AND RATES

Ages Up to 5	Ages 6–15	Ages 16–20	Ages 21 & Up	Senior Citizens
Not Suitable	Not Suitable	☆☆	☆☆	☆☆

Flamingo at a Glance

✉3555 Las Vegas Boulevard South, Las Vegas, NV 89109

✆800-732-2111

✆702-733-3111

✑*www.flamingolasvegas.com*

Room Rate: $$/$$$

There are 4,000 rooms and suites in this hotel, which offers a tropical setting. The 77,000-square-foot casino offers 2,000 slot machines and more than seventy gaming tables. Flamingo offers four fine-dining restaurants as well as four casual restaurants, including the Paradise Garden all-you-can-eat buffet.

Shows and Attractions

Primary shows at the Flamingo include *Bottoms Up*, *Gladys Knight*, *The Second City*, and *George Wallace*. Operated by Caesars Entertainment, Flamingo is a classic resort and casino that is located right on the Strip. Originally conceived and opened by Bugsy Siegel, the Flamingo has been a landmark in Las Vegas since 1946.

 TRAVEL ESSENTIAL

The Flamingo offers everything a vacationer could want, including a wildlife habitat (featuring more than 300 birds) and a fifteen-acre Caribbean-style water playground. The resort also offers tennis courts, a full-service day spa, and its own Las Vegas Monorail station. While this resort is somewhat family-friendly, its primary customers include adult vacationers, conventiongoers, and gamblers.

FLAMINGO: OVERALL RESORT RATING BASED ON AMENITIES AND RATES

Ages Up to 5	Ages 6–15	Ages 16–20	Ages 21 & Up	Senior Citizens
☆	☆	☆	☆☆	☆☆

The New Frontier at a Glance

✉3120 Las Vegas Boulevard South, Las Vegas, NV 89109

✆800-694-6966

✍*www.frontierlv.com*

Room Rate: $$

Offering a Wild West theme, this hotel has 986 rooms. The 41,000-square-foot casino features all of the popular table games, keno, a race and sports book, slot machines, and video poker. What makes this casino special is that it offers ongoing bingo games. There are three casual-dining restaurants.

Shows and Attractions

Live country music is performed at Gilley's Dancehall and Saloon. At Gilley's, adult guests can eat, drink, enjoy the Wild West motif, and ride a mechanical bull. The New Frontier continues to be a classic casino, catering to a clientele that comes to Las Vegas to gamble—not see shows, shop, or experience theme-park attractions. The guest rooms are approximately 400 square feet and are equipped with a nice selection of amenities to insure a comfortable stay at a low price. It also has a swimming pool.

The Frontier was the second casino/gambling hall to open on the Strip, back in 1942. Since then, little has been done to keep up with the times, although the resort has been renovated three times over the years.

THE NEW FRONTIER: OVERALL RESORT RATING BASED ON AMENITIES AND RATES

Ages Up to 5	Ages 6–15	Ages 16–20	Ages 21 & Up	Senior Citizens
Not Suitable	☆	☆	☆☆	☆☆

Golden Nugget at a Glance

✉129 East Fremont Street, Las Vegas, NV 89101

✆800-846-5336

✆702-385-7111

✐*www.goldennugget.com*

Room Rate: $$/$$$

There are 1,907 guest rooms and suites in this classic Las Vegas–style resort and casino. The 36,000-square-foot casino offers all of the popular slot machines, table games, a poker room, and a race and sports book. In July 2004, a newly remodeled high-limit gaming area was opened.

In addition to three fine-dining restaurants, Golden Nugget offers a selection of fast-food and casual-dining options, including a Starbucks and an all-you-can-eat buffet.

Shows and Attractions

The primary show is *Spirit of the Dance*. Well-known headline acts, such as Bruce Willis, Tony Bennett, and Kenny Loggins, appear at the Golden Nugget. Contact the concierge for dates and times of headline shows.

A swimming pool, full-service day spa, and salon are offered. Golden Nugget is located near the downtown area, where the Fremont Street Experience is presented nightly. The Golden Nugget was where the recent Fox Television series *Casino* took place.

GOLDEN NUGGET: OVERALL RESORT RATING
BASED ON AMENITIES AND RATES

Ages Up to 5	Ages 6–15	Ages 16–20	Ages 21 & Up	Senior Citizens
☆	☆	☆☆	☆☆	☆☆

Harrah's at a Glance

✉3475 Las Vegas Boulevard South, Las Vegas, NV 89109

✆800-392-9002

✆702-369-5000

✐*www.harrahs.com*

Room Rate: $$/$$$

This classic Las Vegas–style resort and casino offers 2,579 guest rooms and suites. The 80,000-square-foot casino features eighty gaming tables, 1,200 slot machines (where you can risk between one cent and $500 per play), keno, and a race and sports book.

With seven fine-dining and casual restaurants to choose from, vacationers can enjoy everything from steak and seafood to an all-you-can-eat buffet.

Show and Attractions

Primary shows include *Mac King Comedy Magic Show*, *Skintight*, *Clint Homes*, and *The Improv at Harrah's*.

TRAVEL TIP

Harrah's has its own Las Vegas Monorail stop, a full-service day spa, salon, and swimming pool.

Harrah's is located across from The Mirage and Caesars Palace on the Strip. This is a great place to stay for adult vacationers looking for a classic Las Vegas–style vacation. It doesn't, however, offer too much for kids or teens.

HARRAH'S: OVERALL RESORT RATING BASED ON AMENITIES AND RATES

Ages Up to 5	Ages 6–15	Ages 16–20	Ages 21 & Up	Senior Citizens
☆	☆☆	☆☆	☆☆☆	☆☆☆

Las Vegas Hilton at a Glance

✉3000 Paradise Road, Las Vegas, NV 89109

☎800-732-7117

☎702-732-5111

✍*www.lvhilton.com*

Room Rate: $$$/$$$$

This hotel has 3,000 guest rooms and suites. It is a traditional, rather large Hilton resort that caters mainly to business travelers and conventiongoers. Craps, roulette, blackjack, and virtually every other table game you could want is available within the Hilton's casino. You'll also find more than 1,000 slots and video poker machines in this fully equipped and nicely designed casino.

Six fine-dining restaurants, including a Benihana Japanese Steakhouse (where they cook at your table), as well as several casual-dining options and a buffet are offered. Quark's is a *Star Trek*–theme restaurant and bar that serves up a fun and memorable meal in a recreation of the *Star Trek Deep Space Nine* space station. Kids and teens (along with fans of *Star Trek*) will love this dining experience for lunch or dinner.

▲The Las Vegas Hilton.   Photo ©The Las Vegas News Bureau.

Shows and Attractions

The primary show is *The Dream King*. The Las Vegas Hilton is the home to the popular *Star Trek Experience* (*www.startrekexp. com*), where fans of the *Star Trek* television shows and movies can become part of the adventure. This attraction is exciting, features state-of-the-art technology, and is suitable for anyone over age ten. For young people, there's also a video game arcade. The Las Vegas Monorail has a stop at this resort. Tennis courts, a swimming pool, a full-service day spa, and a salon are also offered here.

**LAS VEGAS HILTON: OVERALL RESORT RATING
BASED ON AMENITIES AND RATES**

Ages Up to 5	Ages 6–15	Ages 16–20	Ages 21 & Up	Senior Citizens
☆	☆☆	☆☆	☆☆☆	☆☆☆

Imperial Palace at a Glance

✉3535 Las Vegas Boulevard South, Las Vegas, NV 89109

☎800-634-3424

☎702-794-3261

www.imperialpalace.com

Room Rate: $$/$$$

This hotel has 2,600 guest rooms and suites. The theme is a taste of the Orient and Hawaii. The 75,000-square-foot casino offers more than 1,500 of the most popular table games and slot machines you'll find in Las Vegas. There's also a poker room, keno lounge, and race and sports book.

Three fine-dining restaurants, including Ming Terrace (Chinese) and Rib House (steaks and prime rib), provide for a wonderful dining experience. For lighter fare, there are three casual restaurants and two Las Vegas-style buffets.

▲The Imperial Palace Resort.   Photo provided by PR Newswire Photo Service.

Shows and Attractions

Primary shows include *Imperial Hawaiian Luau!* and *Legends in Concert*. Imperial Palace has a Las Vegas Monorail stop, along with its own day spa, salon, and swimming pool. The most popular attraction here is the auto collection, featuring more than 350 classic cars on display, many of them available for sale. Open daily from 9:30 A.M. to 9:30 P.M., This is an attraction that kids, teens, and adults who enjoy exotic and classic cars will appreciate. For details, point your Web browser to ✎*www.autocollections.com*.

 TRAVEL ESSENTIAL

Another popular, family-oriented activity is the nightly Imperial Hawaiian Luau, which offers an exciting and memorable dinner show. For the over-twenty-one crowd, the Imperial Palace Karaoke Club offers ongoing singing competitions, a fully stocked bar, and plenty of lighthearted entertainment.

**IMPERIAL PALACE: OVERALL RESORT RATING
BASED ON AMENITIES AND RATES**

Ages Up to 5	Ages 6–15	Ages 16–20	Ages 21 & Up	Senior Citizens
☆	☆	☆	☆☆	☆☆

Monte Carlo at a Glance

✉3770 Las Vegas Boulevard South, Las Vegas, NV 89109

✆800-311-8999

✆702-730-7777

✑*www.monte-carlo.com*

Room Rate: $$/$$$

There are 3,002 guest rooms and suites in this Mediterranean-theme hotel. The casino offers 2,100 slot machines and a wide range of table games. Several fine-dining restaurants, a popular all-you-can-eat buffet, a café that's open twenty-four hours, and several other casual-dining options are available.

Shows and Attractions

Located across from the MGM Grand and next to New York–New York, Monte Carlo is home to Lance Burton, Master Magician (✑*www.lanceburton.com*), who offers an excellent, family-oriented magic show, complete with incredible illusions. With the exception of this show, Monte Carlo is primarily a traditional casino/resort that caters to adult vacationers, conventiongoers, and business travelers. A swimming pool, tennis court, video game arcade, day spa, salon, and fitness center are among this resort's other offerings.

**MONTE CARLO: OVERALL RESORT RATING
BASED ON AMENITIES AND RATES**

Ages Up to 5	Ages 6–15	Ages 16–20	Ages 21 & Up	Senior Citizens
☆	☆	☆	☆☆	☆☆

Palms Casino Resort at a Glance

✉4321 West Flamingo Road, Las Vegas, NV 89109

✆866-725-6773

✆702-942-7777

✍*www.palms.com*

Room Rate: $$$/$$$$

There are 455 guest rooms and suites in this modern, trendy Las Vegas resort. The 95,000-square-foot casino features 1,800 slot machines, plenty of table games, a poker room, a keno lounge, and two high-limit gaming areas.

Eight restaurants and several casual and fast-food dining options offer a wide range of meal selections. The restaurants offer entrées with American, Asian, Italian, and Mexican influences.

Shows and Attractions

The Palms is definitely one of the hippest, trendiest, and most exciting places to be seen in Las Vegas. This resort attracts the over-twenty-one party crowd and offers several well-known and very popular nightclubs, bars, and lounges, including Rain (nightclub) and the Ghost Bar.

🧳 TRAVEL TIP

While the Palms doesn't offer too much in the way of kid-oriented attractions, there is a Kids Quest child care center here, so parents can drop off their kids while they party at any of the nightclubs. The fee is $5.75 or $6.75 per hour, per child. Kid Quest is open to guests and non-guests of the Palms. Contact the resort's concierge for details (✆702-942-7777).

This was the resort featured on MTV's *The Real World* in 2002. It's located a short drive away from the main Strip. In addition to standard guest rooms and suites, the Palms offers several theme suites, including NBA Suites (designed for very tall guests) and *The Real World* suites.

While there is no resident show here, the Palms hosts a wide variety of big-name headline acts, including popular recording artists, who appear almost nightly. For the over-twenty-one crowd, this is definitely a fun and exciting place to stay.

PALMS: OVERALL RESORT RATING BASED ON AMENITIES AND RATES

Ages Up to 5	Ages 6–15	Ages 16–20	Ages 21 & Up	Senior Citizens
☆	☆	☆	☆☆☆	☆☆

Paris Las Vegas at a Glance

⊠3655 Las Vegas Boulevard South, Las Vegas, NV 89109

☎877-796-2096

*www.paris-lasvegas.com*

Room Rate: $$$/$$$$

There are 2,916 guest rooms and suites in this hotel, whose theme is Paris, France. With ninety table games, ranging from blackjack to Three Card Poker, plus plenty of slots, keno, and a race and sports book, Paris offers gamblers plenty of excitement.

Four fine-dining restaurants, seven casual restaurants, and a handful of lounges and bars are yours to choose from. The flagship restaurant here is the Eiffel Tower Restaurant (a fine-dining restaurant that's open for dinner and that offers a spectacular view of the Strip). You can drink and party until 4:00 A.M. at Risqué.

🧳 TRAVEL TIP

If you want a breathtaking view of the Bellagio's Fountain Show (which takes place across the street from the Paris), plan your visit to the top of the Eiffel Tower accordingly and don't forget your camera.

▶ Paris—a taste of France.

Photo PP© Ferras AlQaisi.

Shows and Attractions

The main show at Paris is *We Will Rock You* (the musical by Queen and Ben Elton). The most popular attraction is the replica of the Eiffel Tower, which is a signature of the skyline. This half-scale replica offers an awesome view from its observation area (open 10:00 A.M. to 1:00 A.M.), located 460 feet above the ground. Tickets are priced at $9 or $12 per adult and $7 or $10 for children (prices vary depending on the day). The *We Will Rock You* musical is also family-friendly.

**PARIS LAS VEGAS: OVERALL RESORT RATING
BASED ON AMENITIES AND RATES**

Ages Up to 5	Ages 6–15	Ages 16–20	Ages 21 & Up	Senior Citizens
☆	☆	☆	☆☆☆	☆☆☆

Rio All-Suite Hotel & Casino at a Glance

✉3700 West Flamingo Road, Las Vegas, NV 89109

✆800-752-9746

✆702-777-7777

✎*www.playrio.com*

Room Rate: $$/$$$

Get a taste of Rio at this fun but adult-oriented resort, which offers 2,500 suites. The 100,000-square-foot casino contains 1,200 slot machines, over eighty table games, keno, and a race and sports book.

▲The Rio.   Photo ©The Las Vegas News Bureau.

From the All-American Bar & Grill to the Carnival World Buffet, Rio offers a nice selection of fine-dining restaurants, casual restaurants, bars, lounges, and nightclubs.

Shows and Attractions

Primary shows at this resort include *Chippendales, the Show*; *Penn & Teller*; *Tony 'n' Tina's Wedding*; *The Scintas*; and *Ronn Lucas*.

This "all-suites" resort offers relatively large, 600-square-foot accommodations that are nicely equipped with amenities. Located a short distance from the Strip, this resort, like the Palms, also caters mainly to the over-twenty-one party crowd.

When it comes to entertainment, Rio offers several family-friendly shows. The Ronn Lucas show, for example, is presented every afternoon and features a talented ventriloquist and his puppets. *Penn & Teller* offers a unique brand of comedy and magic that is entertaining and totally suitable for anyone over age sixteen.

For free entertainment, Rio offers the popular *Show in the Sky Parade*, which features colorful floats and performers flying overhead (presented daily at 3:00 P.M., 4:00 P.M., 5:00 P.M., 6:30 P.M., 7:30 P.M., 8:30 P.M., and 9:30 P.M. in the Masquerade Village area).

 TRAVEL TIP

For the over-twenty-one crowd, the Voodoo Lounge, Club Rio, and BiKiNis are nighttime hotspots. Women looking for a fun night out should be sure to check out *Chippendales*.

RIO: OVERALL RESORT RATING BASED ON AMENITIES AND RATES

Ages Up to 5	Ages 6–15	Ages 16–20	Ages 21 & Up	Senior Citizens
☆	☆	☆☆	☆☆☆	☆☆

Riviera at a Glance

✉2901 Las Vegas Boulevard South, Las Vegas, NV 89109
✆800-634-6753
✆702-794-9433
✍*www.rivierahotel.com*
Room Rate: $$/$$$

This Mediterranean-theme resort has 2,075 guest rooms and suites (all recently refurbished). The 100,000-square-foot casino offers all forms of classic Las Vegas–style gaming, from slots to table games.

Steak, Italian food, and a buffet are among the dining options offered here. There's also a popular food court for fast and cheap dining.

Shows and Attractions

Primary shows offered here include *An Evening at La Cage*, *Crazy Girls Las Vegas*, *Splash*, and *The Amazing Jonathan*.

This popular and traditional resort/casino offers a swimming pool, fitness center, day spa, salon, and tennis courts, along with a nice selection of classic Las Vegas-style shows that aren't necessarily suitable for kids or even teens. Riviera does, however, offer adults a wonderful vacation opportunity, especially if you're visiting Las Vegas to gamble. Riviera celebrated its golden anniversary in 2005.

≡FAST FACT

This resort is perhaps best known as the home of *Splash*, a high-energy, topless dance show with state-of-the-art special effects, showgirls in glamorous costumes, ice skaters, motorcycle daredevils, and some of the most entertaining specialty acts on the Strip. Although it's evolved over the years, *Splash* has been a staple in Las Vegas since 1985, when it made its debut. It's suitable for people ages eighteen and up only.

RIVIERA: OVERALL RESORT RATING BASED ON AMENITIES AND RATES

Ages Up to 5	Ages 6–15	Ages 16–20	Ages 21 & Up	Senior Citizens
☆	☆	☆	☆☆☆	☆☆

Sahara Hotel and Casino at a Glance

✉2535 Las Vegas Boulevard South, Las Vegas, NV 89109

✆888-696-2121

✆702-737-2111

✎*www.saharavegas.com*

Room Rate: $/$$/$$$

There are 1,720 guest rooms and suites available in this resort. The theme is a Moroccan desert theme. The 80,000-square-foot casino is nicely equipped with all of the classic Las Vegas gaming action you could want, including table games and slots.

The Sahara Buffet is one of the most popular all-you-can-eat destinations on the Strip. The resort also offers several fine-dining options, plus the NASCAR Café theme restaurant, which is a popular spot for kids, teens, and adult racing fans alike.

Shows and Attractions

The primary show at this resort is *Saturday Night Fever*. The Sahara is another of Las Vegas's historic casinos and resorts. It's been open since 1952 and offers a truly classic Las Vegas–style vacation for adults looking to gamble. A swimming pool, day spa, and salon are some of what's offered here. For family-oriented activities and attractions, Sahara features the popular Cyber Speedway.

═FAST FACT

The Cyber Speedway cars are 7/8 the actual size of authentic stock cars. They're designed to offer the most realistic simulated race car driving experience possible. Each car is equipped with ten driver-adjustable performance parameters to add realism to the virtual driving experience.

Using motion simulation and movie technology, the experience is fun, fast-paced, and truly realistic. During the experience, a 20-foot wraparound screen projects an authentic visual replica of the Las

Vegas Motor Speedway or a course that leads directly down the Las Vegas Strip. You can end your racing experience with a meal at the NASCAR Café. For kids and teens, there's also a video game arcade, featuring more than 120 games.

The resort's resident show, *Saturday Night Fever*, offers plenty of dancing and singing. It's based on the blockbuster film of 1977. The show offers better-than-average family-oriented entertainment.

SAHARA HOTEL & CASINO: OVERALL RESORT RATING BASED ON AMENITIES AND RATES

Ages Up to 5	Ages 6–15	Ages 16–20	Ages 21 & Up	Senior Citizens
☆	☆	☆	☆☆	☆☆

Stardust at a Glance

✉3000 Las Vegas Boulevard South, Las Vegas, NV 89109

✆800-634-6757

✆702-732-6111

✐*www.stardustlv.com*

Room Rate: $$/$$$

There are 1,500 guest rooms and suites in this classic Las Vegas–style casino and resort. The casino is 80,000 square feet and features 1,950 slot and video poker machines, gaming tables, a race and sports book, and a keno lounge. Five restaurants offer a variety of dining options.

Shows and Attractions

Wayne Newton is the main show at this resort. He performs exclusively here forty weeks a year in a 920-seat theater.

Amenities include two swimming pools, a fitness center, and shopping area. Built in the late 1950s, the Stardust is one of the oldest and most recognizable resorts and casinos on the Strip. With its neon exterior, it's hard to miss this rather large complex, especially at night. While the property has undergone renovations over the years, it continues to maintain itself as a classic Las Vegas–style casino that caters primarily to adults looking to gamble.

In recent years, Stardust has added four new restaurants and a shopping mall, along with a day spa and fitness center.

STARDUST: OVERALL RESORT RATING
BASED ON AMENITIES AND RATES

Ages Up to 5	Ages 6–15	Ages 16–20	Ages 21 & Up	Senior Citizens
☆	☆	☆	☆☆	☆☆

Stratosphere Las Vegas at a Glance

✉2000 Las Vegas Boulevard South, Las Vegas, NV 89109

✆800-998-6937

✆702-380-7777

✐*www.stratospherehotel.com*

Room Rate: $$/$$$

There are 2,444 guest rooms and suites in this classic Las Vegas–style resort and casino housed partially within a tower at the edge of the Strip. The 80,000-square-foot casino features fifty table games and 1,500 slot and video poker machines. There's also a race and sports book.

At the Top of the World fine-dining restaurant, you can enjoy a meal while seated 833 feet above the Las Vegas Strip. Located at the top of the Stratosphere Tower, this restaurant offers an incredible view. You'll also find several other fine-dining and casual restaurants within this uniquely shaped resort.

 TRAVEL ESSENTIAL

You can purchase an all-day, unlimited ride ticket for the three thrill rides at Stratosphere for $24.95 per person. Single-ride tickets are priced between $4 and $8. Admission to the observation deck is $9 per person. (Kids and senior citizens receive a $3 discount.)

▲The Stratospere observation deck has amazing views.   Photo ©Ferras AlQaisi.

Shows and Attractions

The primary shows at this resort are *American Superstars*, *Bite*, and *Viva Las Vegas*. *American Superstars* offers family-oriented entertainment. It's an all-out Las Vegas–style dance and variety show featuring a handful of talented celebrity impersonators. *Viva Las Vegas* and *Bite* offer more adult-oriented entertainment for the over-eighteen crowd.

A swimming pool, fitness center, salon, and day spa are some of the amenities offered. In terms of family-oriented attractions, the very top of the Stratosphere Tower is where you'll find several exciting thrill rides. Highroller is a roller coaster that circles around the top of the Stratosphere Tower at thirty-two miles per hour. Big Shot takes riders upward, an additional 921 feet above the top of the tower, then offers a free-fall (fast-drop) experience, complete with the feeling of negative Gs. The X-Scream ride is shaped like a teeter-totter and propels riders over the edge of the Stratosphere Tower.

≡FAST FACT

The Stratosphere Tower, which measures 1,149 feet, is the tallest free-standing observation tower in the United States. It's also the tallest building west of the Mississippi River.

STRATOSPHERE: OVERALL RESORT RATING
BASED ON AMENITIES AND RATES

Ages Up to 5	Ages 6–15	Ages 16–20	Ages 21 & Up	Senior Citizens
☆	☆	☆☆	☆☆	☆☆

Tropicana at a Glance

✉3801 Las Vegas Boulevard South, Las Vegas, NV 89109

✆800-634-4000

✆702-739-2222

✐*www.tropicanalv.com*

Room Rate: $$/$$$

This classic Las Vegas–style resort and casino has 1,878 guest rooms and suites. The 61,000-square-foot casino offers a wide assortment of gaming tables, slots, video poker, race and sports book, and keno. At the swimming pool, Tropicana also offers "swim-up" black-jack tables.

Pietro's and Savanna are among this resort's fine-dining restaurants. There's also a Mizuno's Japanese Steak House and the Tuscany Italian Café. Calypsos is a twenty-four-hour restaurant that offers an extensive menu. Like similar buffets at other resorts, Tropicana's Island Buffet is extremely popular.

Shows and Attractions

The primary shows offered at this resort include *Folies Bergere*, *The Magic of Rick Thomas*, *The Tropicana Bird Show*, *AirPlay*, and *The Comedy Stop*.

Folies Bergere is a classic Las Vegas–style variety show that's complete with showgirls. The early show is family-oriented, while the later show(s) are topless and for audiences over the age of eighteen.

For families, many of Tropicana's other shows, including *The Magic of Rick Thomas*, *AirPlay* (a free show at 11:00 A.M., 1:00 P.M., 3:00 P.M., 5:00 P.M., 7:00 P.M., and 9:00 P.M.), and *The Tropicana Bird Show* (a free show at 11:30 A.M., 1:30 P.M., and 2:30 P.M.), are ideal. There's also a video game arcade for kids and teens.

Tropicana offers a lovely swimming pool area, day spa, and salon. As for attractions, the resort houses the largest collection of casino memorabilia in the world. The Casino Legends Hall of Fame is open from 9:00 A.M. to 9:00 P.M. daily (admission is $6.95 per person).

 TRAVEL TIP

Tropicana is located across from the Excalibur and the MGM Grand. There are walkways connecting these mega-resorts. Even if you're not staying at Tropicana, the free shows are worth dropping in to see.

TROPICANA: OVERALL RESORT RATING BASED ON AMENITIES AND RATES

Ages Up to 5	Ages 6–15	Ages 16–20	Ages 21 & Up	Senior Citizens
☆	☆	☆	☆☆	☆☆

Wynn Las Vegas at a Glance

✉3131 Las Vegas Boulevard South, Las Vegas, NV 89109

✆877-770-7077

✆702-770-7800

✐*www.wynnlasvegas.com*

Room Rate: $$$/$$$$

This resort will have its grand opening in spring 2005. There are 2,700 guest rooms and suites in this resort, which offers pure elegance and luxury at its best. Wynn offers a world-class casino, featuring gaming tables, slots, and a high-limit gaming area. There are eighteen restaurants, along with an array of nightclubs and lounges.

▲Wynn, a new mega-resort, opened in Spring 2005.   Photo ©Ferras AlQaisi.

Shows and Attractions

The primary show featured at the Wynn will be the 2004 Tony Award–winning Broadway show *Avenue Q*. In addition, there will be a new show by Franco Dragone (the person behind *Celine Dion: A New Day . . .*).

In April 2005, the Strip became a bit more crowded when the Wynn Las Vegas opened to the public (more than five years after it was conceived). Stephen Wynn, the creator of this mega-resort, is also responsible for The Mirage, Treasure Island, and the Bellagio.

This 217-acre resort boasts several elegant swimming pools and its own eighteen-hole golf course (designed by Tom Fazio and Steve Wynn). In addition to everything this resort offers, it's conveniently located across the street from the Fashion Show Mall, one of the greatest shopping experiences Las Vegas has to offer.

▲The Fashion Show Mall.   Photo ©The Las Vegas News Bureau.

Wynn Las Vegas is one of the Strip's more upscale resort properties, giving places such as the Bellagio, The Venetian, and the Four Seasons a run for their money in terms of luxury and world-class accommodations. The basic guest rooms offer a comfortable 630 square feet of living space. On the beds, guests are treated to fine European linens, and flat-screen television sets can be found in the living rooms and bathrooms of each suite.

When you're ready to shop, within Wynn you'll find a handful of designer boutiques from Chanel, Louis Vuitton, Dior, Cartier, Jean-Paul Gaultier, Oscar de la Renta, Graff, Brioni, Maserati, and Ferrari. When you're ready to relax, be sure to visit the world-class day spa and salon. Artwork on display throughout the resort come from Steve and Elaine Wynn's personal collection.

Upon entering the resort's main fifty-story tower, it's easy to see why this mega-resort was among the most costly to build, with a price tag of almost $2 billion. Wynn is the ideal vacation destination for couples, families, business travelers, conventiongoers, gamblers, and anyone with the travel budget to afford top-notch accommodations. Not to be outdone by The Mirage or the Bellagio, the free outdoor fountain show at Wynn is sure to become a Las Vegas favorite.

WYNN: OVERALL RESORT RATING BASED ON AMENITIES AND RATES

Ages Up to 5	Ages 6–15	Ages 16–20	Ages 21 & Up	Senior Citizens
☆☆	☆☆	☆☆☆	☆☆☆	☆☆☆

The Evolution of Las Vegas Continues

In the ever-changing evolution of Las Vegas and the Strip, the landmark Hotel San Remo is slated to be transformed into the Hooters Hotel & Casino in late 2005. For information about this new adult-oriented resort, call ✆866-LV-HOOTS.

According to Hooters Management Corporation, "The 711-room hotel and casino resort will remain open as it evolves into an oasis of carefree fun and entertainment for which the famous Hooters brand is so well known. While guests can expect to see Hooters Girls throughout the Hooters Hotel & Casino, alternatives in dining and entertainment will also be featured.

"In addition to a Hooters Restaurant adjacent to the casino floor, a Dan Marino's Fine Food and Spirits Restaurant and its extremely popular Martini Bar will be added, along with the sports fan favorite, Pete & Shorty's Tavern, Book and Bar. A lighter fare health club, sushi bar, and the Hooters Beach Club will be included, to inject Hooters energy and style into the dramatic new tropical pool area."

CHAPTER 19

Indoor Family-Oriented Activities

THE VARIOUS MEGA-RESORTS ARE entertainment complexes unto themselves, designed to offer you unlimited entertainment, twenty-four hours per day. However, on and near the Strip, there are also plenty of family-oriented activities that are totally independent from the mega-resorts, yet are fun and definitely worth checking out. This chapter offers information about the many *indoor* activities families can enjoy, no matter what the weather forecast.

Rain or Shine, There's Plenty to Do!

The weather in Las Vegas is almost always clear, warm, and sunny. After all, it's located in the middle of the desert. In the summers, however, it can get pretty hot during the day, and it does rain occasionally throughout the year. If the weather isn't ideal for outdoor activities, or you'd like to stay inside where it's air-conditioned, there's plenty for the entire family to see and experience indoors throughout the Las Vegas area.

Here's a quick summary of top picks for the best family-oriented activities you'll find *within* the mega-resorts. Details about each of these indoor activities and attractions can be found within Chapters 6 through 18:

Adventuredome, at Circus, Circus

It's America's largest indoor theme park. Kids of all ages will enjoy the excitement that the Adventuredome offers.

AirPlay, at Tropicana

Enjoy the six free acrobatic and high-flying trapeze shows presented each day. This family-friendly atmosphere is a great place to enjoy a breathtaking show.

Auto Collections at the Imperial Palace, at Imperial Palace

Daily from 9:30 A.M. to 9:30 P.M., see a display of more than 350 classic and famous cars, many of which are actually for sale. This is a great place to spend an hour or two if you're a classic car buff.

Bellagio Conservatory & Botanical Garden, at the Bellagio

See an indoor display of nature, landscaping, and waterfalls. It's an indoor park that's absolutely beautiful to stroll through. Enjoy a free, self-paced tour. Open twenty-four hours. This garden was created and is maintained by a team of 100 horticulturists. It's the perfect place to snap a photo, propose marriage, or enjoy a romantic walk. If you're hungry, drop into Aqua for a patio lunch that overlooks the garden.

CBS Television City Research Center, at MGM Grand

You can get a chance to weigh in on the network's decision making and determine what shows should make it on TV and which should get the axe. You watch a screening of a television show and then fill out a survey with your opinions. Open daily between 10:00 A.M. and 10:00 P.M. Suitable for TV viewers over the age of ten. This is a free activity that offers a behind-the-scenes glimpse of TV shows still in development.

Circus Acts, at Circus, Circus

Throughout the entire day and evening (11:00 A.M. to midnight), enjoy free ongoing circus acts presented under the indoor big top. Also see jugglers up close and interact with the clowns.

The Eiffel Tower Experience, at Paris Las Vegas

Take a trip up fifty stories to the top of the Eiffel Tower replica, the landmark that helps the Paris Las Vegas mega-resort stand out along the Strip. Open 10:00 A.M. to 1:00 A.M. daily (weather permitting). Admission is $9 to $12 per adult (depending on the time and day) and $7 to $10 per child. This attraction offers an incredible view of the Las Vegas Strip and the Fountains at Bellagio show. An equally amazing view of the Strip can be found at the top of the Stratosphere Tower.

Fantasy Faire Midway, at Excalibur

Enjoy amusement park–style games and kiosks selling unusual souvenirs. There's also free kid-oriented entertainment throughout the day. Featured here are Merlin's Magic Motion Machines (several motion-simulator rides).

IMAX Experience, at the Palms

This is the latest mega-resort to offer a larger-than-life IMAX movie experience with several movies rotating throughout the day. The Brenden Theaters Las Vegas 14 is also a state-of-the-art traditional movie theater. It features 3,500 luxury rocker high-back seats with lift-up armrests and cup holders; tiered stadium seating; THX digital sound; and wall-to-wall curved screens. For movie listings and show-times, point your Web browser to *www.brendentheatres.com*.

IMAX Theater, at Luxor

Several different IMAX movies are shown daily on a seven-story screen, accompanied by 30,000 watts of sound distributed across six sets of speakers throughout the theater. Recent movies included *NASCAR 3D*, *Adrenaline Rush*, *Haunted Castle Maximum 3D*, and *Ocean Wonderland*.

In Search of the Obelisk, at Luxor

Enjoy a motion-simulator ride that takes you deep into ancient Egyptian pyramids. It's jam-packed with special effects. Open daily.

Madame Tussauds Wax Museum, at The Venetian

This world-famous museum features life-size and extremely lifelike wax replicas of many different celebrities from TV, movies, sports, and music. Plan on spending between one and three hours here, and make sure you bring a camera. One recently added exhibit salutes the hit television show *American Idol* and features talking and animated wax figures of Simon Cowell and Ryan Seacrest.

MGM Grand Lion Habitat, at MGM Grand

Get up close and personal with real-life lions in this free indoor zoolike exhibit. It's open daily from 11:00 A.M. to 10:00 P.M. The best time to catch this is during the posted feeding times.

Shark Reef, at Mandalay Bay

An indoor tank containing 2 million gallons of water (reaching depths up to 22 feet) houses 2,000 different species of aquatic life, including sharks, exotic fish, sea turtles, and many other sea creatures. This is an extremely impressive attraction that shouldn't be missed. Open 10:00 A.M. to 11:00 P.M. daily. Admission: $11.95 (adults) and $9.95 (children).

Star Trek: The Experience, at the Las Vegas Hilton

Experience four *Star Trek* attractions in one. First, there's the world's largest *Star Trek* museum, featuring costumes and props from the various *Star Trek* TV series and movies. Next, you can experience two different, state-of-the-art rides/attractions—*Borg Invasion 4D* and *Klingon Encounter*—that literally put you into an exciting *Star Trek* adventure where you'll come face-to-face with the

Borg or the Klingons. Both are immersive attractions that combine 3-D film, live actors, and special effects. Klingon Encounter also offers motion simulation technology.

≡ FAST FACT

Star Trek: The Experience features costumes and props from the various *Star Trek* TV series and movies. Fans of the show will love looking at the real thing.

Finally, enjoy lunch, dinner, or a snack at Quark's, a theme dining experience that re-creates the Deep Space 9 space station. It's a must-see attraction for all ages; however, young children might find portions a bit scary.

Admission is $29.99 (adults) and $26.99 (children). Hours of operation are 11:00 A.M. to 11:00 P.M. Get to this attraction easily using the Las Vegas Monorail. Get off at the Las Vegas Hilton stop. You'll exit the monorail right in front of the attraction's main entrance.

The Secret Garden, at Mirage

See an indoor, zoolike exhibit featuring Siegfried and Roy's beautiful white tigers and lions. The outdoor portion of this attraction features an up-close look at bottlenose dolphins. Open daily from 11:00 A.M. to 7:00 P.M. (opens at 10:00 A.M. on weekends). Admission to both attractions costs $12 per person.

Time Traveler: The Ride, at The Venetian

These are the latest in virtual reality, motion simulation, thrill-ride experiences that last about eight-and-a-half minutes each. Three different rides/attractions are available. Admission is $7 or $9 per person, depending on the presentation. Open daily from 10:00 A.M. to 11:00 P.M. (midnight on weekends). Discounted multiticket packages are available.

Wildlife Habitat and Bird Show at the Flamingo, at Flamingo

This free wildlife exhibit features dozens of flamingos, penguins, and other birds on display, twenty-four hours per day. The best time to visit, however, is when the flamingos are fed daily at 8:25 A.M. and 2:55 P.M. While visiting this mega-resort, be sure to check out the live *Tiana Caroll's Bird Show*, featuring the professional bird trainer showing off her colorful feathered friends. The free twenty-minute shows take place daily at 11:30 A.M., 1:30 P.M., and 2:30 P.M. (except Thursdays).

Indoor Activities

The rest of this chapter contains details about activities the entire family can enjoy on or around the Strip that aren't necessarily affiliated with a mega-resort.

Bowling

Here's a listing of Las Vegas area bowling alleys. With plenty of lanes to choose from, you can bowl a few frames anytime day or night.

Gold Coast Bowling
✉4000 West Flamingo Road
✆702-367-4700
Enjoy seventy lanes, open twenty-four hours per day.

The Orleans
✉4500 West Tropicana Avenue
✆702-365-7400
Enjoy seventy lanes, open twenty-four hours per day.

Sam's Town
✉5111 Boulder Highway
✆702-454-8022
Enjoy fifty-six lanes, open twenty-four hours per day.

Suncoast

✉9090 West Alta Drive (Summerlin)

✆702-636-7111

Enjoy sixty-four lanes, open twenty-four hours per day.

Local Indoor Attractions

There are a number of local indoor activities you and your family can take advantage of while on vacation in Las Vegas. Listed below are just some:

Ethel M's Chocolate Factory

✉Two Cactus Garden Drive, Henderson

✆702-433-2500

✐*www.ethelm.com*

If you want a firsthand look (and taste) of how candy is made, take a fifteen-minute drive from the Strip (about five miles) and experience a free, self-guided tour of Ethel M's Chocolate Factory. You'll see the entire candy-making process firsthand, plus get free samples. Outside the factory, you can explore the beautiful and unusual cactus garden. Open daily, 8:30 A.M. to 7:00 P.M. If you're taking a drive to the Hoover Dam, this is a fun stop along the way, but it also makes an ideal morning or afternoon activity itself.

ETHEL M'S CHOCOLATE FACTORY

Ages Up to 5	Ages 6–15	Ages 16–20	Ages 21 & Up	Senior Citizens
☆	☆☆	☆☆☆	☆☆☆	☆☆☆

Fastlap Indoor Kart Racing

✉4288 South Polaris Street

✆702-736-8113

✐*www.fastlaplv.com*

Seven days per week, starting at noon, for about $20 per person you can experience the thrill of wheel-to-wheel racing in race karts. "Arrive and Drive" races are split into ten-minute heats (approximately twenty laps each) with up to thirteen karts racing together. These karts are faster and more powerful than your run-of-the-mill go-carts. This attraction is suitable for anyone over age ten. Getting to Fastlap Indoor Kart Racing requires a ten-minute drive from the Strip.

FASTLAP INDOOR KART RACING

Ages Up to 5	Ages 6–15	Ages 16–20	Ages 21 & Up	Senior Citizens
Not Suitable	★★★	★★★	★★★	★

Flyaway Indoor Skydiving

✉200 Convention Center Drive

✆702-731-4768

✐*www.flyawayindoorskydiving.com*

If you've ever wanted to experience the thrill of skydiving but didn't like the idea of jumping out of an airplane, Flyaway Indoor Skydiving offers the ultimate alternative. For about $50 per person, you'll receive a twenty-minute training session, followed by a fifteen-minute flight session that's shared with up to five fliers. (Actual flying time is about three minutes per person.) All necessary equipment is provided. Indoor skydiving is designed to create the feeling of skydiving without much of the risk.

 TRAVEL TIP

For an additional fee, a videotape of your diving experience can be purchased. Flyaway Indoor Skydiving is open seven days per week, starting at 10:00 A.M.

The facility uses a large electric motor and propeller that can create wind speeds up to 120 miles per hour. The skills needed to fly the tunnel are basically the same skills needed to skydive. Reservations aren't required but are recommended to avoid long waits.

FLYAWAY INDOOR SKYDIVING

Ages Up to 5	Ages 6–15	Ages 16–20	Ages 21 & Up	Senior Citizens
Not Suitable	Not Suitable	☆☆☆	☆☆☆	☆

GameWorks

✉3769 Las Vegas Boulevard—Next to MGM Grand

✆702-432-4263

✐*www.gameworks.com*

Originally conceived by the video game designers at Sega in conjunction with producers from Dreamworks SKG and Universal Studios, GameWorks has evolved into the ultimate virtual reality theme park and video game arcade.

Suitable for kids, teens, and adults alike, GameWorks offers a huge video game arcade, a wide range of virtual reality and other state-of-the-art activities, plus a snack shop, full bar (for ages twenty-one and over), and 75-foot-tall indoor rock-climbing wall.

The price of video games is between $.50 and $4 per play. A debit card–style "SmartCard" system is used instead of tokens or quarters to pay for the games. Anyone who enjoys video games will have a blast here!

GAMEWORKS

Ages Up to 5	Ages 6–15	Ages 16–20	Ages 21 & Up	Senior Citizens
Not Suitable	☆☆	☆☆☆	☆☆	☆

═FAST FACT

Local law within Las Vegas stipulates that kids (under age eighteen) cannot be in an arcade after 10:00 P.M. (weekdays) or midnight (weekends) unless they're accompanied by an adult.

💼 TRAVEL TIP

If you're looking for additional video game arcades, you have plenty of options. ESPN Zone offers sports-oriented video games, while Bally's, Circus, Circus, Excalibur, Hard Rock Hotel & Casino, Luxor, MGM Grand, Monte Carlo, New York–New York, Orleans, Riviera, Sahara, and Stratosphere all offer impressive video game arcades.

M&M's World

✉3785 Las Vegas Boulevard South—Next to MGM Grand

✆702-736-7611

✐*http://shop.mms.com/service/lasvegas.asp*

Image a place the size of a major department store that is chock-full of toys, clothing, souvenirs, collectibles, and everything else having to do with M&M's candy. Well, that's what M&M's World offers, in addition to a free twenty-minute 3-D movie featuring the M&M's characters. It's definitely a fun place to explore.

In recent years, the "tour" aspect of this attraction has been scaled down a bit, but it's still worth checking out. M&M's World opens daily at 9:00 A.M. and remains open until 11:00 P.M. or midnight (depending on the day of the week).

M&M'S WORLD

Ages Up to 5	Ages 6–15	Ages 16–20	Ages 21 & Up	Senior Citizens
☆☆	☆☆	☆☆	☆	☆

World of Coca-Cola

✉3785 Las Vegas Boulevard South—Next to MGM Grand

✆702-597-3122

Originally a full-scale attraction similar to the World of Cola-Cola attraction in Atlanta, Georgia, the Las Vegas location has been transformed into a giant multilevel department store selling products, collectibles, and merchandise having to do with the popular soft drink. It's a fun place to explore, but when you get right down to it, it's just a large retail store.

WORLD OF COCA-COLA

Ages Up to 5	Ages 6–15	Ages 16–20	Ages 21 & Up	Senior Citizens
☆	☆	☆	☆	☆

Movies

When you're in the mood to see a movie, you have several options. First, you can go to a traditional movie theater and catch one of the latest blockbusters. Las Vegas has several large movie theater complexes that are easy to get to, including several right on the Strip. There are also IMAX theaters, which offer a more spectacular moviegoing experience.

Most of the resort and hotel rooms in the Las Vegas area offer pay-per-view movies right on your room's television set. For a flat fee, you can choose your movie from an on-screen menu and enjoy it anytime from the comfort and convenience of your hotel room.

 TRAVEL TIP

Located in the same complex as World of Coca-Cola, GameWorks, and M&M's World you'll find the United Artist Cinemas (featuring the latest blockbuster movies). If you're staying somewhere along the Strip, this is one of the closest movie theater complexes.

Finally, if you have a portable DVD player or a DVD drive built into your laptop computer, you can visit a local video store, such as Blockbuster, and rent movies that you can watch anytime. There are several Blockbuster locations within one mile of the Strip.

Catch the Latest Blockbuster

To discover what's playing and exact movie times at any of these theaters, call the theater's box office directly, call Fandango (✆800-326-3264/✎*www.fandango.com*), or visit the Moviefone (✎*www.moviefone.com*) or Movies.com (✎*www.movies.com*) Web sites and enter "Las Vegas" as the city name or "89109" as the zip code. You can also check the local newspaper or ask your hotel's concierge.

Brenden Las Vegas 14
✉4321 West Flamingo Road
✆702-507-4849

Century Orleans 18
✉4500 West Tropicana
✆702-227-3456

Century Sam's Town 18
✉5111 Boulder Highway
✆702-547-7469

Century Stadium 16 Rancho Santa Fe
✉5101 North Rainbow Boulevard
✆702-645-5518

Century 16 Suncoast
✉9090 Alta Drive
✆702-341-5555

Crown Neonopolis 14
✉450 Fremont Street
✆702-383-9600

Regal Cinemas Boulder Station 11
✉4111 Boulder Highway
✆702-641-7505

Regal Cinemas Colonnade 14
✉8880 South Eastern Avenue
✆702-948-2900

Regal Cinemas Village Square
✉9101 West Sahara Avenue
✆702-221-2283

Tropicana Cinemas
✉3330 East Tropicana Avenue
✆702-450-3737

United Artists Rainbow Promenade
✉2321 North Rainbow Boulevard
✆702-636-2869

United Artists Showcase Cinemas
✉3769 Las Vegas Boulevard South
✆702-470-4511

Not Your Typical Museums

Not everyone, especially among kids and teens, enjoys visiting museums. However, many of the museums in Las Vegas are nothing like traditional museums. Many are extremely kid- and family-friendly, plus offer fun, exciting, interactive, and sometimes educational exhibits. In addition to the museums and interactive exhibits housed in the various mega-resorts, the following are a few stand-alone museums worth checking out.

Elvis-A-Rama Museum
✉3401 Industrial Drive
✆702-309-7200
✑*www.elvisarama.com*

See an Elvis impersonator perform several times daily and check out the newly expanded, $5 million Elvis-related exhibits. Interactive displays include three of Elvis's cars (including the famous '55 Concert Tour Limo), stage-worn jumpsuits (including the famous Peacock Suit), and more than $500,000 worth of Elvis-worn jewelry.

You'll also see some of Elvis's movie wardrobe, plus personal documents and handwritten letters. A free shuttle bus is available from the Strip. The museum is open daily from 10:00 A.M. to 8:00 P.M. and costs $9.95 to get in (children 12 and under get in free). The gift shop offers the largest selection of Elvis merchandise, collectibles, and tribute items in the world.

ELVIS-A-RAMA MUSEUM

Ages Up to 5	Ages 6–15	Ages 16–20	Ages 21 & Up	Senior Citizens
Not Suitable	☆	☆☆	☆☆	☆☆

Liberace Museum
✉1775 East Tropicana
✆702-798-5595
🖋*www.liberace.org*

On display are glittering costumes, jewels, pianos, and exotic cars that were all once owned by Liberace. The Liberace Museum was founded April 15, 1979, by the late entertainer. A free shuttle bus is available. Open daily from 10:00 A.M. to 5:00 P.M. (Sundays from noon to 4:00 P.M.). Admission: $12 (adults) and $8 (senior citizens and children).

LIBERACE MUSEUM

Ages Up to 5	Ages 6–15	Ages 16–20	Ages 21 & Up	Senior Citizens
Not Suitable	Not Suitable	☆	☆☆	☆☆☆

Las Vegas Art Museum
✉9600 West Sahara Avenue
✆702-360-8000

Suitable more for adults and those who appreciate fine art, this museum is affiliated with the Smithsonian and features monthly rotating exhibits. If you're interested in seeing fine art, also be sure to visit the Gallery of Fine Art (✆702-693-7871/🖎*www.bgfa.biz*) located within the Bellagio Hotel and Casino (see Chapter 6 for more details).

≡FAST FACT

In 2004, the Bellagio featured *Claude Monet: Masterworks from the Museum of Fine Arts* as its primary exhibit.

There's also a fine art gallery within the new Wynn Las Vegas. For a listing of all art galleries in the Las Vegas area, point your Web browser to 🖎*www.ftguide.com.*

LAS VEGAS ART MUSEUM

Ages Up to 5	Ages 6–15	Ages 16–20	Ages 21 & Up	Senior Citizens
Not Suitable	Not Suitable	★★	★★★	★★★

GALLERY OF FINE ART AT THE BELLAGIO

Ages Up to 5	Ages 6–15	Ages 16–20	Ages 21 & Up	Senior Citizens
Not Suitable	Not Suitable	★★	★★★	★★★

Las Vegas Natural History Museum
✉900 Las Vegas Boulevard North
✆702-384-3466
🖎*www.lvnhm.org*

Open daily from 9:00 A.M. to 4:00 P.M., visitors can learn about Las Vegas's history. This museum also offers exhibits featuring desert life and how animals have genetically evolved to withstand the desert heat. Other exhibits showcase dinosaur fossils, marine life, and Africa. Admission is $6 per adult and $3 per child.

LAS VEGAS NATURAL HISTORY MUSEUM

Ages Up to 5	Ages 6–15	Ages 16–20	Ages 21 & Up	Senior Citizens
Not Suitable	☆☆	☆☆	☆☆	☆☆

Neon Museum
✉East end of Fremont Street Experience—Downtown area
✆702-387-NEON
✐*www.neonmuseum.org*

Located in the historic downtown area, the Neon Museum showcases some of the neon signs that have made Las Vegas famous. Stroll around three acres' worth of exhibits, some of which are on display twenty-four hours per day and are best viewed after dark. The Neon Boneyard also features classic neon signs from around the world. This exhibit is free, self-paced, and worth checking out if you're in the downtown area.

NEON MUSEUM

Ages Up to 5	Ages 6–15	Ages 16–20	Ages 21 & Up	Senior Citizens
Not Suitable	☆☆	☆☆	☆☆	☆☆

Planetarium and Observatory
✉3200 East Cheyenne Avenue, Suite 1A
✆702-651-4SKY
✐*www.ccsn.nevada.edu*

In the late afternoons and evenings only, visitors can experience a wide range of shows and presentations offered on a rotating basis throughout the year. The cost is a mere $5 per adult; kids are free.

PLANETARIUM AND OBSERVATORY

Ages Up to 5	Ages 6–15	Ages 16–20	Ages 21 & Up	Senior Citizens
Not Suitable	Not Suitable	☆☆	☆☆	☆☆

Ron Lee's World of Clowns

✉330 Carousel Parkway, Henderson

✆702-434-1700

✐*www.ronlee.com*

Located twenty minutes southeast of the Strip, this free attraction showcases an impressive collection of Ron Lee sculptures, including Ron's Clown Collection. The wonderful Emmett Kelly Jr. Collection, Warner Brothers Looney Tunes figurines, and the complete Disney Showcase Collection (with more than 115 Disney character sculptures) are on display and for sale.

Enjoy the free, self-guided tour, and visit the Ron Lee Gallery to purchase the sculptures. As an artist and sculptor for more than twenty-five years, Ron Lee has created the world's largest collection of limited-edition clown figurines.

TRAVEL ESSENTIAL

Sculptures for Disney, Warner Brothers, and Universal Studios and his selection of clown figurines are valued by collectors around the world. Every sculpture is hand painted and mounted on an onyx base.

Hours of operation are 8:30 A.M. to 4:30 P.M., Monday through Friday. Closed on Saturdays, Sundays, and holidays.

RON LEE'S WORLD OF CLOWNS

Ages Up to 5	Ages 6–15	Ages 16–20	Ages 21 & Up	Senior Citizens
Not Suitable	Not Suitable	☆	☆☆	☆☆

Lied Children's Museum

✉833 North Las Vegas Boulevard

☎702-382-3445

✐*www.ldcm.org*

With more than 100 innovative, hands-on exhibits in 25,000 square feet, the museum is one of the largest children's museums in the United States. Since its opening in 1990, more than a million children and adults have visited the museum. Exhibits rotate throughout the year. Almost all of the exhibits are interactive. While teens and adults wouldn't want to visit this museum alone, it's a great place to bring kids. Open daily from 10:00 A.M. to 5:00 P.M. (closed Mondays during non-summer months). Admission is $7 per adult, $5 per child.

LIED CHILDREN'S MUSEUM

Ages Up to 5	Ages 6–15	Ages 16–20	Ages 21 & Up	Senior Citizens
☆☆	☆☆☆	☆☆	☆	☆

Shop till You Drop!

Those who love to shop will think they're in heaven when they get to Las Vegas! Here you'll find some of the best shopping anywhere in the world, whether you're looking for the best bargains or the most exclusive designer fashions. In many cases, the malls themselves are tourist attractions.

Fashion Outlets

☎888-424-6898

✐*www.folv.com*

Visit a selection of more than 100 outlet stores, including Coach, Versace, Burberry, Polo, Old Navy, Gap, Banana Republic, and dozens of others. There's a free shuttle bus that departs seven times daily from the Strip.

Las Vegas Premium Outlets

✉875 South Grand Central Parkway

✆702-474-7500

✐*www.premiumoutlets.com*

Features 120 discount outlets for popular mall chain stores, such as A/X, the Gap, Calvin Klein, Eddie Bauer, Izod, Jockey, Nike, Timberland, Tommy Hilfiger, and Wilson's Leather. The drawback to this mall is that it's outdoors, so there's no air conditioning as you travel from store to store looking for the best deals. This shopping area is also located about five minutes past the Stratosphere (toward the downtown area), so expect a $10 to $20 cab ride to get there if you don't have a rental car.

Las Vegas Outlet Center

✉7400 Las Vegas Boulevard South

✆702-896-5599

✐*www.LasVegasOutletCenter.com*

More than 130 stores can be found here, many offering incredible bargains.

Fantastic Indoor Swap Meet

✉1717 South Decatur at Oakey

✆702-877-0087

✐*www.fantasticswap.com*

Located two miles from the Strip, this swap meet is open every Friday, Saturday, and Sunday from 10:00 A.M. to 6:00 P.M., and features hundreds of shops and vendors.

The Boulevard

✉3528 South Maryland Parkway

✆702-732-8849

Features 150 shops, including Macy's, JC Penney, Dillard's, and Sears.

Desert Passage

☎702-866-0710

Located at the Aladdin Resort & Casino, Desert Passage offers more than 140 specialty stores and more common mall stores right on the Strip.

Fashion Show Mall

✉3200 Las Vegas Boulevard

☎702-369-0704

⌨*www.thefashionshow.com*

The Fashion Show Mall, located on the Strip, is an extremely large indoor mall containing more than 250 shops and restaurants. Department stores include Neiman Marcus, Saks Fifth Avenue, Macy's, Robinsons-May, and Nordstrom. Plan on spending several hours here! This mall recently underwent a $1 billion expansion. It now features a stage, fashion show runway, and regularly scheduled free shows, concerts, and special events for shoppers.

The Forum Shops at Caesars

☎702-893-4800

Even if you hate shopping, this is one of the most unusual indoor malls in the world—and also one of the most popular, so don't miss it! It features more than 110 shops and restaurants plus several indoor attractions, including the free *Fountain of the Gods* show. Every day, 50,000 to 70,000 people visit the mall, which offers a wonderful shopping experience for the whole family. Definitely plan on spending several hours here! If you're a savvy shopper, you can often find amazing deals on top-name designer fashions. The Forum Shops are open daily from 10:00 A.M. until 11:00 P.M. or midnight. See Chapter 7 for more information. For a listing of shops and restaurants, point your Web browser to ⌨*www.caesars.com*. In October 2004, dozens of new designer shops opened as part of a major expansion of this incredible, one-of-a-kind mall.

Galleria at Sunset

✉1300 Sunset Road

☎702-434-0202

✐*www.caesars.com*

This is another of Las Vegas's world-class malls, featuring 140 shops, including a handful of popular department stores such as Dillard's, Robinson-May, JC Penney, and Mervyn's.

Mandalay Place

☎702-632-9333

This indoor shopping mall links Mandalay Bay and Luxor. It features more than forty stores and boutiques, and stays open late (until 11 P.M. on Sunday through Thursday, and midnight on Friday and Saturday).

The Tower Shops

☎702-383-5319

Located in the tower of the Stratosphere Las Vegas Hotel and Casino, this mall features fifty shops. If you're in the area, check it out, but there's certainly plenty of other shopping more conveniently located along the Strip.

Via Bellagio

☎702-693-7111

If you're looking for designers such as Gucci, Prada, Chanel, or Tiffany & Co., this is the place to shop. This mall is small, but very upscale.

Sporting Events and Major Concerts

When it comes to major sporting events, comedy shows, and concerts featuring some of the best-known athletes, comedians, recording artists, and entertainers in the world, Las Vegas offers something for everyone. Virtually every night of the year, there's some type of major headliner or special event happening at one or more of the mega-resorts.

For more information and event listings, contact Ticketmaster (℡702-474-4000/✑*www.ticketmaster.com*), the venues directly, or point your Web browser to ✑*www.vegas.com* and check out the "Upcoming Events" listing on the main page.

The Las Vegas Convention and Visitors Authority's Web site (✑*www.lasvegas24hours.com*) is also a great place to find information about special events, shows, and activities.

A Chance to Pamper Yourself and Relax

If you're an adult looking for the ultimate way to relax, unwind, and pamper yourself, be sure to visit one of the many world-class day spas now open in the popular mega-resorts. Enjoy a massage, body wrap, facial, or more exotic treatment. Las Vegas has become home to some of the most exclusive and luxurious day spas in the world. People from all over travel to Las Vegas just to visit the Canyon Ranch SpaClub (℡877-220-2688/✑*www.canyonranch.com*) at The Venetian, for example.

In addition to offering state-of-the-art fitness and salon facilities, the Canyon Ranch SpaClub is known for its specialized massages and treatments, such as Euphoria (a 100-minute aromatherapy scalp massage and warm botanical body mask), Canyon Stone Massage, Canyon Ranch Mango Sugar Glo (body scrub), and Tibetan Bowl Healing treatments.

It's open daily from 5:30 A.M. to 10:00 P.M. Nobody under age eighteen is admitted. Advance reservations for spa treatments and fitness classes are definitely recommended. This is one of the most beautiful, well-equipped, and customer-service-oriented day spas in the Las Vegas area. The prices aren't low, but the experience is well worth it! After your treatments and/or workout, enjoy a healthy meal at the spa's café.

Nightlife for Adults Only

Every night, 365 days per year, Las Vegas becomes the place to be if you want to experience incredible nightlife activities, with more than forty nightclubs to choose from, all located on or near the Strip. Dance, drink, and party throughout the night. Some clubs have special themes, such as Studio 54 (✆702-891-7254/the mega-popular club from the 1970s is back, at the MGM Grand) or BiKiNis (✆702-992-7970/at the Rio, offering a beach party theme).

Other popular hotspots include:

- **Seven** (✆702-992-7970/3724 Las Vegas Boulevard South)
- **Coyote Ugly** (✆702-992-7970/New York–New York Hotel & Casino)
- **RA** (✆702-992-7970/Luxor)
- **Ice** (✆702-992-7970/200 East Harmon Avenue)
- **Rain** (✆702-992-7970/the Palms—This is the club made popular on MTV's *The Real World Las Vegas*)
- **Jillian's** (✆702-759-0450/450 Fremont Street—Downtown)

 TRAVEL TIP

Like all major cities, Las Vegas offers clubs and bars (over a dozen) that cater to a gay/lesbian clientele, such as the Gipsy (✆702-731-1919/4605 Paradise Road), Free Zone (✆702-794-2300/610 East Naples Drive), and Backstreet Bar & Grill (✆702-876-1844/5012 Arville Street). For a more complete listing of these bars and clubs, point your Web browser to ✑*www.gayvegas.com* or ✑*www.digitalcity.com/lasvegas/gaylocalscene.*

Nightclubs and lounges located in the various mega-resorts are described within Chapters 6 through 18. All clubs and bars cater to the eighteen- or twenty-one-and-over crowd. Contact the clubs directly or speak with your hotel's concierge to learn about special events and baby-sitting services for your kids. Each club has a cover charge. For a complete listing of nightclubs in Las Vegas, point your Web browser to *www.vegas.com.*

For the ultimate experience in Las Vegas, check out VIPVegas. com (*www.vipvegas.com*) or BachelorBlowOut.com (*www. bachelorblowout.com*) to receive help planning the ultimate vacation itinerary. These services will arrange for VIP transportation during your entire stay in the Las Vegas area, plus arrange for you to have VIP access to the most exclusive nightclubs. You'll also be able to get your hands on tickets to shows, fights, and concerts, even if they're sold out. While you'll pay extra for these services, you'll experience Las Vegas the way the celebrities and high rollers do. These services are also ideal if you need help planning a bachelor or bachelorette party, or if you're visiting Las Vegas with a group of adults.

See Attractions at a Discount

The PowerPass Card (☏800-490-9330/*www.powerpasscard.com*) is a one-, two-, three-, or five-day pass that offers unlimited entry into nineteen popular Las Vegas-area attractions, plus special discounted offers at dozens of restaurants.

Some of the attractions you'll have unlimited access to while your pass is valid include:

- Elvis-A-Rama
- Guggenheim Hermitage Museum
- In Search of the Obelisk
- King Tut Museum
- Las Vegas Art Museum
- Las Vegas Zoo
- Liberace Museum
- Madame Tussauds
- Manhattan Express roller coaster
- *Star Trek*: The Experience
- Stratosphere Tower observation deck and rides

To get the most out of this pass, you'll want to schedule your time wisely, so you can visit as many of the participating attractions as possible in a single day (or during the days your pass is valid).

POWERPASS CARD PRICES

One-Day Pass	Two-Day Pass	Three-Day Pass	Five-Day Pass
$55 Adult	$85 Adult	$100 Adult	$140 Adult
$35 Child	$65 Child	$80 Child	$110 Child

Explore the Great Outdoors

The next chapter describes a wide range of outdoor family-oriented activities in and around the Las Vegas area. You'll also learn about exciting tours to the Grand Canyon and Hoover Dam, for example, which, time permitting, should not be missed. Taking a helicopter tour of the Grand Canyon is something the entire family will remember for a lifetime.

Whether you enjoy golf, tennis, swimming, hiking, rock climbing, sky diving, bungee jumping, car racing, or a wide range of other outdoor activities, you'll discover what there is to do *outside* during your vacation. On a particularly hot day, your kids and teens will enjoy spending a few hours at the Wet 'N Wild water park, for example, or just kicking back at your hotel or resort's swimming pool.

CHAPTER 20

Outdoor Family-Oriented Activities

ON AVERAGE, YOU CAN EXPECT 310 sunny days per year in Las Vegas. In the summertime, temperatures can soar to over 100 degrees Fahrenheit. Even in the winter, however, during the day the temperature is often in the sixties or seventies. Thanks to this fine year-round weather, it doesn't really matter when you visit Las Vegas. Chances are, the weather will be ideal for many different types of outdoor activities.

Outdoor Sports and Recreation

This chapter offers details about many of the outdoor activities you and your family can enjoy in and around the Las Vegas area. As you already know, all of the mega-resorts offer swimming pools. Many also offer tennis, golf, and other outdoor activities. If you travel beyond the mega-resort properties, however, you'll find countless additional outdoor activities suitable for the whole family.

It's Tee Time: Golf Courses

Golfers from all over the world travel to Las Vegas in order to experience the city's more than thirty award-winning championship courses. Be sure to reserve your tee times in advance, especially during peak travel times. The following is a list of golf courses in the Las Vegas area, including many that are right on or near the

Strip. Additional courses can be found in nearby Boulder City and Henderson. Prices range from under $50 to well over $200, depending on the course and season.

TRAVEL ESSENTIAL

Before departing for *any* outdoor activity, make sure you pack plenty of drinking water. It's easy to become dehydrated from the heat. Also, bring along sunblock, a hat, comfortable shoes (yes, you'll be doing *a lot* of walking), and sunglasses for everyone. For some activities, bringing along a jacket or change of clothes is advisable.

For additional information about specific courses, rates, and tee times, contact the course directly or point your Web browser to ✑*www. vegas.com*. In many situations, tee times can be booked online.

Angel Park
✉100 South Rampart Boulevard
✆702-254-4633
Features: Four courses and thirty-six holes

Badland's Golf Club
✉9119 Alta Drive
✆702-363-0754
Features: Twenty-seven holes, par seventy-two

Bali Hai
✉5160 Las Vegas Boulevard
✆702-450-8000
Features: Championship golf course right on the Strip

Bear's Best
✉11111 West Flamingo Road
✆702-804-8500

Features: Eighteen holes, par seventy-two; designed by Jack Nicklaus.

Desert Pines
✉3415 East Bonanza Road
☎702-450-8000
Features: Eighteen holes, par seventy-one

Eagle Crest
✉2203 Thomas Ryan
☎702-240-1320
Features: Eighteen holes, par sixty

The Greens of Las Vegas
✉4813 Paradise Road
☎702-740-PUTT

Highland Falls
✉10201 Sun City Boulevard
☎702-254-7010
Features: Eighteen holes, par seventy-two

Las Vegas Golf Club
✉4300 West Washington Avenue
☎702-646-3003
Features: Eighteen holes, par seventy-two

Las Vegas National Golf Club
✉1911 East Desert Inn Road
☎702-734-1796
Features: Eighteen holes, par seventy-one

Painted Desert
✉5555 Painted Mirage Way
☎702-645-2570

Features: Eighteen holes, par seventy-two

Reflection Bay
✉605 Lake Las Vegas Parkway)
✆702-740-GOLF
Features: Eighteen holes, par seventy-two; designed by Jack Nicklaus

Rhodes Ranch Country Club
✉20 South Rhodes Ranch Parkway
✆702-740-4114
Features: Eighteen holes, par seventy-two

Royal Links
✉5995 East Vegas Valley Road
✆702-450-8000
Features: Eighteen holes, par seventy-two

Shadow Creek
✉3 Shadow Creek Drive, North Las Vegas
✆702-399-7111
Features: This is one of the world's top 100 rated courses, but you can only play if you stay at one of the MGM Grand hotel properties.

Siena Golf Club
✉10575 Siena Monte Avenue
✆702-341-9200
Features: Eighteen holes

Silverstone
✉8600 Cupp Drive
✆702-562-3770
✍*www.silverstonegolfclub.com*
Features: Twenty-seven holes

Stallion Mountain
✉5500 East Flamingo Road
☎702-450-8000
Features: Three eighteen-hole courses

Wildhorse
✉2100 West Warm Springs Road
☎702-434-9000
Features: Eighteen holes, par seventy-two

 TRAVEL TIP

Many of the Las Vegas area golf courses offer a golf shop, lessons, and equipment rentals. If you choose to bring your own clubs, remember that you must check them as luggage on the airplane. (Clubs cannot be brought onto the aircraft as a carry-on.)

Racquet and Tennis Clubs

Following is a partial listing of tennis courts in the Las Vegas area. Be sure to call in advance to reserve court time. Equipment can often be rented and lessons from pros are available for a fee. You do not have to be a guest at any of the mega-resorts to reserve court time, though prices tend to be higher for non-guests.

Bally's
☎702-967-4598
Prices: $10 to $15 per hour for court rentals. Open daily from 8:00 A.M. to 5:00 P.M. Lessons and equipment rentals are available.

Flamingo
☎702-733-3111
Prices: $12 to $20 per hour for court rentals. Open daily from 7:00 A.M. to 7:00 P.M. Lessons and equipment sales and rentals are available.

Monte Carlo

✆702-730-7411

Prices: $12 to $15 per hour. Open daily from 10:00 A.M. to 7:30 P.M. Lessons and equipment rentals are available. A tennis clinic is held daily.

Riviera

✆702-794-9679

Prices: Free for guests, $10 for two hours for non-guests.

TRAVEL ESSENTIAL

Additional mega-resorts that offer tennis courts include Alexis Park, Caesars Palace, Desert Inn, Flamingo Hilton, MGM Grand, The Mirage, New Frontier, Paradise Park, Stardust, Sunset Park, Budget Suites of America, and Tropicana.

Swimming

Virtually all of the mega-resorts and hotels in the Las Vegas area offer at least one swimming pool. Many offer multiple pools, kiddy pools, and hot tubs. When visiting your hotel's pool, never leave your kids unattended, even if a lifeguard is on duty. Bring your own sunscreen. Depending on where you're staying, towels may be provided poolside (meaning that it won't be necessary to remove towels from your room or suite). For pool hours, call your hotel's front desk or concierge.

Horseback Riding

Take a trip back to the Old West by driving about fifteen miles outside of Las Vegas to Bonnie Springs Ranch in Old Nevada. This ranch offers horseback riding, a petting zoo, stagecoach rides, and other activities throughout the day. The ranch was originally built in 1843, but has been a tourist destination since 1952. Hours of operation are 9:00 A.M. to 5:00 P.M. or 6:00 P.M., depending on the season.

 **TRAVEL TIP**

For additional horseback-riding opportunities and tours, contact the Grand Canyon tour providers listed later in this chapter.

Other horseback-riding opportunities in the Las Vegas area include:

Cowboy Horseback Tours
✉800 North Rainbow Boulevard
✆702-948-7061

Las Vegas Horseback Tours
✉SageBrush Ranch 12000 West Ann Road (about forty-five minutes from the Strip)
✆702-641-5536
✐*www.lasvegashorsebacktours.com*

Lost Wages Tours
✆888-888-7501
✐*www.lostwagestours.com*)

Mount Charleston Riding Stables
✆702-948-7061
✐*www.mountcharlestonridingstables.com*

Local Area Attractions

Whether you're traveling with kids, teens, or a group of adults, the majority of the outdoor attractions located on or near the Strip are exciting, fun, and well worth experiencing.

The Fremont Street Experience
✉Fremont Street—Downtown Las Vegas
✐*www.vegasexperience.com*

The Fremont Street Experience is a one-of-a-kind entertainment venue in the heart of Las Vegas's historic downtown area. It comprises a 900-foot-high, four-block-long canopy of electric lights used to create visually stunning shows.

These nightly shows are free and deliver an incredible array of musical adventures, utilizing the world's largest electric sign and over 550,000 watts of concert-quality sound. Nearby is a popular pedestrian mall, home to Las Vegas's most legendary casinos and hotels. In addition, the pedestrian mall has numerous stages and venues presenting a wide range of shows, musical ensembles, and concerts.

The Fremont Street Experience district entertains over 15 million visitors annually. It's been featured in dozens of movies, television shows, and commercials. In June 2004, Viva Vision made its debut. This dazzling $17 million spectacle of lights and sounds delights visitors of all ages with beautiful computer-generated animations, integrated live video feeds, and perfectly synchronized music.

TRAVEL TIP

Traveling from anywhere on the Strip to the Fremont Street Experience is easy and takes less than fifteen minutes. Take the trip downtown by boarding the Las Vegas Monorail to the Sahara Station. From there, hop on the Monorail/Downtown Connector Bus (route 551), which brings you right to the Fremont Street Experience. The shuttle bus follows the path of the planned monorail extension, between the Sahara Station and Downtown Transit Center, slated for completion in 2007.

Once the sun goes down, visitors simply need to look upward to experience over 12.5 million synchronized LED modules displaying crisp, high-resolution images and impressive special effects.

Shows presented on the Viva Vision screen include *The Drop*, a mythical underwater journey, and *Area 51*, a peek at a fantastical alien world. The shows are free and can be viewed from just about any angle along the four-block promenade.

The Fremont Street Experience should be experienced after dark. It's suitable for the entire family.

THE FREMONT STREET EXPERIENCE

Ages Up to 5	Ages 6–15	Ages 16–20	Ages 21 & Up	Senior Citizens
Not Suitable	★★★	★★★	★★★	★★★

Zoological Botanical Park

✉1775 North Rancho Drive

✆702-647-4685

✑*www.lasvegaszoo.org*

This family-oriented zoo allows you to see a wide range of exotic cats, birds, and reptiles, along with chimpanzees and wallabies, among other critters. There's also an exhibit showcasing every species of venomous reptile native to southern Nevada. The zoo itself is open daily from 9:00 A.M. to 5:00 P.M.

Admission is $7 per adult and $5 per child. (Children are admitted free if you print out an online coupon available from the zoo's Web site.) For a more educational half-day or full-day experience, the zoo offers special Eco-Tours, starting at $109 per person. A shuttle bus is available from the Strip.

ZOOLOGICAL BOTANICAL PARK

Ages Up to 5	Ages 6–15	Ages 16–20	Ages 21 & Up	Senior Citizens
★★	★★★	★★	★	★

Sirens of TI (Treasure Island)

From South Las Vegas Boulevard in front of Treasure Island, catch this free show every night at 7:00 P.M., 8:30 P.M., 10:00 P.M., and 11:30 P.M. Complete with special effects, music, dance, acrobats, and larger-than-life sets, *Sirens of TI* is a twelve-minute show that takes place on an underwater "stage" the size of four football fields.

SIRENS OF TI

Ages Up to 5	Ages 6–15	Ages 16–20	Ages 21 & Up	Senior Citizens
Not Suitable	Not Suitable	☆☆	☆☆	☆☆

Fountains at Bellagio

The large fountains located in front of the Bellagio come to life for special shows that are synchronized with colored lights and music. At a cost of $40 million to create, these visually impressive shows are held Monday through Friday between 3:00 P.M. and midnight, and on Saturdays and Sundays between noon and midnight.

Weather permitting, catch a free show from in front of the mega-resort (while standing along South Las Vegas Boulevard) every half hour before 8:00 P.M. and every fifteen minutes after 8:00 P.M. It's a popular attraction that's suitable for the entire family.

FOUNTAINS AT BELLAGIO

Ages Up to 5	Ages 6–15	Ages 16–20	Ages 21 & Up	Senior Citizens
☆☆	☆☆☆	☆☆☆	☆☆☆	☆☆☆

Gondola Rides (The Venetian)

You'll feel as if you've left Las Vegas and traveled to Italy as you ride in a real gondola piloted by a gondolier who will serenade you. The man-made canal flows around The Venetian property (outside) as well as through the mega-resort's shopping area (indoors).

This ride can be extremely romantic or just plain fun if you're with kids. Boats operate daily from 10:00 A.M. to 11:00 P.M. (midnight on weekends).

GONDOLA RIDES

Ages Up to 5	Ages 6–15	Ages 16–20	Ages 21 & Up	Senior Citizens
☆☆	☆☆☆	☆☆☆	☆☆☆	☆☆☆

Roller Coaster Roundup

Along the Strip, you'll find a handful of exciting thrill rides and roller coasters, many of which are unlike any other theme park rides in the world. Whether you're looking for speed, twists, drops, loops, incredible views, or just breathtaking thrills, these rides have it all . . . and more!

Manhattan Express, at New York–New York

Enjoy the thrill of a roller coaster that takes you in, around, and above the fabulous New York–New York Hotel and Casino. This coaster offers a fantastic view of the Strip—plus an extreme rush! Admission is between $10 and $12.50, depending on the day. Open daily, 10:00 A.M. until 11:30 P.M. on weekdays and until midnight on weekends.

To save money, consider purchasing the All-in-One-Fun-Pass. For $39.95, riders receive unlimited access to the roller coaster for a day, lunch, a souvenir photo, a souvenir T-shirt, a clown doll, plus 500 prize points that can be redeemed at the arcade. There's also an all-day pass (without the extras) for $25. Riders of the roller coaster must be at least 54 inches tall. It's a rather turbulent thrill ride that's not for the timid.

MANHATTAN EXPRESS

Ages Up to 5	Ages 6–15	Ages 16–20	Ages 21 & Up	Senior Citizens
Not Suitable	☆	☆☆☆	☆☆☆	☆

Sling Shot, at Circus, Circus

Enjoy this relatively new free-fall ride within the Adventuredome theme park. This is just one of a handful of serious thrill rides at Circus, Circus, so plan on spending between one and four hours here—preferably *before* you eat lunch or dinner, since some of these rides will shake you up.

SLING SHOT

Ages Up to 5	Ages 6–15	Ages 16–20	Ages 21 & Up	Senior Citizens
Not Suitable	☆	☆☆☆	☆☆☆	☆

Speed: The Ride, at Sahara

Take a whirlwind trip at seventy miles per hour along a track with sharp turns and a breathtaking loop, then travel upward at a ninety-degree angle to 224 feet in the air. Open daily, starting at noon, the ride closes at 9:00 P.M. on weekdays and Sundays and at midnight on Saturdays.

SPEED: THE RIDE

Ages Up to 5	Ages 6–15	Ages 16–20	Ages 21 & Up	Senior Citizens
Not Suitable	☆	☆☆☆	☆☆☆	☆

Big Shot, High Roller, and Project X-Scream, at Stratosphere

These thrill rides have been built at the very top of the Stratosphere Tower. When you ride the Big Shot, you'll be shot an additional 160 feet into the air, only to be dropped as you experience a free fall. The High Roller roller coaster whips around the top perimeter of the Stratosphere at thirty-five miles per hour, offering an incredible view. This is the world's highest (but not fastest) roller coaster.

Project X-Scream is a thrill ride that sends riders 27 feet over the edge of the Strip's tallest tower (900 feet above the ground). Open daily, between 10:00 A.M. and 1:00 A.M. (until 2:00 A.M. on Fridays, Saturdays, and holidays).

BIG SHOT, HIGH ROLLER, AND PROJECT X-SCREAM

Ages Up to 5	Ages 6–15	Ages 16–20	Ages 21 & Up	Senior Citizens
Not Suitable	☆	☆☆☆	☆☆☆	☆

Activities for Thrill-Seekers

If you're looking for more than just the thrill of a roller coaster, Las Vegas definitely has what you're looking for! Keep in mind that some of these attractions and activities are *not* suitable for kids. In almost every case, all necessary equipment is either provided or available for rent.

Bungee Jumping

For all you daredevils out there, bungee jumping may be just the activity for you. Take in the beautiful view just before you make the plunge.

AJ Hackett Bungee Jumping
✉810 Circus Circus Drive
✆702-385-4321
See an awesome view of Las Vegas from 171 feet in the air before bungee jumping downward. Open daily from 11:00 A.M. until 8:30 P.M. (Saturdays until 10:00 P.M.).

Rock Climbing

Test your endurance as you scale ever higher during a rock-climbing tour. Not for the faint of heart, these adventures are offered close to the Strip and transportation is often included.

American Alpine Institute
✆800-424-2249
✐*www.aai.cc*
Go rock climbing in Red Rock Canyon. Half- and full-day trips and guided climbs are available. Transportation to and from the Strip is provided.

Hike This!
✆702-393-4453
✐*www.hikethislasvegas.com*
Experience a half-day hiking and rock-climbing adventure in the majestic Red Rock Canyon. Transportation to and from the Strip is provided.

Sky's the Limit

☎702-363-4533

☎800-733-7597

✑*www.skysthelimit.com*

Rock climbing, hiking, mountaineering, and other outdoor tours and expeditions are offered for novice and experienced thrill-seekers. Your adventure will begin just minutes away from the Strip.

Hot-Air Balloon Rides

This is a perfect way to enjoy the beautiful views that Las Vegas has to offer. These thrilling rides offer a once-in-a-lifetime experience.

Las Vegas Balloon Rides

☎702-248-7609

✑*www.lasvegasballoonrides.com*

For $150 per person, enjoy the thrill and beauty of a hot-air balloon ride at sunrise or sunset. Includes a champagne toast upon landing.

Race Car Driving and Go-Carts

If you're a NASCAR fan or you've ever wanted to drive as fast as you could without worrying about getting a speeding ticket, your need for speed will be satisfied when you participate in one of these driving programs. You must have a valid driver's license and be over the age of eighteen to participate. As you'll see, at the Las Vegas Motor Speedway, a variety of racing schools and programs are available to everyday people.

Richard Petty Driving Experience

☎800-BE-PETTY

✑*www.1800bepetty.com*

Starting at $99, you can ride along with a professional driver and race around the track in an actual racing car. For between $199 and $249, you'll have a thrilling race experience. You'll sit in the passenger's seat and ride for six to ten laps, from flag to flag, as you experience side-by-side racing, drafting, passing, pit stops, and more. Other packages and programs are also available.

Derek Daly Performance Driving Academy

✆888-GO-DEREK

✑*www.derekdaly.com*

Experience the thrill of being a professional race car driver. For a really over-the-top experience, sign up for a three-day racing school program ($3,500 per person). One-day ($1,200) and two-day ($2,500) programs are also available. Courses and driving takes place at the Las Vegas Motor Speedway.

Las Vegas Mini Grand Prix

✉1401 North Rainbow Boulevard

✆702-259-7000

✑*www.lvmgp.com*

This is an indoor/outdoor family fun center, complete with several types of go-carts and tracks, plus video games, slides, a mini roller coaster, and more. Open daily from 10:00 A.M. until 10:00 P.M. (11:00 P.M. on Fridays, Saturdays, and Sundays). This is a great place to bring kids and teens for several hours of fun.

Mario Andretti Racing School

✆877-ANDRETTI

✑*www.driving101.com*

Racing superstar Mario Andretti and a team of instructors offer the ultimate racing experience. The Mario Andretti Pace Car Ride ($75 per person), for example, places you in the passenger seat with one of Andretti's professional instructors as you race around the Las Vegas Motor Speedway track for six laps, at speeds up to 145 miles per hour in a 600 horsepower race car. The Mario Andretti Champ Ride ($129) allows you to be in the passenger seat for a qualifying run as you race at speeds up to 180 miles per hour. The Mario Andretti Qualifier experience ($399) puts you in the *driver's* seat for six heart-pounding laps around the track. These experiences last between thirty minutes and three hours, and are offered throughout the day at the Las Vegas Motor Speedway.

Skydiving

Why settle for seeing Las Vegas from the ground when you can hop on a plane, get a bird's-eye view, and then jump out of the plane and parachute to the ground? Several different skydiving programs are available, particularly for first-time jumpers. All instruction and equipment is supplied.

Sky Dive Las Vegas

℡702-759-3483

℡800-U-SKYDIV

✑*www.skydivelasvegas.com*

With over thirteen years in the business, Sky Dive Las Vegas offers free ground training before taking you up in an airplane and allowing you to enjoy the thrill of a tandem jump from 15,000 feet up, dropping at 200 miles per hour for a full sixty-second free fall and up to a seven-minute parachute ride. A free video of your experience is provided with your first jump. Free shuttle bus service is available from the Strip. Skydivers must be over the age of eighteen. Prices start at about $200 per jump; however, various types of discounts are offered.

Vegas Extreme Skydiving

℡866-398-5867

✑*www.vegasextremeskydiving.com*

Allow the experts at Las Vegas Extreme Skydiving to show you the city . . . from a different dimension. View the Strip from two miles above the earth at 120 miles per hour for the greatest adrenaline-charged adventure of your life. The company offers tandem skydiving for beginners and solo skydiving for experienced jumpers. Prices for first-time jumpers start around $200. Skydivers must be over age eighteen and weigh under 250 pounds.

Helicopter Tours

Maverick Helicopter Tours (888-261-4414/✐*www.maverick helicopters.com*) and Las Vegas Helicopters (888-779-0800/✐*www. lvhelicopters.com*) offer relatively inexpensive helicopter rides along the Las Vegas Strip and the downtown area. For under $70 per person, you can enjoy a twelve- to fifteen-minute helicopter ride and see all of the mega-resorts from a new and exciting perspective. The nighttime flights allow you to see all of the lights that make the Strip world famous.

More extensive Grand Canyon and Hoover Dam tours are also available. One great thing about Las Vegas Helicopters' tours is that you take off and land from the company's own heliport, located right on the Las Vegas Strip (3712 Las Vegas Boulevard). Keep your eyes out for the red, white, and blue helicopters flying overhead.

All-Terrain Vehicle Tours and Rentals

Explore the desert that surrounds the Las Vegas Strip by driving in an all-terrain vehicle.

Valley of Fire ATV Adventure

✆702-631-3091

✆800-405-6288

✐*www.lvgct.com*

The Valley of Fire features fiery red rock formations, an abundance of desert plants, exotic wildlife, and Native American petroglyphs. After an orientation and outfitting in protective gear, you will take to the trails for an exciting two-and-a-half-hour ride. The entire experience, including the lunch that is provided, lasts just under six hours. Tours depart at 8:00 A.M. and 5:00 P.M. and cost $155 to $165 per person. Riders under age eighteen must have a parent sign a waiver; kids age fifteen and under must ride on a two-seat ATV with a guide or parent.

The Grand Canyon and Hoover Dam

A tour of the Hoover Dam and Grand Canyon is something that you'll remember for a lifetime. These sights are utterly magnificent! The very best way to see these sights, if you have time in your itinerary to do so, is by taking a helicopter tour from McCarran International Airport. Less expensive bus tours are also available, or you can always rent a car and experience a self-guided tour.

Once you're at the Grand Canyon, consider taking a horseback riding tour to round out your adventure. Another exciting option is a mild Colorado River rafting tour, offered by Black Canyon Adventures. This allows you to see the Hoover Dam and Grand Canyon from a very different perspective than you would from a helicopter, car, or tour bus.

As you'll discover, each of the tour companies described in this section offers many different types of tours and options for seeing the Hoover Dam, Grand Canyon, and neighboring attractions. Ground tours start at around $49 per person and typically take up the entire day, while helicopter tours start at over $150 per person (but are well worth it) and require only between two and five hours to see and do everything.

Helicopter Tours

As soon as you get to Las Vegas, you'll see countless ads for a wide range of Grand Canyon and Hoover Dam tours, as well as for helicopter rides that'll give you an incredible view of the Strip for a lot less money. If you plan to take one of the helicopter rides along the Strip, the very best time to experience this is at sunset or after dark.

For those who have more money in their travel budget and who are looking for a truly memorable experience, taking a more elaborate helicopter tour to the Hoover Dam and/or the Grand Canyon from a well-respected and established company, such as HeliUSA (✆800-359-8727/702-736-8787/✑www.heliusa.com), is well worth the cost.

Since it was established, HeliUSA has flown over 700,000 passengers in its fleet of luxurious, climate-controlled, A-Star jet helicopters. Not only are the pilots skilled at flying, they're also extremely friendly and knowledgeable. From the moment you take off from the Executive Air Terminal at McCarran International Airport (shuttle bus transportation is provided to and from your hotel), your pilot will offer entertaining and informative narration throughout your flight, providing history, trivia, and a wide range of information about Las Vegas and your ultimate destinations.

To make your helicopter adventure even more memorable, HeliUSA offers several tours that include a half-day or a full-day's worth of activities. In addition to seeing spectacular views of the Hoover Dam, the Grand Canyon, Lake Mead, and the Strip, HeliUSA offers a midday stop at a real-life ranch located in the heart of the Grand Canyon. Here, you'll have lunch with real cowboys and can experience an optional horseback riding tour, stagecoach ride, or cattle drive while visiting the 106,000-acre Grand Canyon West Ranch (✎*www.grandcanyonranch.com*), which is nestled under Spirit Mountain. Overnight stays at the ranch are also available.

For under $75 per person, much shorter nighttime flights above the Las Vegas Strip are also available from HeliUSA.

TRAVEL ESSENTIAL

> When embarking on any type of helicopter tour that includes a stop in or near the Grand Canyon, be sure to dress appropriately for the outdoors. Bring a hat, sunblock, and sunglasses. If you'll be horseback riding, consider wearing jeans or slacks as well as comfortable shoes, boots, or sneakers (not sandals).

The Helicopter and Ranch Adventure, which lasts for five memorable hours and provides for countless photo opportunities, is priced starting at $319 per adult and $219 per child. Prices for other tours from HeliUSA vary, but are all an excellent value. Reservations for these popular tours should be made in advance.

HELIUSA'S HELICOPTER AND RANCH ADVENTURE

Ages Up to 5	Ages 6–15	Ages 16–20	Ages 21 & Up	Senior Citizens
★★	★★★	★★★	★★★	★★★

Other helicopter tour operators in the Las Vegas area include:

- All American Adventure Tours (✆702-631-3091)
- Discount Helicopter Tours (✆702-471-7155)
- Las Vegas Tour & Travel (✆702-739-8975)
- Magic Tours (✆702-380-2206)
- Papillon Grand Canyon Helicopters (✆702-736-6322/✍*www. papillon.com*)

Bus Tours

This is a perfect way to take in everything Las Vegas has to offer. Prices and destinations vary, but the whole family will enjoy a bus tour.

All American Adventure Tours

✆702-631-3091

This company offers more than a dozen different tours, including several inexpensive bus tours to the Grand Canyon, Lake Mead, and/ or the Hoover Dam. Helicopter, Hummer, rafting, airplane, and all-terrain vehicle tours can also be booked through this company.

Gray Line Bus Tours

✆800-634-6579

✆702-384-1234

✍*www.grayline.com*

These relatively inexpensive bus tours typically last between five and nine hours. Visit the Hoover Dam, Grand Canyon, Red Rock Canyon, Lake Mead, and a few other nearby tourist destinations. Prices start at $31.99 per adult and go up to $109.99, depending on the tour. One fun tour for families is the Lake Mead Cruise & Dam Combo. You'll drive out to Lake Mead, then float along the Colorado River on a two-hour cruise aboard the Desert Princess (a 300-passenger Mississippi-style paddle-wheeler). This is a full-day tour that's priced at $61.99 per person. The Colorado River Raft Tour ($109.99 per person) includes the bus tour to and from the Hoover

Dam, plus an eleven-mile float along the Colorado River in a river raft. All buses are fully air-conditioned. When booking your tour, ask for the AAA or AARP discount if you're a member of one of these organizations.

Grand Tours Las Vegas

✆702-368-5100

✉*www.grandtourslv.com*

Enjoy a magnificent tour of the Hoover Dam, spend several hours at the Grand Canyon, and add an optional helicopter ride or horseback-riding adventure. Several partial-day and full-day tours are available at affordable prices.

Las Vegas Tour & Travel

✆702-739-8975

This company offers more than sixteen different tours, including several inexpensive bus tours to the Grand Canyon, Lake Mead, and/or the Hoover Dam. Helicopter, Hummer, airplane, and all-terrain vehicle tours can also be booked through this company.

Rafting Tours

A relaxing and inspiring adventure awaits you when you take advantage of a rafting tour. This is one the whole family will love.

Black Canyon Adventures

✆800-455-3490

✉*www.blackcanyonadventures.com*

Enjoy a scenic and smooth-water raft ride that starts at the base of the Hoover Dam and winds along the Colorado River in the Black Canyon. It's a beautiful, twelve-mile journey.

TRAVEL TIP

One way to explore the Strip is to rent scooters from Sin City Scooters (℡702-303-1833/*www.sincityscooters.com*). You must have a valid driver's license to rent a scooter. Ask about special "rent-two-hours, get one-hour-free" promotions between Monday and Thursday. Rates range from $18 to $29 per hour, with excellent discounts offered for full-day rentals.

Find Additional Information

Need more help deciding how to spend your time in Las Vegas? In addition to surfing the Web (to Web sites such as *www.vegas.com*, *www.vegasfreedom.com*, and *www.lvcva.com*) for details about the many attractions and things to do, be sure to ask your hotel's concierge for recommendations.

Throughout the Las Vegas area, there are also numerous tourist information counters and kiosks staffed by knowledgeable personnel who can answer your questions.

You can obtain a free visitor information packet, either by mail or in person, by contacting or visiting the Las Vegas Visitor Information Center, 3150 Paradise Road, Las Vegas, NV 89109-9096, or by calling ℡702-892-7575 or ℡877-VISIT-LV. The office is open daily from 8:00 A.M. to 5:00 P.M.

CHAPTER 21

Finding What You Need in Las Vegas

IT'S IMPOSSIBLE TO PLAN for every situation, especially when you're traveling with kids or teens or have to deal with an unexpected work-related emergency when you're on vacation. This section will help you find the services and resources you need while in the Las Vegas area, should the unexpected happen.

Baby-Sitting Services and Child Care

While your resort or hotel's concierge or front desk attendant can help you find and hire a reliable, private, in-room baby-sitter who will watch your kids in the comfort of your hotel room, the following child care services are available that allow you to drop off your children.

These child care centers offer a wide range of activities and services for kids. Each caters to a slightly different age group and has different requirements and maximum lengths of stay per day, so be sure to call the center, in advance, prior to dropping off your child.

Kid's Tyme Child Care at the Suncoast

✉9090 Alta Drive

✆702-636-7300

Open seven days a week, for children ages two-and-a-half to twelve. Children must be completely potty trained and out of diapers or Pull-Ups. The center features a jungle gym, a movie room, arts and crafts activities, interactive play, and much more. Hours: 9:00 A.M. to 11:30 P.M. (or 12:30 A.M. on weekends). Rates: $6 per hour, per child. Open to resort guests and non-guests, on a first-come basis.

Kid's Tyme Child Care at the Goldcoast

✉4000 West Flamingo Road

✆702-367-7111

Open seven days a week, for children ages two-and-a-half to twelve. Children must be completely potty trained and out of diapers or Pull-Ups. The center features a jungle gym, a movie room, arts and crafts activities, interactive play, and much more. Hours: 9:00 A.M. to 11:30 P.M. (or 12:30 P.M. on weekends). Rates: $6 per hour, per child. Open to resort guests and non-guests, on a first-come basis.

Kids Quest at Boulder Station Hotel

✉4111 Boulder Highway

✆702-432-7569

✍*www.kidsquest.com*

Kids Quest is a professionally supervised children's activity center with a secure environment that features thousands of square feet of play areas, creative activities, and the latest interactive electronics for children six weeks to twelve years old. Rates range from $6 to $7.25 per hour, per child, depending on the day of the week and child's age. Open daily from 9:00 A.M. to 11:00 P.M. (until 1:00 A.M. on Fridays and Saturdays). Maximum stay per visit is three and a half hours. Open to resort guests and non-guests on a first-come basis.

Kid's Tyme Child Care Center at the Orleans

✉4500 West Tropicana

✆702-365-7300

Open seven days a week, for children ages two-and-a-half to twelve. Children must be completely potty trained and out of diapers or Pull-Ups. The center features a jungle gym, a movie room, arts and crafts activities, interactive play, and much more. Hours: 9:00 A.M. to

11:30 P.M. (or 12:30 A.M. on weekends). Rates: $6 per hour, per child. Open to resort guests and non-guests, on a first-come basis.

The Four Seasons Baby-Sitting Services

With two hours' notice, the Four Seasons staff can arrange reliable baby-sitting services for hotel guests only. They refer only experienced, bonded, and licensed baby-sitters. There is an hourly fee for this service. Contact the concierge for details.

The Palms Kids Quest Center

✉4321 West Flamingo Road

☏702-942-7777

✐*www.kidsquest.com*

Open 10:00 A.M. to 11:00 P.M. (Monday through Thursday) and until 1:00 A.M. on Fridays, Saturdays, and Sundays. Rates range from $5.75 to $6.75 per hour, per child. Accepts children ages three to twelve who are toilet trained. Open to resort guests and non-guests on a first-come basis.

Medical Emergencies

If you experience any type of medical-related emergency, virtually every mega-resort has a team of medical professionals on-site and available to assist you, any time day or night. In addition, there are local hospitals, doctor's offices, dentists, eye doctors, and other medical specialists in the Las Vegas area who can assist you. This section will help you find the medical assistance you need.

TRAVEL ESSENTIAL

In an emergency that requires urgent police, fire, or medical attention, use any telephone and dial 9-1-1. The non-emergency hotline number is 3-1-1.

Las Vegas–Area Emergency Services

The following is a list of Las Vegas-area emergency services.

Federal Bureau of Investigation
Las Vegas Office
✆702-385-1281

Las Vegas Fire and Rescue Headquarters
✆702-383-2888

Las Vegas Metropolitan Police Department
✆702-385-5555
✍*www.lvmpd.com*

The Office of the Sheriff
✆702-229-3231

University Medical Center–Emergency Room
✉1800 West Charleston Boulevard
✆702-383-2000
This is the closest hospital and emergency room to the Strip.

Dentist Referrals

Either of these two services can help you locate a Las Vegas-area dentist to deal with a dental emergency, such as a toothache, loose filling, or cracked tooth or cavity. Some dentists are available to deal with emergencies twenty-four hours per day.

Dental Find
✍*www.dentalfind.com*

800-DENTIST
✆800-DENTIST
✍*www.1800dentist.com*

Doctor and Pediatrician Referrals

A Web site called HealthGrade Reports (*⊘www.healthgrades reports.com*) is a free service that provides you with the information and tools you need to identify and choose leading Las Vegas-area doctors. This is an efficient method of finding and researching doctors to ensure that you receive the highest quality care. Using this Web site, you can research a doctor's credentials and find a referral based on a wide range of medical specialties.

TRAVEL TIP

For referrals relating to any type of service, especially if it's an emergency, be sure to consult the concierge or front desk attendant at your hotel.

Direct Doctor's Plus offers a free "Doctor Referral Service," available online at *⊘www.desertspringshospital.net* or by calling ✆702-388-4888. This service is available by phone weekdays between 8:00 A.M. and 8:00 P.M. and on Saturdays between 9:00 A.M. and 3:00 P.M.

Another doctor referral service you can reach by telephone is operated by the University Medical Center. Call ✆702-383-1904.

Eye Doctors/Eyeglasses

If you lose or break your prescription eyeglasses or sunglasses or need to replace your contact lenses, within many of the malls along the Strip you'll find a Lenscrafters (*⊘www.lenscrafters.com*) or Pearle Vision Center (*⊘www.pearlevision.com*) location with optometrists on staff during mall operating hours.

At Lenscrafters or Pearle Vision Centers, you can have a new pair of prescription eyeglasses made or repaired, usually in one hour. These locations all employ at least one Doctor of Optometry, who can provide an eye exam and determine your prescription, if necessary. Walk-in appointments are typically available.

 **TRAVEL TIP**

If you need your disposable contact lenses replaced quickly, order them from 1-800-CONTACTS (*www.1800contacts.com*) and have them sent directly to your hotel via Federal Express. You or your eye doctor will need to fax the company your prescription. You can then pay using any major credit card.

Eye Care Centers

The following is a list of local eye care centers.

Lenscrafters
✉3614 South Maryland Parkway
✆702-737-8893

Lenscrafters
✉The Fashion Show Mall, 3200 Las Vegas Boulevard South
✆702-732-8233

Lenscrafters
✉Galleria at Sunset Mall, 1300 West Sunset Drive, Henderson
✆702-436-0040

Lenscrafters
✉Meadows Mall, 4300 Meadows Lane
✆702-877-6779

Lenscrafters
✉Lake Mead Pavilion, 7361 West Lake Mead Boulevard
✆702-360-8070

Pearle Vision Center
✉230 North Nellis Boulevard
✆702-452-3414

Pearle Vision Center
✉506 South Decatur Boulevard
✆702-870-8121

Pearle Vision Center
✉3993 South Maryland Parkway
✆702-734-1551

Las Vegas-Area Hospitals

The following is a listing of Las Vegas-area hospitals and emergency rooms. From the Las Vegas Strip, the University Medical Center (✆702-383-2000/1800 West Charleston Boulevard) is the closest hospital and emergency room.

TRAVEL ESSENTIAL

When visiting any hospital bring your driver's license or passport, if possible, along with your health insurance membership card or insurance information.

Boulder City Hospital
✉901 Adams Boulevard, Boulder City, NV 89005
✆702-293-4111
✑*www.bouldercityhospital.org*

Desert Springs Hospital Medical Center
✉2075 East Flamingo Road, Las Vegas, NV 89119
✆702-733-8800
✑*www.desertspringshospital.net*

Kindred Hospital–Las Vegas
✉5110 West Sahara Avenue, Las Vegas, NV 89146
✆702-871-1418
✑*www.kindredhospitallvs.com*

MountainView Hospital
✉ 3100 North Tenaya Way, Las Vegas, NV 89128
✆ 702-255-5000
✐ www.mountainview-hospital.com

St. Rose Dominican Hospitals–Rose deLima Campus
✉ 102 East Lake Mead Drive, Henderson, NV 89015
✆ 702-616-5000
✐ www.strosecares.com

Sunrise Children's Hospital
✉ 3186 Maryland Parkway, Las Vegas, NV 89109
✆ 702-731-8000
✐ www.sunrisehospital.com

Sunrise Hospital & Medical Center
✉ 3186 Maryland Parkway, Las Vegas, NV 89109
✆ 702-731-8000
✐ www.sunrisehospital.com

University Medical Center
✉ 1800 West Charleston Boulevard, Las Vegas, NV 89102
✆ 702-383-2000
✆ 702-383-2661 (Emergency Room)
✐ www.umc-cares.org

Valley Hospital Medical Center
✉ 620 Shadow Lane, Las Vegas, NV 89106
✆ 702-388-4000
✐ www.valleyhospital.net

Pharmacies

Within five miles of the Las Vegas Strip, there are more than ten Walgreen's pharmacies (✐ www.walgreens.com), including several located right on the Strip. Contact your hotel's concierge (or front desk attendant) or check the local Yellow Pages for information about other local area pharmacies.

Walgreen's
✉1101 South Las Vegas Boulevard
✆702-471-6844

Walgreen's (open 24 hours)
✉2280 North Las Vegas Boulevard
✆702-649-1415

Walgreen's
✉495 Fremont Street
✆702-385-1284

Walgreen's
✉3025 Las Vegas Boulevard South
✆702-836-0820

Walgreen's
✉3030 Las Vegas Boulevard North
✆702-642-5318

Walgreen's (open 24 hours)
✉4470 Bonanza Road
✆702-531-8006

Walgreen's
✉451 South Decatur Boulevard
✆702-870-1626

Walgreen's
✉4470 Bonanza Road
✆702-531-8006

Walgreen's
✉3400 Boulder Highway
✆702-432-6940

Walgreen's
✉2882 South Maryland Parkway
✆702-866-6213

Walgreen's
✉900 North Rancho Drive
✆702-646-4651

Coin-Operated Laundromats

All of the mega-resorts and hotels offer a full-service laundry and dry cleaning service. Garments will be picked up from your hotel room, laundered and/or dry-cleaned, then returned to your room several hours later or the following morning. The cost for this pickup and delivery service is typically extremely high.

 TRAVEL TIP

To locate any type of business or service in the Las Vegas area, check the Yellow Pages in your hotel room or point your Web browser to one of the online Yellow Pages services, such as ✑*www.411.com,* ✑*www. 555-1212.com,* ✑*www.las.vegas.ypcity.info,* ✑*www.switchboard.com,* or ✑*www.yellowpages.com.*

There are several less-expensive options if you need clothing laundered or dry-cleaned during your Las Vegas trip. Especially if you're traveling with kids or teens, if you plan on utilizing a nearby self-service, coin-operated Laundromat, you can pack less clothing for your trip.

The following are a few self-service, coin-operated Laundromats near the Las Vegas Strip:

Amy's Laundry Basket
✉1923 North Decatur Boulevard
✆702-646-5059

City Center Laundromat
✉719 Fremont Street
✆702-366-0742

Coin Laundry & Cleaners
✉4940 West Tropicana Avenue
✆702-451-6100

Cora's Coin Laundry
✉1097 East Tropicana Avenue
✆702-736-6181

Parkway Laundromat
✉1234 East Sahara Avenue
✆702-792-4570

Sahara Laundry
✉4601 West Sahara Avenue
✆702-871-1281

Washboard
✉4137 South Maryland Parkway
✆702-732-0998

Full-Service Dry Cleaners

The following are a few local dry cleaning services in the Las Vegas area where you can drop off garments to be cleaned. Same-day or next-day service is typically available. Many of these businesses also do alterations.

Amy's Cleaners & Laundry
✉7756 West Sahara Avenue
✆702-233-3902

Cantrell's Cleaners
✉1532 North Street
✆702-648-2756

Canyon Gate Cleaners
✉8145 West Sahara Avenue
✆702-360-3666

Comet Cleaners
✉4965 West Tropicana Avenue
✆702-253-0111

Dry Clean Express
✉3715 West Flamingo Road
✆702-222-1852

Fast 'N Fresh Cleaners
✉2548 East Desert Inn Drive
✆702-735-6860

Las Vegas Cleaners
✉550 South Decatur Boulevard
✆702-258-0090

One Hour Martinizing Cleaners
✉3230 East Flamingo Drive
✆702-451-7727

Palms Cleaners
✉4557 West Flamingo Drive
✆702-252-6901

Phillips the Cleaners
✉3620 West Sahara Avenue
✆702-873-8220

Phillips the Cleaners
✉6194 West Flamingo Road
✆702-367-8383

Phillips the Cleaners
✉6980 West Tropicana Avenue
✆702-252-0609

Royalty Cleaners
✉1830 North Martin L. King Boulevard
✆702-631-3028

The Cleaners & Alterations
✉3160 East Desert Inn Drive
✆702-693-4719

TRAVEL ESSENTIAL

When booking your hotel or resort accommodations, ask if self-service laundry facilities are available on-site. This will ultimately offer the most convenience. Many of the resorts and hotels located on and right off the Strip offer self-service laundry facilities available to guests, along with a vending machine or a gift shop that sells detergent and fabric softener.

Banking and ATM Machines

Within every mega-resort and hotel on or near the Strip is at least one ATM machine. Unless the ATM machine is part of a network your own bank is affiliated with, you will typically be charged a transaction fee of between $1 and $3.50 for each withdrawal from an ATM while you're traveling. ATMs not directly affiliated with a bank or financial institution often charge higher service fees. Many hotels, however, offer a check-cashing service for their registered guests.

 TRAVEL TIP

If you need to have money wired to you, there's a Western Union desk or office located within each of the mega-resorts on or near the Strip. Call Western Union at ✆800-325-6000 or visit the company's Web site (✐www.westernunions.com) for details about how to send or receive money using this service.

Located right off the Strip are dozens of full-service banks, including branches for Bank of America, Bank of Commerce, First Republic Bank, Chase Manhattan Bank, Citibank, Colonial Bank, U.S. Bank, Washington Mutual Bank, and Wells Fargo Bank. Call your bank directly to determine whether there's a branch in the Las Vegas area. Your hotel's concierge or front desk attendant can direct you to the nearest full-service bank.

Lost or Stolen Credit Cards or Traveler's Checks

If your major credit card, debit card, or traveler's checks get lost or stolen during your trip, it's important to report this immediately to the appropriate credit card company or the financial institution that issued the traveler's checks. If it's a debit card, call your bank.

The emergency service phone numbers listed in Table 21-1 for each credit card company are available twenty-four hours per day every day and offer help relating to the following services:

- Reporting a lost or stolen card
- Obtaining an emergency card replacement
- Requesting an emergency cash advance
- Locating the closest ATM
- Accessing account-related information
- Accessing or learning about applicable card benefits

TABLE 21-1
CREDIT CARD COMPANY CONTACT INFORMATION

Credit Card Company	Phone Number to Report a Lost or Stolen Card	Web Site
MasterCard	800-MC-ASSIST	www.mastercard.com
Visa	800-847-2911	www.visa.com
American Express	800-AXP-1234	www.americanexpress.com
American Express Traveler's Checks	800-525-7641	www.americanexpress.com
Diners Club	800-234-6377	www.dinersclub.com

Business Services

Whether you're visiting Las Vegas on business to attend a convention or you're on vacation and have a work-related emergency, just about every type of business-related service you could possibly need is available in the Las Vegas area.

For example, if you need access to a computer with a high-speed Internet connection or a Wi-Fi hotspot so you can surf the Web using your laptop computer, or if you need to ship a package or make copies, the following are some useful resources. Keep in mind that most mega-resorts and hotels also have business centers available to guests located on-site.

Computer Rentals

Las Vegas hosts some of the largest conventions in the world, not to mention having millions of businesspeople visit the city each year on vacation. If you find yourself in need of a computer, you can visit a local cybercafé, visit any of the FedEx/Kinko's locations and rent a PC by the minute, or rent a fully equipped computer system and have it delivered directly to your hotel room. The following are two computer rental companies located in the Las Vegas area:

ABC Rentals
📞800-256-6087
📞702-368-7784
✉*www.abcrentals.net*

Comp-U-Rent Las Vegas
📞702-838-8536
✉*ww.comp-u-rent-lasvegas.com*

═FAST FACT

Need to purchase a new laptop computer, software, or computer supplies? There's a CompUSA Superstore located at 3535 West Sahara Avenue (📞702-252-0149). There's also a Best Buy located at 3820 South Maryland Parkway (📞702-732-8283) and a Circuit City located at 5055 Sahara Avenue (📞702-367-9700).

Cellular Phone Companies

Every national cell phone service provider has a customer service center or authorized agents in the Las Vegas area. Following are the toll-free phone numbers for the most popular cellular phone service providers.

If you don't currently have a cellular phone with a nationwide calling plan, but you need a cell phone while in Las Vegas, consider purchasing a phone with a "pay as you go" plan, so you can make and receive calls without racking up roaming and long-distance fees. If your cell phone is lost or stolen, you can also use the following phone numbers to report it to your service provider.

AT&T Wireless
☎866-293-4634
✎*www.attwireless.com*

Cingular
☎800-331-0500
✎*www.cingular.com*

Nextel
☎800-639-6111
✎*www.nextel.com*

Sprint PCS
☎888-788-4727
✎*www.sprintpcs.com*

T-Mobile
☎800-T-MOBILE
✎*www.t-mobile.com*

Verizon Wireless
☎800-922-0204
✎*www.verizonwireless.com*

FedEx/Kinko's Locations

Whether you need printing, copying, package shipping, access to a computer to send or receive a fax, access to a high-speed Internet connection or a Wi-Fi hotspot, there are five full-service FedEx/Kinko's locations in Las Vegas, shown in Table 21-2. Several of these locations are open twenty-four hours per day. If you're shipping a package or overnight letter, FedEx shipping supplies are available at these locations.

For general information, package pickup, or package tracking, call FedEx at ✆800-238-5355 or point your Web browser to ✑*www. fedexkinkos.com.*

TABLE 21-2
FEDEX/KINKO'S LOCATIONS

FedEx/Kinko's Address	Phone Number	Hours
830 South 4th Street	702-383-7022	Weekdays: 7:00 A.M. to 10:00 P.M. Closed Weekends
395 Hughes Center Drive	702-951-2400	Open 24 hours
4750 West Sahara Avenue	702-870-7011	Open 24 hours
4440 South Maryland Parkway, Suite 107	702-735-4402	Daily: 7:00 A.M. to 11:00 P.M.
2288 South Nellis Boulevard	702-431-5076	Weekdays: 7:00 A.M. to 10:00 P.M. Saturdays: 7:00 A.M. to 5:00 P.M. Sundays: Closed

United States Post Office Locations

There are five United States Post Office locations in the Las Vegas area, listed in Table 21-3. For general information or package tracking, call ✆800-275-8777, or point your Web browser to ✑*www.usps.com.*

TABLE 21-3
U.S. POST OFFICE LOCATIONS

United States Post Office Location	Phone Number	Hours
Strip Station, 3100 Industrial Road	702-735-8519	Weekdays: 8:30 A.M. to 5:00 P.M.
Post Office Express, 4801 Spring Mountain Road, Station A	702-362-3951	Weekdays: 10:30 A.M. to 7:00 P.M. Saturdays: 11:00 A.M. to 7:00 P.M. Sundays: 11:00 A.M. to 7:00 P.M.

United States Post Office Location	Phone Number	Hours
University Station, 4632 South Maryland Parkway	702-736-7649	Weekdays: 9:00 A.M. to 4:30 P.M.
Paradise Valley Station, 4975 Swenson Street	702-736-7649	Weekdays: 8:30 A.M. to 5:00 P.M.
Garside Station, 1801 South Decatur Boulevard	702-220-8454	Weekdays: 8:30 A.M. to 5:00 P.M. Saturdays: 9:00 A.M. to 3:00 P.M.

The UPS Store—United Parcel Service

For general information, package tracking, or pickup service, call ✆800-PICK-UPS, or point your Web browser to ✑*www.ups.com.* There are five full-service UPS Store shipping locations in the Las Vegas area, shown in Table 21-4. Packaging materials, such as boxes, labels, and packing tape, are available for an additional fee.

TABLE 21-4
UPS STORE LOCATIONS

The UPS Store Address	Phone Number	Hours
1306 West Craig Road	702-639-6222	Weekdays: 8:00 A.M. to 6:00 P.M. Saturdays: 8:00 A.M. to 4:00 P.M. Sundays: Closed
2550 East Desert Inn Road	702-369-5920	Weekdays: 9:00 A.M. to 6:00 P.M. Saturdays: 9:00 A.M. to 5:00 P.M. Sundays: Closed
3540 West Sahara	702-367-6252	Weekdays: 7:30 A.M. to 5:30 P.M. Saturdays: 8:00 A.M. to 4:00 P.M. Sundays: Closed
4255 East Charleston	702-641-0605	Weekdays: 8:00 A.M. to 6:00 P.M. Saturdays: 9:00 A.M. to 5:00 P.M. Sundays: Closed
740 North Martin L. King	702-742-5877	Weekdays: 8:30 A.M. to 5:30 P.M. Weekends: Closed

Packing List

UNLESS YOU'RE ACCUSTOMED TO traveling on a regular basis, it's very common to forget important items when packing for a trip. While in Las Vegas, you can, of course, purchase any items you forget, but to save time and money, detailed packing checklists follow in Tables A-1 through A-5 to help insure that you bring along the most commonly needed items and articles of clothing.

To begin, run down this list and place a check mark (✓) in the Needed column for the items you'd like to pack. Calculate the quantity of each item you'll need, based on how long you'll be traveling. For example, if you'll be traveling for three days, make sure you pack at least three pairs of socks for each person.

Later, as you're actually packing, place a check mark (✓) in the appropriate Packed column for items as they're placed in your suitcase or carry-on bag.

Remember, due to enhanced security at all U.S. airports, all luggage is subject to being x-rayed and/or hand-searched by the airline or TSA (Transportation Security Administration). If you choose to lock your bag(s), be sure to use luggage locks that are TSA approved to avoid having the locks cut so your bags can be searched.

Also, never pack any items that are forbidden by the TSA. For details about items that cannot be checked as baggage or carried onto an airplane, point your Web browser to *www.tsa.gov*. Failing to abide by the packing guidelines created by the TSA will cause major delays as you attempt to check your bags at the airport and/or pass through security.

CASUAL WEAR

Item/Garment	Needed ✓	Quantity Needed	Packed for You ✓	Packed for Spouse ✓	Packed for Kids ✓
Belt(s)					
Casual shirts					
Handkerchiefs					
Hat/cap					
Jacket/ windbreaker					
Lingerie					
Pajamas/sleep-wear/nightgown					
Purses					
Sandals					
Scarf					
Shorts					
Sneakers					
Socks					
Stockings					
Sweater/ sweatshirt					
Trousers (pants, jeans, etc.)					
T-shirts					
Underwear					
Walking shoes					
Other item:					
Other item:					
Other item:					

FORMAL WEAR (OR BUSINESS ATTIRE)

Item/Garment	Needed ✓	Quantity Needed	Packed for You ✓	Packed for Spouse ✓	Packed for Kids ✓
Blouses					
Cufflinks					
Dress belt					
Dress purse					
Dress shirt(s)					
Dress shoes					
Dress socks					
Dresses/gowns					
Men's suit/ sport coat					
Necktie					
Undershirt					
Other item:					
Other item:					
Other item:					

BEACH/POOL/OUTDOOR WEAR

Item/Garment	Needed ✓	Quantity Needed	Packed for You ✓	Packed for Spouse ✓	Packed for Kids ✓
Bathing suits					
Beachwear					
Flip-flops/sandals					
Hat					
Sunblock					
Sunglasses					
Umbrella					
Other item:					
Other item:					
Other item:					

MISCELLANEOUS

Item/Garment	Needed ✓	Quantity Needed	Packed for You ✓	Packed for Spouse ✓	Packed for Kids ✓
Batteries					
Camera, film, and accessories					
Deodorant					
Golf clubs					
Hairbrush, comb, and hair care products					
Make-up/ cosmetics					
Moisturizer					
Perfume/cologne					
Shaver (razor), shaving cream, extra blades, etc.					
Tampons					
Tennis racket					
The Everything® Family Guide to Las Vegas (this book)					
Toothbrush, toothpaste, and dental floss					
Video camera and accessories					
Other item:					
Other item:					
Other item:					

CARRY-ON

Item/Garment	Needed ✓	Quantity Needed	Packed for You ✓	Packed for Spouse ✓	Packed for Kids ✓
Airline tickets, travel documents, itinerary and confirmation letter for hotel, rental car, etc.					
Baby and toddler items (if applicable) —food, diapers, bottles, pacifier, baby wipes, car seat, stroller, baby carrier, sippy cups, bibs, toys, formula, change of clothing, etc.					
Books/magazines					
Cash					
Cell phone and charger					
Credit cards					
Driver's license/ government ID					
Eyeglasses/ contact lenses (and related supplies)					
Handheld video game system (Game Boy)					
Jewelry/valuables					
Laptop computer					
Over-the-counter medications (pain-killers, allergy medications, vitamins/ supplements, antacids, etc.)					

Item/Garment	Needed ✓	Quantity Needed	Packed for You ✓	Packed for Spouse ✓	Packed for Kids ✓
Personal electronics (PDA, etc.)					
Portable DVD player and movies					
Prepaid phone card(s)					
Prescription medications					
Toys/activities for the kids					
Traveler's checks					
Walkman/iPod (MP3 player) and headphones					
Wallet					
Watch					
Other item:					
Other item:					
Other item:					

Before Leaving Home Checklist

The following to-do list will help you prepare your home or apartment before leaving on vacation.

BEFORE LEAVING HOME CHECKLIST

Completed	✓
Adjust the thermostat.	
Arrange for care and feeding of your pets while you're away.	
Confirm that all needed articles of clothing and items are packed in your luggage.	
Contact the U.S. Post Office to put a hold on your mail.	
Leave your travel itinerary with a relative and/or your employer, in case of an emergency.	
Lock your windows and doors.	
Make your home look "lived in" while you're away by putting one or two lights on timers.	
Pay your household bills—utilities, mortgage, rent, etc.	
Remove the trash.	
Set the burglar alarm system.	
Stop deliveries to your home while you're away. Ask a neighbor to take in delivered newspapers and packages so they don't pile up at your door and alert potential criminals that you're on vacation.	
Throw out items in your refrigerator that will spoil.	
Turn off all unnecessary lights and appliances.	
Turn on your telephone answering machine.	
Water your plants.	
Other:	
Other:	
Other:	

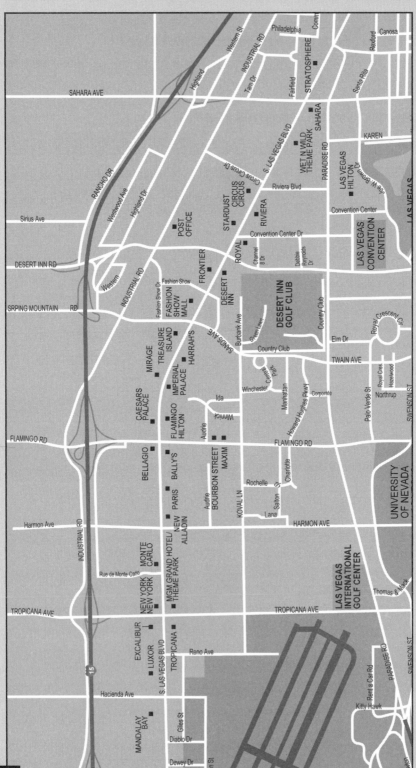

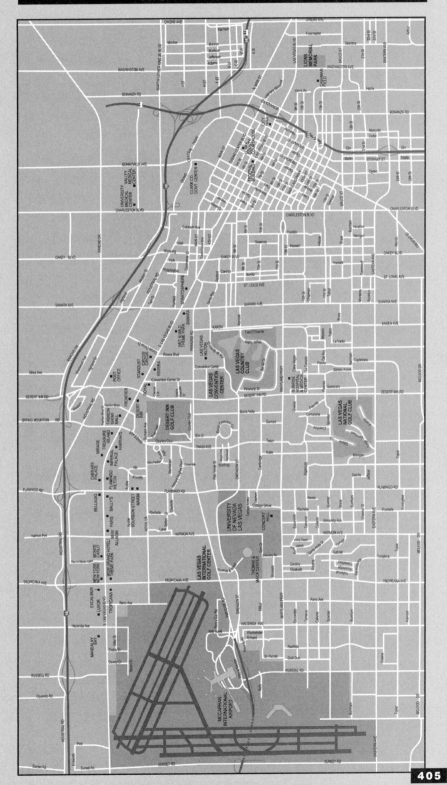

Index